# Taking Center Stage

## A Commitment to Standards-Based Education for California's Middle Grades Students

# Publishing Information

*Taking Center Stage* was developed under the direction of the Middle
Grades and High School Networks Office, Education Support and
Networks Division, California Department of Education. It was prepared
for printing by the staff of CDE Press, California Department of Education,
working in cooperation with Mary Ann Overton and Barbara Castillo,
Consultants, Middle Grades and High School Networks Office. The
publication was edited by Edward O'Malley and Bob Klingensmith, the
cover and interior design were prepared and created by Cheryl McDonald,
and the typesetting was done by Jeannette Huff and Carey Johnson. It was
published by the Department, 721 Capitol Mall, Sacramento, California
(mailing address: P.O. Box 944272, Sacramento, CA 94244-2720) and was
distributed under the provisions of the Library Distribution Act and
*Government Code* Section 11096.

ISBN 0-8011-1503-5

## Ordering Information

Copies of this publication are available for $13.50 each, plus shipping and
handling charges. California residents are charged sales tax. Orders may
be sent to the California Department of Education, CDE Press, Sales
Office, P.O. Box 271, Sacramento, CA 95812-0271; FAX (916) 323-0823.
See page 272 for complete information on payment, including credit card
purchases and an order form. Prices on all publications are subject to
change.

A partial list of other educational resources available from the Department
appears on page 271. In addition, an illustrated *Educational Resources
Catalog* describing publications, videos, and other instructional media
available from the Department can be obtained without charge by writing
to the address given above or by calling the Sales Office at (916) 445-1260.
Notice

The guidance in *Taking Center Stage* is not binding on local educational
agencies or other entities. Except for the statutes, regulations, and court
decisions that are referenced herein, the document is exemplary, and
compliance with it is not mandatory. (See *Education Code* Section
33308.5.)

# Contents

# Message from the State Superintendent of Public Instruction

They are not our youngest students. They are not our oldest students. They are those students who are in the center—our *middle grades students*. They are also those students who are often living through the most confusing, uncertain times of their lives.

This handbook, *Taking Center Stage: A Commitment of Standards-Based Education for California's Middle Grades Students*, looks at the needs of middle grades students against a backdrop of standards, assessment, and accountability. It provides guidance for California's educators to help them successfully implement a standards-based education for our young adolescents.

Clearly, students are facing a challenging period in their development. As a result, those educators who have been charged with the important task of educating these students have an *equally* challenging task. It is a time of ups and downs, successes and setbacks, and bold exploration juxtaposed against anxieties and insecurities. In fact, the adolescent years can be so tumultuous that some of us—when we reflect back on our own experiences—are enormously thankful that we do not need to relive those years.

To guide us in our efforts to provide a world-class education for these students, I established the Middle Grades Task Force,

and I want to thank the educators who served on this group. I greatly appreciate all their hard work and the many hours they spent on this project. Their charge was to build upon the earlier work of *Caught in the Middle*, the 1987 California Department of Education middle grades report. Moving forward from that previous document, *Taking Center Stage* specifically addresses how to implement standards and to explore their implications for the school as a whole.

The middle grades have always been a critical and pivotal link for students in the education chain. This linkage takes on an even greater significance with the *High School Exit Examination* looming in the future of every middle grades student. Our middle school educators are vital to the standards-based learning that will prepare students for the future.

I hope you find this document a useful tool, and I look forward to working with you as we continue building a world-class, standards-based education in California for *all* students.

*[signature]*

DELAINE EASTIN
*State Superintendent of Public Instruction*

# Preface

*Taking Center Stage: A Commitment to Standards-Based Education for California's Middle Grades Students* has been written primarily for teachers and principals, most of whom consider implementing standards-based education one of their most compelling professional challenges. Examining standards-based education from several perspectives, the document focuses on what some observers refer to as the technology of standards: What are they? How do we work toward meeting them? How do we measure them? What do we do with the results?

This publication contains helpful information for school personnel about what they need to know and do to make standards-based education a success. Accordingly, it examines such issues as school culture, classroom organization, differentiated instruction, accelerated learning opportunities, an emotionally and physically safe school environment, and the specific knowledge and skills teachers and principals need to work effectively in a standards-based middle school.

Each chapter concludes with thought-provoking professional reflections, intended to challenge teachers and principals to think deeply about the issues presented, and one or more appendixes containing material related to the chapter. Notes and additional references are provided at the back of the publication.

Analytical, reflective, and informative, *Taking Center Stage* avoids the danger of assuming that everyone understands or is committed to standards-based education in the same way. The reader is provided with a substantial amount of information, together with the logic behind standards, assessment, and accountability for unleashing greater levels of professional commitment to reforms in standards-based education.

LESLIE FAUSSET
*Chief Deputy Superintendent*
*Policy and Programs*

SONIA HERNANDEZ
*Deputy Superintendent*
*Curriculum and Instructional Leadership Branch*

WENDY HARRIS
*Assistant Superintendent and Director*
*Education Support and Networks Division*

THADDEUS DUMAS
*Administrator*
*Middle Grades and High School Networks Office*

ROZYLNN WORRALL
*Administrator*
*Middle Grades and High School Networks Office*

# Acknowledgments

The California Department of Education extends special appreciation to the Middle Grades Task Force, the authors of *Taking Center Stage: A Commitment to Standards-Based Education for California's Middle Grades Students,* and numerous individuals in the Department who collaborated on this publication. Their combined efforts have resulted in a practical, grade-span document for middle grades educators that emphasizes the importance of a student-centered, middle grades philosophy as a strong and compatible foundation for standards-based education in California.

## Middle Grades Task Force

**Frank Adelman,** Superintendent, Mt. Shasta Union School District, Mt. Shasta

**Ernest Anastos,** Principal, Rancho del Rey Middle School, Sweetwater Union High School District, Chula Vista

**Robert Coble,** Teacher, Gambetta Middle School, North Monterey County Unified School District, Moss Landing (Representative, California Federation of Teachers)

**Cecilia Costas,** Principal, Maclay Middle School, Los Angeles Unified School District, Los Angeles

**James Fenwick,** Consultant, Fenwick Associates, Inc., San Diego

**Carole Firestone,** Teacher, Lindero Canyon Middle School, Las Virgenes Unified School District, Calabasas

**Irvin Howard,** Professor, California State University, San Bernardino; and President, California League of Middle Schools, Redlands

**Linda MacDonell,** Director, Instructional Services, Orange County Office of Education

**Gary Mantey,** Principal, Washington Middle School, La Habra City Elementary School District, La Habra

**Craig Nelson,** Consultant, California Teachers Association, Burlingame

**Charles Palmer,** Trustee, West Region, National Middle School Association, Los Angeles

**Cathy Seighman,** Teacher, Imperial Middle School, La Habra City Elementary School District, La Habra

**Ginny Krauzer Sharp,** Instructor, California State University, San Marcos

**Lois Statum,** Teacher, Charles M. Goethe Middle School, Sacramento City Unified School District, Sacramento

**Peter Watson,** Superintendent, Upland Unified School District, Upland

**Carl Zon,** Consultant, Sunnyvale

## Authors

**James Fenwick**, Primary Author and author of *Caught in the Middle*, Member of the Middle Grades Task Force, Fenwick Associates, Inc., San Diego

**Rozlynn Worrall**, Contributing Author, Administrator of Middle Grades and High School Networks Office, California Department of Education

**Diane Levin**, Contributing Author, Education Policy Advisor to the Chief Deputy Superintendent, Accountability and Administration, California Department of Education

Appreciation is extended to James Fenwick for interrupting his retirement and being the driving force behind the development of this publication. Mr. Fenwick's expertise, integrity, and uncommon commitment to middle grades education are reflected throughout the book.

During the development of this publication, the educational landscape in California changed drastically. The system of standards, assessment, and accountability matured and became technically more complex. In addition, new California initiatives directly affecting middle grades schools outpaced the document's currency.

The Department also extends appreciation to Rozlynn Worrall and Diane Levin, who put forth an extraordinary effort to update the document. Their collective expertise and background as middle grades educators, writers, and consultants in standards, assessment, and accountability are reflected in the initial chapters of this book.

## California Department of Education Staff

Thanks are also due to the following consultants in the Middle Grades and High School Networks Office who contributed to the development of this document:

**Barbara Castillo**
**Saundra Davis**
**James Miller**
**Mary Ann Overton**
**Margaret Park**

# Introduction

## Report from the Superintendent's Middle Grades Task Force

I n September 1998 State Superintendent of Public Instruction Delaine Eastin convened the Middle Grades Task Force to develop a grade-span sequel to the 1987 publication *Caught in the Middle: Educational Reform for Young Adolescents in California Public Schools.* Superintendent Eastin also asked the task force to move beyond that earlier work and to focus on standards, assessment, and accountability and their implications for middle school instruction.

Shortly after, on January 18, 1999, the State Board of Education and Superintendent Eastin issued a joint public statement defining policy and administrative commitments to standards-based education:

> A shortcoming of [school reform] up to this point has been the lack of focus on rigorous academic standards. The desire to improve student achievement . . . lacked a comprehensive, specific vision of what students actually needed to know and be able to do. . . . For the first time we are stating explicitly the content that students need to acquire at each grade level through grade eight and in grades nine and ten and in grades eleven and twelve. These standards are rigorous. With student mastery of this content, California schools will be on a par with those in the best educational systems in

other states and nations. . . . Fifteen years from now, we are convinced, the adoption of standards will be viewed as the signal event that began "a rising tide of excellence" in our schools. No more will the critical question "What should my child be learning?" be met with uncertainty of knowledge, purpose, and resolve. These standards answer the question. They are comprehensive and specific. They represent our commitment to excellence.

The report of the findings and recommendations of the Middle Grades Task Force affirms the relationship between a sound middle school philosophy and the goals of standards-based education.

The task force approached this work with the utmost seriousness. *Taking Center Stage* outlines the conditions for implementing standards-based middle grades education, including specific recommendations on such issues as the following:

- Professional accountability
- Reports of standards-based performance to students and parents
- Creation of a school culture capable of sustaining standards-based education
- Effective use of time through the scheduling of strategies that emphasize deep learning, complex reasoning, and differentiated instruction

- After-hours programs designed to support academic learning in response to content and performance standards
- Site-based professional development designed to provide teachers with the knowledge and skills needed to work effectively in a standards-based middle school

*Taking Center Stage* includes more than two hundred references, including the work of major scholars and middle-level educators.

Throughout its work the Middle Grades Task Force has been driven by an intense desire to develop a document and recommendations that:

- Reflect the philosophy and policy of the State Board of Education and State Superintendent Eastin.

- Support and build on the student-centered middle school philosophy for young adolescents.
- Speak directly to the needs of teachers and principals as they incorporate new knowledge and skills into their day-to-day professional practices.
- Guide instructional and assessment practices designed to help all students meet or exceed defined academic proficiency levels.

The Middle Grades Task Force and the California Department of Education have identified key elements *and* recommendations needed to implement standards-based education and support student academic achievement. The seven key elements and the 16 recommendations are as follows:

## Key Elements and Recommendations

### Key Element I  Rigorous Academic Content and Performance Standards

To ensure the success of all students:

Recommendation 1: Implement rigorous and consistent standards while maintaining a dynamic student-centered culture. (See Chapters 1, 2, 5, and 10.)

Recommendation 2: Provide sustaining resources and support for standards-based education. (See Chapters 2, 3, 5, 7, 8, 10, and 12.)

### Key Element II  Curriculum and Instruction

To ensure the success of all students:

Recommendation 3: Demonstrate commitment to essential elements of the middle grades philosophy. (See Chapters 1, 5, 6, 7, 8, 9, and 12.)

Recommendation 4: Align curriculum, instruction, and assessment practices with the California content and performance standards. (See Chapters 2, 3, and 14.)

| Recommendation 5: | Connect the contributions of California's diverse multicultural population as standards are implemented. (See Chapters 6, 10, 12, and 14.) |
| Recommendation 6: | Use technology as a tool to improve and increase student academic achievement. (See Chapters 6 and 14.) |
| Recommendation 7: | Examine the use of time to provide students and teachers opportunities to plan, integrate, teach, and learn. (See Chapters 7, 9, and 11.) |
| Recommendation 8: | Work with feeder elementary schools and destination high schools to provide consistent expectations and seamless transitions. (See Chapters 2, 4, 11, and 13.) |

## Key Element III  Assessment and Accountability

To ensure the success of all students:

| Recommendation 9: | Relate performance standards to content standards to define levels of academic excellence and proficiency. (See Chapters 2, 3, and 4.) |
| Recommendation 10: | Develop classroom and local assessment data systems that are used to determine appropriate instructional practices. (See Chapters 3, 4, and 8.) |
| Recommendation 11: | Hold all stakeholders accountable for high academic and behavioral expectations. (See Chapters 1, 2, 4, and 11.) |

## Key Element IV  Student Interventions

To ensure the success of all students:

| Recommendation 12: | Provide appropriate accelerated interventions based on the results of relevant assessment instruments. (See Chapters 3, 10, 11, 12, and 14.) |

## Key Element V  Professional Development

To ensure the success of all students:

| Recommendation 13: | Provide relevant and appropriate school-based, comprehensive, ongoing professional development. (See Chapters 7 and 14.) |

**Key Element VI    Parent and Community Partnerships**

To ensure the success of all students:

Recommendation 14:    Engage families and the community to support student achievement. (See Chapters 9, 12, and 13.)

**Key Element VII    Health and Safety**

To ensure the success of all students:

Recommendation 15:    Create and sustain safe school environments. (See Chapters 6, 8, 12, and 13.)

Recommendation 16:    Provide access to health and social services to maximize student well-being. (See Chapter 13.)

As middle schools have evolved and grown in number and research continues to validate the unique and vital role that middle schools play in the development of young adolescents, the next major advance—standards-based middle grades education—will challenge every middle-level educator in California. Standards-based education in the middle grades is the dominant theme around which this document is organized. Many observers of the middle school movement believe that it is now possible to implement a powerful model for schooling young adolescents in the middle grades and to make the educational experience even more dynamic and effective. A passion on the part of teachers, principals, and parents for academic excellence as well as a deep commitment to opportunities for engaging young adolescents during their formative stages of development will count most in preparing them for successful productive citizenship in the new millennium.

The seven key elements frame for the reader the meaning and importance of standards-based middle grades education. Throughout the document the recommendations of the Superintendent's Middle Grades Task Force are noted with a star and band of blue on the first page of every chapter. These notations will assist in locating material specific to each recommendation.

*"A total commitment is paramount to reaching
the ultimate in performance."*

—Tom Flores

# California's Middle Schools: Poised for World-Class Performance

I n any performance all eyes are
fixed on center stage. When the
players take center stage, they
enter the spotlight—the focal
point where the foremost action
takes place. With expectation
the audience watches.

Education is always in the spotlight
because of its unquestionable value to a literate
and responsible citizenry. At center stage in the
continuum of grade spans are the middle
grades, a pivotal period between elementary
school and high school. Within the middle
grades a number of key constructs share the
spotlight:

- ***Standards-based education takes center
  stage.*** Both content and performance
  standards are central to the shift from a
  curriculum-based paradigm to one highlighting standards.
- ***Assessment takes center stage.*** Meaningful
  student assessments are central to effective
  instruction. From assessment results,
  teachers determine what needs to be taught
  and, perhaps, what needs to be taught
  again. A variety of assessment tools are
  used: statewide and local, formal and
  informal. Standards-aligned assessments
  are essential in determining whether
  students have achieved standards.
- ***Accountability takes center stage.*** Teachers, administrators, students, and parents
  are all essential stakeholders and partners
  responsible for student success.

A student-centered philosophy occupies
the stage in the middle grades. It provides a
rich setting and context for initiatives that lead
to higher levels of student achievement for all
students. *Taking Center Stage* addresses each
of the fundamental components within a
context relevant to California's middle schools,
a central grade span well poised for world-
class performance. But first a historical perspective of middle grades philosophy as well
as the key events and initiatives leading to
standards-based education in California must
be provided.

 Recommendations 1, 3, 11

Tom Flores, former National Football League coach

## Historical Perspective: Setting the Stage for California's Middle School Reform Movement

Those who were engaged in middle-level education during the latter half of the twentieth century are familiar with the debate over the most appropriate kind of schooling to be provided for young adolescents. During that period deep concerns developed over the failure of many junior high schools to respond adequately to the unique developmental characteristics of middle-level students. The typically rigid organization of junior high schools, which mimicked the departmentalized structure of secondary education, rendered young adolescents unprepared for the transition from the emotionally safe haven of elementary schools to the demands of the junior high schools.

Two things became increasingly clear. First, students in grades six, seven, and eight required schools that would focus on the students' physical, social, and emotional development. Second, they needed schools that would respond effectively to the students' rapidly developing intellectual abilities. Unfortunately, the staffs in many junior high schools in California were ill prepared by training or inclination to take on that dual requirement. Nor were conventional elementary schools, kindergarten through grade eight, prepared to alter their self-contained classroom structures to provide for a more rigorous academic emphasis, particularly in mathematics and science, even though their nurturing student-centered focus was laudable. In short, young adolescents found themselves caught in the middle.

Concerns about meeting the needs of those students led to the publication in 1987 of *Caught in the Middle: Educational Reform for Young Adolescents in California Public Schools,*[1] which captured the essence of a new kind of school for young adolescents. Before its publication many California educators and parents saw the middle school years as a period of time to be endured rather than celebrated. But much of that mentality has disappeared with the advent of middle schools. Because of concerted efforts by middle school principals to hire teachers who embrace this more positive philosophy, a much higher number of those teaching in middle grades schools today do so by choice, not by chance. Teachers with specialized training in core subjects are attracted to middle schools that emphasize high academic standards. At the same time, school administrators have been successfully recruiting teachers with serious interest in the promise rather than the problems of early adolescence.

Early adolescence is one of the most exciting periods of intellectual, physical, social, and emotional development in the human life span. To energize the education of the state's young adolescents, hundreds of new middle schools have emerged throughout California during the past decade. The resulting changes that have occurred in middle-level education constitute one of California's most successful educational reform efforts.

Combining demands for academic proficiency and enlightened responsiveness to the physical, emotional, social, and intellectual challenges of students in the middle grades, teachers and principals have created middle schools in which students are no longer caught in the middle. Their efforts, together with those of approximately 500 middle grades partnership schools in the California Middle Grades Partnership Network, have produced dynamic new learning environments (see also Appendix 1-A, "California Middle Grades Partnership Network," at the end of this chapter).

A research-based report funded by the Carnegie Corporation of New York, *Turning Points 2000: Educating Adolescents in the 21st Century,*[2] documents the progress made by middle schools in the last decade. The first *Turning Points* report and recommendations, published in 1989,[3] called on middle schools to "transmit a core of common, substantial knowledge to all students in ways that foster curiosity, problem solving, and critical thinking." *Turning Points 2000* reshapes and adds precision to that recommendation and the others, having based the new recommendations on practices found to be effective.

The new recommendations call for "middle grades schools that:[4]

- Teach a curriculum grounded in rigorous public academic standards for what students should know and be able to do relevant to the concerns of adolescents and based on how students learn best. . . .
- Use instructional methods designed to prepare all students to achieve higher standards and become lifelong learners. . . .
- Staff middle grades schools with teachers who are expert at teaching young adolescents and engage teachers in ongoing, targeted professional development opportunities. . . .
- Organize relationships for learning to create a climate of intellectual development and a caring community of shared educational purpose. . . .

- Govern democratically, through direct or representative participation by all school staff members, the adults who know the students best. . . .
- Provide a safe and healthy school environment as part of improving academic performance and developing caring and ethical citizens. . . .
- Involve parents and communities in supporting student learning and healthy development. . . ."

The *Turning Points 2000* recommendations are consistent with those of California's Middle Grades Task Force (see Introduction). California's Middle Grades Task Force's recommendations reflect the best of middle grades philosophy (including equal access to the most demanding curricula, interdisciplinary team teaching, active and cooperative learning, flexible scheduling, inclusive classrooms, multicultural education, complex reasoning, and differentiated instruction, along with mentoring, tutoring, and counseling experiences) and an increased emphasis on academic expectations through standards-based education. The task force's recommendations relevant to the content in each chapter are highlighted on the first page of each chapter.

## A Shift in California's Educational Paradigm

For a better understanding of the rationale behind California's shift to a standards-based system, it is important to take a look back at some of the milestones of the past decade. What took place in the 1990s to warrant a change in the delivery system for education?

What events precipitated the call for standards-based education?

In 1991 the U.S. Secretary of Labor's Commission on Achieving Necessary Skills (SCANS) in *What Work Requires of Schools*[5] called for schools to produce students better prepared to transition to a workplace environment significantly changed from an industrial model to a knowledge-based, technology model. The emerging jobs and workplace were calling for employees with sophisticated critical thinking and higher-reasoning skills as well as basic skills in reading, writing, mathematics, speaking, and listening. The SCANS report also emphasized the importance of interpersonal skills and the ability of incoming employees to work on teams and with people from culturally diverse backgrounds. The expected workplace and foundation competencies were to begin in kindergarten and grow throughout a student's educational career (see also Appendix 1-B, "SCANS Workplace Know-How," at the end of this chapter).

The American-based New Standards Project[6] began in 1993 to collect and analyze standardized tests and documents from other countries whose students were performing well on international tests and whose highly skilled citizens tended to hold jobs that paid well. A major finding of this analysis—of prevailing significance—is that schools are successful when they set clear, consistent, demanding standards that make sense in the culture of the local school community and the nation. Use of performance assessments to determine academic proficiency in relation to standards is also a common feature of successful schools.

A major factor sounding an alarm for California to reevaluate its instructional and curricular practices was the showing of its students on the National Assessment of Educational Progress (NAEP). In the mid-1990s, the results of NAEP tests in reading and mathematics revealed that California's students ranked near the bottom when compared with students from other participating states. Additionally, the results of statewide assessments in California indicated that, collectively, the state's students were not demonstrating high levels of academic achievement.

California also needed to develop a plan to respond to its socioeconomic and culturally diverse population, ensuring access to rigorous standards for all of its students. Forty-eight percent of California's children live near or below the poverty line, the majority of California's children are minorities, and one in every four California students (1.4 million) speaks little or no English.[7] Significant changes would have to take place to close the achievement gap and prepare California's children for the knowledge-based technological economy that awaited them.

In the spring of 1995, one of the first acts of newly elected State Superintendent of Public Instruction Delaine Eastin was to convene a Reading Task Force and a Mathematics Task Force. The purpose of the task forces was to (1) determine some of the potential causes for the less-than-satisfactory assessment results; and (2) make specific recommendations that would collectively serve to raise achievement levels.

### Reading

The efforts of the Reading Task Force culminated with the report titled *Every Child a Reader*.[8] Published in 1995, the document was pivotal in promoting "balanced and comprehensive" language arts instruction. The report also touted multiple solutions to the very complex challenge of improving reading achievement, among which were the following:

- A new language arts framework to articulate fully the notion of "balanced and comprehensive" instruction
- The establishment of academic content standards in the language arts (reading, writing, speaking, and listening) for every grade level, kindergarten through grade twelve
- An assessment system aligned with standards
- Intensive professional development at the in-service and preservice levels
- A high-quality preschool experience to be available to all children
- Appropriate instructional materials (textbooks)
- Class-size reduction minimizing the student/teacher ratio to promote more effective classroom instruction
- Intervention strategies to prevent reading deficiencies before they become too great to overcome
- Prioritization of reading instruction at every school site
- Increased funding and resources to promote the recommendations

### Mathematics

In 1995 the Mathematics Task Force published its own report titled *Improving Mathematics Achievement for All California Students*.[9] Like the Reading Task Force's report, the mathematics document included a variety of recommendations designed to advance mathematics achievement in the state:

- Rigorous, balanced content and performance standards in mathematics
- The establishment of a stable, coherent, and informative system of assessment
- High-quality instruction for all students, including adequate time, adequate instructional materials, mathematically powerful teachers, and additional time in the school day and school year
- Research to improve mathematics education along with the improvement of the *Mathematics Framework*
- Parents as partners: supporting the role of parents in their children's education

In 1997 the U.S. Department of Education issued a white paper prepared for U.S. Secretary of Education Richard W. Riley and titled *Mathematics Equals Opportunity*.[10] It reaffirmed the need for states to adopt rigorous standards in mathematics with the conclusion:

> In the United States today, mastering mathematics has become more important than ever. Students with a strong grasp of mathematics have an advantage in academics and in the job market. The eighth grade is a critical point in mathematics education. Achievement at that stage clears the way for students to take rigorous high school mathematics and science courses— keys to college entrance and success in the labor force.

### The Advent of Standards and a New Role for the Frameworks

In the first year of Delaine Eastin's superintendency, a rigorous set of voluntary standards in every core subject area, including foreign language, visual and performing arts, physical education, health, and career-technical subjects, was developed for each grade level. The standards emphasize critical thinking and many of the workplace competencies called for in the SCANS report. The first standards were a catalyst and the forerunners to the State Board–approved content standards in the four core academic subject areas.

In the fall of 1995, Assembly Bill 265 mandated the creation of a statewide assessment system that would be fully aligned to a set of content and performance standards. It further authorized the development of a four-core set of academic content standards and performance standards to be approved by the State Board of Education. English–language arts and mathematics were identified as the first content areas to be developed and to be followed by history–social science and science.

The California Standards Commission, composed of a demographic cross-section of teachers, administrators, and educational associations representing kindergarten through grade twelve, developed the content standards. After two years of work and numerous public hearings, the commission presented the standards to the State Board of Education for adoption.

In 1997 academic content standards in English–language arts and mathematics were adopted by the California State Board of Education. In the following year standards were adopted in two other important curricular areas, science and history–social science.

With the publication of the standards came a legislative mandate calling for every curriculum framework produced from that point forward to be fully aligned with the adopted standards. Furthermore, the frameworks would have to take on a very different role. Unlike frameworks of the past, new frameworks would serve an entirely new purpose, one that would link them inextricably to standards. To understand the new role of the new frameworks, one must first understand the role of standards.

As stated in the Introduction to each set of content standards: "Standards describe what to teach, not how to teach it." The standards serve to articulate those things that students at each grade level must know and be able to do by the end of that grade. However, the standards themselves are devoid of any discussion about the kind of instruction needed to lead students to master the standards. To that end the frameworks have been designed to provide an instructional context for the standards; they contain recommendations for instruction that are aligned with the standards.

Each content area framework uses the California standards as its curricular platform and aligns curriculum, assessment, instruction, and organization to provide a comprehensive, coherent structure for teaching and learning. Additionally, the frameworks guide the implementation of the standards through specifications for the design of instructional materials, curriculum, instruction, and professional development. They provide guidelines and selected research-based approaches for implementing instruction to ensure optimal benefits for all students, including students with special learning needs.

## Adoption of Instructional Materials

Instructional materials aligned to the standards is an essential tool for teachers. The following discussion excerpted from *Fact Book 2000: Handbook of Education Information* explains the adoption and funding process for instructional materials.

Primary adoptions [of textbooks] (i.e., the first adoption following the approval of a new state framework) are conducted every six years for the four core curriculum areas. . . . Primary adoptions in foreign language, visual and performing arts, and health are to be conducted every eight years. In all cases a follow-up adoption (using the same evaluation criteria) is to be scheduled between adoptions. . . .

Evaluation criteria based on the framework and the content standards are developed by the Curriculum Commission and adopted by the State Board. Following a statewide recruitment and thorough application process, the Curriculum Commission recommends and the State Board appoints two panels, the Instructional Materials Panel (IMAP) and the Content Review Panel (CRP). The IMAP is composed primarily of classroom teachers (but also includes other participants, such as administrators, curriculum specialists, university faculty, and parents) who evaluate materials according to all elements of the criteria. The CRP is composed of subject matter experts who review materials according to content criteria and ensure that the materials are accurate, aligned with State Board-adopted content standards in the four curricular areas, and contain current and confirmed research. The CRP serves as a resource for the IMAP.

The IMAP's and CRP's recommendations are forwarded to the Curriculum Commission. The Commission then develops a written report to the State Board containing its recommendation on each submission. . . . The State Board considers the Curriculum Commission's recommendations, related documents, and public comment prior to adopting or not adopting each submission.

### Instructional Materials and Funds

The Instructional Materials Fund (IMF) was established as ". . . a means of annually funding the acquisition of instructional materials" (*Education Code* Section 60240). For kindergarten through grade eight, the IMF is allocated to local educational agencies based on the average daily attendance. The IMF for grades nine through twelve is based on total enrollment. Section 60242 authorizes the State Board to establish a policy governing IMF expenditures for kindergarten through grade eight. This policy states that:

- At least 70 percent of IMF funds must be spent on state-adopted instructional materials.
- Up to 30 percent of IMF funds may be spent on nonadopted instructional materials that have passed the state legal compliance review; instructional materials that are exempt from a legal compliance review, such as trade books, maps and globes, reference materials (including dictionaries), mathematics manipulatives, and hand-held calculators; and instructional materials that are designed for use by pupils and their teachers as a learning resource [and] are integral to a program as defined in *Education Code* Section 60010(h) but do not contain print or pictures and, therefore, do not need a legal compliance review.
- Of the 30 percent, up to 5 percent of the total IMF funds may be spent on any instructional material which has passed a state-level or local-level legal compliance review; instructional television and distance learning; tests (*Education Code* Section 60242[a][3]);

in-service training (*Education Code* section 60242[a][5]); and/or binding basic textbooks (*Education Code* Section 60242[a][4]).[11]

With the curriculum frameworks and the content standards that they embody as the foundation, adoptions are a powerful leverage point for educational reform and improvement in student achievement. Instructional materials funding underscores the emphasis of State Board–approved, content standards-based materials as the foundation for student learning.

## Relevant Legislative Initiatives and Background

In an effort to move California toward a standards-based system of education mirroring national-level efforts, several key pieces of California legislation have been written and enacted in recent years. Collectively, these new laws form the foundation for the state's system of standards, assessment, and accountability. Figure 1-1 highlights that legislation.

## Comparison of California with Other States

A comparison of California's educational accomplishments with those of other states reveals that California is one of:

- Forty-nine states that have adopted standards in the core academic subjects of English–language arts, mathematics, history–social science, and science
- Fifty states that administer a statewide testing program
- Forty states that provide for annual report cards on the performance of individual schools

- Twenty-seven states that evaluate and issue public ratings of schools
- Fourteen states that reward successful schools in some way
- Twenty-one states that identify low-performing schools as part of their accountability system, requiring schools to write or revise a school improvement plan and obtain assistance to improve academically
- Eighteen states with legislative authority to close, take over, or reorganize a school that continues to underperform academically

## Summary of the Chapter

Calls for middle grades reform began in the late 1980s. Both *Caught in the Middle* and *Turning Points* focused their recommendations on creating a caring student-centered culture that would support high academic achievement.

A strong student-centered educational philosophy is entirely compatible with high academic expectations. This type of philosophy is a hallmark of excellence in schools which serve the middle grades. It is important to affirm the conviction that education in the middle grades should take place in a setting specifically designed to meet the academic, personal, and social needs and goals of students. Responding to the intensity of this challenge, while maintaining a clear perspective about the fundamental academic mission of public schooling, requires a firm hand on the helm in schools which serve young adolescents.[12]

Many of the recommendations in those publications have been implemented in schools in California and nationally as a result and are still valid today.

Subsequent research in the 1990s called for more precision and consistency in defining and

| California legislation | Approved/ chaptered | Summary of components addressed |
|---|---|---|
| Assembly Bill 265<br>*Education Code* sections 60600–60618 | October 1995 | Calls for a statewide assessment system, including both local and state tests; requires development of state content and performance standards |
| Senate Bill 376<br>*Education Code* sections 60640–60644 | October 1997 | Modifies the local portion of the statewide assessment system to instead require the use of a single state-selected, nationally normed test as part of the Statewide Testing and Reporting (STAR) Program; requires the nationally normed test to be augmented with test items aligned to the California content standards |
| Assembly Bill 1626<br>*Education Code* Section 48070 | August 1998 | Requires all school districts to adopt promotion and retention policies that require students to demonstrate basic proficiency in certain subjects and certain grades before they progress to the next grade |
| Senate Bill 1X<br>*Education Code* sections 52050–52058 | April 1999 | Establishes the Public School Performance Accountability Program, the *Academic Performance Index (API)*, the Immediate Intervention and Underperforming Schools Program (II/USP), and the Governor's High Achieving/Improving Schools Program; establishes the Public Schools Accountability Act |
| Senate Bill 2X<br>*Education Code* sections 60850–60856 | April 1999 | Authorizes the development of the *High School Exit Examination (HSEE)* (Beginning with the graduating class of 2004, California public school students must pass the *HSEE* to receive a high school diploma.) |
| Senate Bill 366<br>*Education Code* Section 60605.5 | October 1999 | Modifies the definition, development, and calendar for performance standards to include a system of levels, descriptors, and exemplars; sets November 2001 as the timeline for State Board of Education adoption of performance standards for all core content areas |
| Assembly Bill 2812<br>*Education Code* sections 60642.5 and 60649 | August 2000 | Modifies the statewide assessment system to eliminate an assessment of applied academic skills (matrix test); separates the *California Standards Tests* from the nationally normed test; refines the testing window for the STAR Program to ensure comparability of results for accountability purposes |
| Senate Bill 1354<br>*Education Code* Section 51224.5 | September 2000 | Requires all California students to pass Algebra 1 (or the equivalent) in order to graduate from high school beginning with the graduating class of 2004 |

measuring the expectations of "high academic achievement" and what students need when they move from school to the workplace. Reading and mathematics were identified as the enabling core for other content areas.

During the past decade California has taken significant steps to respond to the call for action. The response, relatively swift, has expectedly placed many new demands on educators and students for which they may not be ready. These changes are uncomfortable and fraught with unknowns. As educators, policymakers, parents, students, and communities move forward together, all will have a hand in clarifying and implementing the initiatives.

In a sense there is no conclusion to this chapter because there is no end to being responsive to the needs of our children. California's educators, kindergarten through grade twelve, are committed to the students they serve. Middle grades educators take center stage in their continuing and future efforts in guiding young adolescents through a pivotal period of human development and propelling them to high academic achievement.

# California's Middle Schools:
# Poised for World-Class Performance

- **Periodic review of a school's mission and vision statements provides direction and focus for all staff.** Is your school vision consistent with the middle grades philosophy and standards-based education? Has your staff had the opportunity to review *Caught in the Middle* and *Turning Points 2000?* Share your thoughts about what it means to have a student-centered standards-based program.

- **Recent state legislation has been enacted to move California schools to standards-based education.** How has the legislation (see Figure 1-1) affected the ways in which you plan course offerings? How has your staff organized to increase reading levels in your school? In what ways have you and your staff considered algebra preparation for *all* your students? Have collaborative discussions and planning with feeder elementary schools and destination high schools taken place about what students should know and be able to do in reading and mathematics?

- **Content area teachers know the value of articulation with high school staff.** Has your staff been a part of discussions with high school staff about *High School Exit Examination* criteria? What is (would be) the role and responsibility of each? Have mathematics teachers discussed how to get all students prepared for algebra? What new strategies will be required to ensure success on the *High School Exit Examination* for struggling students? Accelerated students? Students with special needs?

- **The California Middle Grades Partnership Network has played a major role in implementing standards-based middle grades reform.** Have you had opportunities to review the frameworks and standards and share issues, challenges, and concerns about standards-based education with colleagues at your site? With colleagues in your district? Middle grades educators in your county? How can sharing with colleagues help your school implement the findings and recommendations found in *Taking Center Stage?* Become a state-of-the-art middle school? Explore knowledge and research about increased academic and intellectual development for your students? (See Appendix 1-A.)

- **As middle schools respond to the various state initiatives, a need will arise to clarify new roles for educational stakeholders.** How have you helped students, their families, and community supporters understand the transition to standards-based education and assessment? What will it mean to hold everyone accountable? Teachers and administrators? Students and families? Policymakers and community supporters? What will you need from each to ensure student success?

# Appendix 1-A

# California Middle Grades Partnership Network

*". . . leaders in collaborative networking for student success"*

Schools do not need to implement middle grades philosophy and standards-based education in isolation. Nor do they have to reinvent the same wheel. The California Middle Grades Partnership Network's multischool professional development activities can have a liberating effect on administrators and teachers who feel part of a greater collegial effort.

Middle schools that network are able more effectively to:

- Improve student achievement through standards-based education.
- Promote research and knowledge about young adolescent learning.
- Initiate collegial dialogue across school and district boundaries.
- Share the successes and challenges of managing, operating, and teaching in a middle school.

- Pool and share resources to leverage others who affect middle grades education.
- Serve as a resource to the school, the community, and other education stakeholders.
- Implement the initiatives of the California Department of Education and national initiatives (e.g., *Taking Center Stage, Turning Points 2000,* eighth-grade algebra, middle grades reading, and other student support interventions).
- Prepare students for the rigors of high school and beyond.

For more information about the California Middle Grades Partnership Network, telephone the Middle Grades and High School Networks Office, California Department of Education, at (916) 322-1892.

# Appendix 1-B

# SCANS Workplace Know-How

The U.S. Department of Labor, through the Secretary's Commission on Achieving Necessary Skills (SCANS), has published a now-famous report that addresses personal abilities needed for employment and effective ways to assess them. Included in the report are *thinking skills* and *personal qualities.* Some of the competencies can be reformatted under the *study skills* and *emotional and social growth* categories of school report cards. (See the "Prototype Performance Report Card" in Chapter 2, Figure 2-3).

## Workplace Competencies

Effective workers can productively use:

- *Resources.* They know how to allocate time, money, materials, space, and staff.
- *Interpersonal skills.* They can work on teams, teach others, serve customers, lead, negotiate, and work well with people from culturally diverse backgrounds.
- *Information.* They can acquire and evaluate data, organize and maintain files, interpret and communicate, and use computers to process information.
- *Systems.* They understand social, organizational, and technological systems; they can monitor and correct performance; and they can design or improve systems.
- *Technology.* They can select equipment and tools, apply technology to specific tasks, and maintain and troubleshoot equipment.

## Foundation Skills

Competent workers in the high-performance workplace need:

*Basic Skills:* The student reads, writes, performs arithmetic and mathematical operations, listens, and speaks:

- *Reading*—locates, understands, and interprets written information in prose and in documents such as manuals, graphs, and schedules
- *Writing*—communicates thoughts, ideas, information, and messages in writing; and creates documents such as letters, directions, manuals, reports, graphs, and flowcharts
- *Arithmetic/mathematics*—performs basic computations and approaches practical problems by choosing appropriately from a variety of mathematical techniques
- *Listening*—receives, attends to, interprets, and responds to verbal messages and other cues
- *Speaking*—organizes ideas and communicates orally

*Thinking Skills:* The student thinks creatively, makes decisions, solves problems, visualizes, knows how to learn, and reasons:

- *Creative thinking*—generates new ideas
- *Decision making*—specifies goals and constraints, generates alternatives, considers risks, and evaluates and chooses best alternative
- *Problem solving*—recognizes problems and devises and implements a plan of action
- *Seeing things in the mind's eye*—organizes and processes symbols, pictures, graphs, objects, and other information

From *What Work Requires of Schools: A SCANS Report for America 2000.* Washington, D.C.: U.S. Department of Labor, 1991.

- *Knowing how to learn*—uses efficient learning techniques to acquire and apply new knowledge and skills
- *Reasoning*—discovers a rule or principle underlying the relationship between two or more objects and applies it when solving a problem

*Personal Qualities:* The student displays responsibility, self-esteem, sociability, self-management, and integrity and honesty:

- *Responsibility*—exerts a high level of effort and perseveres toward goal attainment

- *Self-esteem*—believes in . . . self-worth and maintains a positive view of self
- *Sociability*—demonstrates understanding, friendliness, adaptability, empathy, and politeness in group settings
- *Self-management*—assesses self accurately, sets personal goals, monitors progress, and exhibits self-control
- *Integrity and honesty*—chooses ethical courses of action

*"Imagine a school . . . in which all children excel to high levels, regardless of their background. Imagine a school that treats all children as gifted and builds on their strengths through enrichment strategies, independent research, problem solving, science, writing, music, and art. Imagine a school in which all members of the school community develop a vision of their ideal school and in which they collaborate to achieve that dream by making major decisions about curriculum, instructional strategies, and school organization. Imagine a school where ideas count. Let your imagination go as far as it can."* [That school is within our reach.]

—Accelerated Schools Project

# Standards-Based Education Takes Center Stage: Content and Performance Standards

hen a new play is to be produced, each actor gets the same script from which to work. And when a new game is to be played, each player gets the same set of rules because fairness requires common understanding, expectations, and a willingness to play by the rules. Chaos would occur on the stage if every actor worked from a different script and on the playing field if every team played by a different set of rules. Mutual understanding and expectations do not decrease the actor's ability to be creative or the athlete's ability to be spontaneous and respon-

Recommendations 1, 2, 4, 9, 11

sive. In fact, these common sets of rules and expectations heighten the experience for all participants. When everyone knows the parameters, the challenge and energy are focused on the means to achieve the end.

## A Promise for Increased Academic Achievement

Equity and excellence in education also require a common set of expectations and a willingness to play by the rules. Standards-based education holds the promise of fairness and increased academic achievement for all students because of its rigorous, uniform expectations. Although educational goals for students have long existed, they have not always been rigorous or consistent and have been subjected to interpretation and misinterpretation by teachers, parents, and the general public. When the expectations and outcomes are clear and consistent, teachers are able to focus their professional attention on delivering a rich standards-based curriculum and responding to the targeted needs of their students.

Instead of perceiving that process as a top-down approach, many middle-level teachers see it as a liberating feature of standards-based education that defines the curriculum more precisely. Because the most important knowledge and skills are identified in the standards, teachers no longer feel pressured to cover all the content presented in many textbooks and therefore become more confident and comfortable in their work.

Higher achievement through standards-based education holds promise for all students regardless of their socioeconomic or ethnic backgrounds; those who are gifted; those with disabilities; those who speak English well and for those who are learning the language. Standards-based education promises equity in a student's access to consistent, high expectations provided by teachers employing a rich, standards-driven curriculum.

A school is measured by the achievement of all its students. Standards-based reform, a system of standards, assessments, and accountability, not only holds the promise of moving all students toward high, consistent expectations but also attempts to close the achievement gap between those who have been advantaged and those who have not through targeted assessment and immediate interventions. Most instruction takes place in inclusive, heterogeneous classrooms in which differentiated instruction is the

norm. Appropriate intervention strategies would include targeted, flexible grouping within a classroom or team teaching; targeted, accelerated assistance to struggling students as a supplement to their regular classrooms; and targeted, supplemental acceleration for advanced students requiring more challenges outside a heterogeneous classroom.

Establishing content and performance standards in schools that expect high achievement of all students begins with specific efforts to weed out policies and practices that divide students into those who have had advantages and those who have not. Any differentiation among learning opportunities that may produce negative consequences for students is counterproductive and inappropriate. A high-quality middle school is measured by the achievement of all its students as opposed to that of its best students or even the average performance of all its students.

Teachers and principals must ensure that the gap between high performance and low performance is as narrow as possible. Higher expectations for all students can exaggerate the gap for students at risk if support and early interventions are not provided for the latter. Students with learning deficits, specific disabilities, or limited-English proficiency require differentiated instruction and early interventions to succeed.

Just as educators were led by compelling arguments to initiate middle grades reform throughout California in the 1980s, they are now challenged to increase academic achievement for all students and to close the achievement gap by implementing standards-based education. The strength of a middle grades philosophy, together with the practice of standards-based education, offers an unprecedented opportunity for increased student achievement within a school culture that is focused on the needs of the young adolescent.

Both content and performance standards are central to the shift from a curriculum-based paradigm to one highlighting standards. At center stage in a standards-based education system are the statements of desired learning results, known as *content standards,* and descriptions of student achievement and proficiency, known as *performance standards.* Each standard, integral to a standards-based system, will be discussed more fully.

## Content Standards

Content standards define for each subject and grade level the most important knowledge that students must acquire and the skills that they must master. Standards are the clear and consistent targets toward which educators are expected to aim and students are expected to reach. The most widely used definition of a content standard is "what students should know and be able to do." Exemplary standards usually have specific characteristics. Figure 2-1 shows characteristics of exemplary content standards.

The characteristics listed in Figure 2-1 control the following discussion and generate questions about the issues and concrete applicability of standards in the middle grades.

### Content Standards: Concerned with Big Ideas (1)

Big ideas and essential concepts are the foundation on which the curriculum is built and lessons are planned. Through collaborative planning and teaching, students are given many opportunities in many contexts to become proficient in using the standards for which they are held accountable.

Middle grades philosophy promotes a demanding, relevant curriculum and interdisciplinary team teaching. Collaborative lesson planning that incorporates big ideas across the curriculum and shares responsibility for essential standards can consolidate the workload and provide students with more time for in-depth learning. All classes can support academic core standards to some degree. The degree to which academic and nonacademic classes support the core standards should be an essential part of collaborative staff discussions.

Initiatives of the 1990s underscore the importance of teaching the core standards. The California State Testing and Reporting (STAR) Program is composed of a norm-referenced test (the *Stanford Achievement Test, Ninth Edition, Form T* [*SAT 9*]) and the *California Standards Tests. The California Standards Tests* are aligned directly with the core standards and when fully developed will be the state's primary, large-scale assessment of standards performance in grades two through eleven.

The *High School Exit Examination (HSEE),* given to California's high school students as early as grade nine, is aligned with the state standards in English–language arts for grades nine and ten, and to key Algebra 1 and mathematics standards for grades six and seven. Early student success on the *High School Exit Examination* reflects preparation in the middle grades more than in the first year of high school.

Teaching middle grades students to be proficient in their grade-level standards in the four core academic areas with an initial emphasis on English–language arts and mathematics has the highest priority. The core academic subjects of science and history–social science will eventually become part of the *Academic Performance Index (API)* and may eventually become a part of the *HSEE*.

The science and history–social science standards are the last components to be folded into the accountability system. However, their importance in the curriculum or the instructional attention they receive should not be diminished. It would be very shortsighted to concentrate on English–language arts and mathematics and exclude science and history–social science. Teachers should not direct their instruction to a particular assessment or

---

**Figure 2-1    Characteristics of Content Standards**

1. **Content standards are concerned with big ideas.** Standards should contain the major concepts and essential ideas that students must master in order to grasp the content. Being able to understand mathematics by making inferences is different from memorizing formulas.

2. **Content standards are accurate and sound.** Standards should reflect the most recent, widely accepted scholarship in the discipline. Because facts and concepts change rapidly today, when new information is constantly being generated, maintaining accuracy and balance among the important concepts requires continual revision. Documents related to content learning should be updated regularly.

3. **Content standards are clear and useful.** Standards should be specific enough to drive the curriculum. They should not be written in language so abstract or technical that teachers, parents, and students cannot easily understand them.

4. **Content standards are parsimonious.** Standards should reflect the depth of learning. Standards should be few and brief and short enough to be memorable because they are strong, bold statements, not details of content description (the details are in the curriculum).

5. **Content standards are built by consensus.** Standards must be arrived at by most of the constituency who will use them. Conversations about standards are as important as the standards themselves.

6. **Content standards are assessable.** Standards should have verbs that indicate an assessable action. Words like "compare," "explain," or "analyze" are useful for assessments. Words like "understand" or "appreciate" are not.

7. **Content standards are for students.** Standards should evidence a clear sense of increased knowledge and sophistication of skills. Standards that simply repeat content and specify "more" at successive levels are not useful. Benchmarks, or target levels for assessment, should indicate developmentally appropriate content knowledge and skills.

8. **Content standards are visionary.** Standards should be the goal of student learning. They should not describe "what is" or "this is where we are" but rather, "this is where we want our students to be."[1]

component of the *Academic Performance Index* but should use a balanced, long-term approach, integrating the big ideas and key standards across the four core areas. They should teach to the standards, and the students should work to become proficient in meeting those standards. Assessments and indexes simply measure and analyze progress toward that goal.

Exploratory and elective classes play an important role in the lives of adolescents. As they pass from childhood to young adulthood, students need to develop a broader schema of opportunities and assess their interests and talents beyond traditional core subjects. Often, they become motivated to learn academics when they pursue the adjunct curriculum. However, because of the focus on the academic core content standards, particularly those for mathematics and English–language arts, valid concern exists among teachers in the middle grades and in high school that other classes might be ignored and resources might be deleted. Included might be classes in foreign languages, the visual and performing arts, health, technology, adolescent skills, vocational-career technical, and service learning.

Educators and local communities should address this important challenge together and find ways to maintain elective classes. Many schools are defending their elective programs by demonstrating how their elective curriculum supports the core academic standards. If the links to core standards are lacking, some schools are providing more opportunities for developing skills in problem solving, reading, writing, speaking, listening, and delivering presentations. Other schools are maintaining their electives by creating alternative interven-

tion programs for struggling students by organizing programs before and after school and on Saturdays.

The academic core standards and the big ideas are at center stage. As the stars of the show, they capture the spotlight. Although supporting roles and side acts add interest and vitality to the curriculum, they should not detract from the focus, but add to it.

### Content Standards: Parsimonious, Clear and Useful, Accurate and Sound (2, 3, 4)

Collectively, these characteristics mean that a few key standards are provided for each subject at each grade level. Those standards are well articulated and are specific enough to be useful to teachers but are also easily understood by parents. In the English–language arts standards for grade seven, for example, there are 15 reading standards, 12 writing standards related to strategies and applications, seven related to conventions (grammar, mechanics, punctuation, spelling), 12 related to listening and speaking strategies and applications (see also Appendix 2-A, "The New California Curriculum Frameworks," at the end of this chapter). Standards in the other core areas are similarly few and concise. In comparison with the phone-book-size scope and sequence curriculum binders that most teachers have in their classrooms, the content standards represent a short, concise version of what students should know and be able to do at each grade level in each core content area.

Many teachers have the standards posted in their classrooms. Because the standards are written at an adult reading level, some teachers have rephrased the standards for emerging readers. Provided that the content standards are not compromised or misinterpreted, they may be simplified to prevent misunderstanding in communicating with students, parents, and the general public.

California's standards are not excessively detailed, usually containing only a few pages per content area within a grade level. Nonetheless, they call for deep learning and academic rigor through the highest levels of cognitive thinking. Collectively, the standards in the academic core areas make a powerful statement about what is expected of students at each grade level. In California the state frameworks, detailed documents that reflect current scholarship and strategies for teaching the standards to all students, serve as the instructional context for the standards.

Middle grades classrooms organized to integrate curriculum and team teaching may be best prepared to handle the demands of the standards. Although the standards are few and concise, they must be looked at collectively to clarify what each standard means and in what context it can best be taught. Collaborative discussion helps answer the question of how standards might be effectively organized and taught so that they do not overwhelm staff and students. The author of *Making Standards Work*, Douglas Reeves, suggests identifying power standards and clustering others under them.[2]

### Content Standards: Built by Consensus (5)

California's content and performance standards have been forged through rigorous debate and a process involving a cross-section of stakeholders, including educators, content experts, and the public. Involvement of the

stakeholders at the state and local levels is an important aspect of any reform effort. Consensus stretches beyond the initial development and adoption of content standards. For standards-based education to be effective at local levels, mutual understanding and support of standards-based education by the stakeholders (policymakers, administrators, teachers, staff, parents, students, and community) is an ongoing process. Consensus building and communication align expectations, garner support, connect resources, and establish accountability.

The leadership of superintendents and principals in standards-based education is essential to successful reform. Through such leadership, the stakeholders are brought together to explore issues, develop proactive programs, build capacity to support classroom instruction, and solve problems.

If classroom teachers are to be successful in standards-based instruction, they need broad-based support from their schools, school districts, and communities. Standards-based education requires collaborative, time-intensive work by teachers beyond daily preparation and direct contact time with students. A few of the important responsibilities beyond the classroom of the standards-focused teacher and the school principal are participating in professional development and collaborative planning, matching lessons and standards, developing performance tasks and scoring criteria, evaluating student work, analyzing data, and planning focused interventions.

School districts and schools are held accountable for improved student achievement. Schools that consistently fail to meet their growth targets are subject to state sanctions; those that meet their targets are rewarded. Teachers are encouraged, coached, and evaluated by principals familiar with the standards and who are in turn supported by superintendents who are also familiar with them. Struggling students are provided with ongoing targeted interventions to help them achieve proficiency, and parents are asked to support student participation in supplemental learning opportunities. Growth and accountability are expected of all participants. Emphasis is given continually to communicating the purposes of standards-based education to parents and the general public. Ample opportunity should also be provided to develop professional and public consensus about content standards as an ongoing process.

Education based on the standards should be undertaken in full cooperation with teachers' unions and other professional organizations. Any change as sweeping and intense in its implications for teachers' professional practice as standards-based education can prosper only with the sustained support of those entities.

Middle grades students, their parents, and their teachers are caught up in the daily challenges of young adolescents. Quicksilver emotions, adolescent perceptions, and behavior that tests the boundaries can be the breeding ground for misunderstanding. If ever in a child's life consistent, clear expectations and communications are needed, it is during the middle school years. Keeping middle grades parents, students, and the community informed and involved is vital. Regular communications to the home, opportunities for parents to visit

the school and participate, and public recognition of the achievements of young adolescents foster a positive climate in which standards-based education thrives.

## Content Standards: Assessable (6)

Assessability is an important transitional characteristic of a content standard that leads to performance standards. The statements of expectation are written with active verbs that students can demonstrate and teachers can measure.

Merely the *knowing* of how to do something is passive. However, application of that knowledge is active and observable. There is a saying that "knowledge is power." In fact, knowledge without application is essentially powerless. It is the application of what we know, the "doing" part of the content standard, that is powerful. Knowledge is the lowest level of a cognitive taxonomy. "Doing" stretches adolescent minds into the higher levels of thinking. The ability to assess what students know and can do is the foundation for diagnosing, building on strengths, and eliminating weaknesses in student learning and in instruction (see Chapter 3).

Middle grades students abound with kinetic energy. Those who teach at the middle levels know that active, hands-on learning has strong appeal for young adolescents. The "doing" part of content standards lends itself to projects and activities that students can work on in groups or as individuals. When the "do" part of the standard is explicit, students understand clearly what is expected of them, and it is an instructional target the teacher can assess.

## Content Standards: Designed for Students (7)

The content standards are student-centered and describe what students should know and be able to do at each grade level. The standards are developmental and increase in complexity and sophistication with each instructional year. Teachers who fail to teach to their grade-level standards begin a pattern of curriculum slippage.

Curriculum slippage creates an insidious problem for students and for their subsequent teachers. Students are ultimately held accountable for being proficient in grade-level standards, and it is the educators' responsibility to provide students the opportunity to learn the grade-level standards for which students will be held accountable. If students are moved to the next grade level without all the requisite knowledge and skills, they become disadvantaged. Teachers feel compelled to remediate the deficit from the previous year(s) at the expense of their own grade-level standards, and the pattern of curriculum slippage continues. Accelerated intervention and instructional strategies for students who lack the requisite skills are discussed in Chapters 11 and 12.

Instructional time is always a scarce commodity requiring expert maximization. Classroom time on task for students is highly valued. If, however, the task is not related to becoming proficient at grade-level content standards, one must question the use of time. There are, of course, many lessons students must learn and teachers want to teach that are not explicitly a part of the standards. Skillful teachers weave these adjunct lessons into a curriculum without sacrificing valuable standards-based instructional time. As teachers engage in standards reform, reflection and critical review of lessons and activities should be their basis for making

necessary changes (see also Appendix 2-B, "Face to Face with Content Standards: An Interview with a Teacher," at the end of this chapter).

Most teachers are surprised when matching (calibrating) lessons to standards. Much of what good teachers already teach is standards-based. In calibrating lessons, even good teachers will make discoveries about minimal exposure to some standards and overexposure to other standards (particularly earlier grade-level standards) and activities that are not connected to standards in any way. A critical reflection on one's lessons is the basis for deciding what stays, what goes, and what needs to be reshaped or enhanced (see also Appendix 2-C, "Curriculum Calibration, Lessons Learned from Underperforming Schools," at the end of this chapter).

Middle grades educators have a particularly difficult challenge because the minds of young adolescents can be resistant to academic rigor. For students of this particular age group, peer relationships often have a higher priority than academics. Adolescent social, emotional, and behavioral needs may conflict with the teachers' needs to deliver increasingly complex and sophisticated content.

Good middle grades teachers are masters at capturing the attention of these youngsters and delivering a high-interest, youth-centered curriculum based on standards. Effective teachers produce measurable results. Staffing middle grades schools with caring, competent, standards-based teachers takes a special commitment by districts. The skills and strategies to manage classrooms, maximize instructional time, and plan and deliver engaging, lively youth-focused, standards-based instruction does not just happen. Opportunities for ongoing professional development, coaching, and collaborative work should be the hallmarks of a standards-based school.

## Content Standards: Visionary (8)

Few would argue that the California standards and expectations are not high enough. The standards are "forward-focused" and reflect where we want our students to be so that they can ultimately become successful and responsible adults. It is painfully obvious from national and statewide test scores, the *Academic Performance Index,* and local assessment measures that educators and students have much work to do and progress to make. The gap in achievement and the gap between reality and vision can be significantly closed with a committed focus to standards at every grade level.

Middle grades students are not only young adolescents with a unique set of transitional emotional and social behaviors; they are the educational products of elementary education. When students come to the middle grades, many do not possess the requisite skills and knowledge to get them to where we want them to be within the short time (two or three years) that they spend in the middle grades. The *High School Exit Examination* adds a high-stakes urgency to what is to be accomplished in the middle years. In the short term, middle grades cannot wait for the current wave of elementary students to catch up. Interim interventions need to be planned and implemented to equip middle grades students for the forward-focused standards they will be required to master for high school graduation. There will very likely be increased support and initiatives from the state to assist middle grades educators in helping

students achieve and be prepared for the rigors of high school.

Short-term and long-term articulation with feeder elementary schools and destination high schools is of paramount importance, particularly in nonunified districts. Several questions will undoubtedly arise: How can we get teachers at all levels to teach to the standards so that the grade-level transition of students lacking proficiency in earlier standards is only a temporary problem? What measures will we use to evaluate students' mastery of standards as they exit elementary school, enter middle school, exit middle school, and enter high school? What can we do to accelerate remediation now? What can we do to assist students with immediate and ongoing interventions? How can we use business and community resources to help in this effort? How can we "package" the academic rigor for young adolescents in ways that motivate, inspire, and connect them to the bigger picture?

Understandably, schools may differ in the progress they make in implementing standards-based education. The implementation process is arduous and time intensive, and progress is made in increments. Most districts have adopted the California State Board of Education's content standards in English–language arts, mathematics, history–social science, and science for kindergarten through high school. Some districts have used the State Board's content standards to develop their own standards that meet or exceed the State Board's standards. This is a permissible practice, but it may create a challenge for a district trying to align its standards to state assessments and state-adopted instructional materials.

## Performance Standards

California's comprehensive system of standards, assessment, and accountability calls for a coordinated system of content standards and performance standards. The most widely used and somewhat abstract definition of a performance standard is that it answers the question, How good is good enough? The content standards describe what students should know and be able to do. Their demonstrable learning is measured against a performance standard that determines the degree to which the student has mastered the content.

The state's performance standards represent a system that includes multiple, interdependent components:

- Performance levels—labels for each level of student achievement
- Descriptions of student performance (performance descriptors)—descriptive narratives about student performance at each performance level
- Examples of student work (exemplars)— samples of student work that are pulled from a representative sample of all students and that illustrate the range of performance within each level
- Cut scores on assessments—designated scores that separate one performance level from the next

The performance standards will categorize student performance only on the *California Standards Tests*. The English–language arts assessment will be the first in which students are measured against the performance standards. Mathematics will follow.

The State Board of Education has examined a variety of existing performance standard models and has selected the following performance levels:

- Advanced
- Proficient
- Basic
- Below basic
- Far below basic

The statewide standards-setting process will determine California's specific cut scores on the *California Standards Tests* for each of the performance levels. The State Board is expected to set the "proficient" level as the target level for all students.

Performance standards at the state level are summative (end-of-year). They are broad and refer to an entire set of standards in a content area as opposed to specific content standards. Performance standard results from broad, summative assessments are an appropriate means of providing trend data for school and district accountability purposes and general planning. It does not, however, provide formative (ongoing) feedback to students about their progress toward mastery of specific content standards. A formative performance standard system at the local level is critical to measuring student achievement. If local performance levels are linked with the state's, the expectations provide a consistent target for teachers and students.

## Performance Standards at the Local Level

The content standards are rigorous, and students attain mastery of them by degrees. While students are learning and acquiring the necessary skills, they should be informed continually of their progress in specific terms. A performance standard system developed at a local level provides important feedback to students, reports progress to parents, informs instructional practice, and serves as a basis for policymakers and administrators to allocate services and resources where they are most needed.

A local performance standard system should have the same integral, component parts as the state's performance standard system: performance levels, descriptors, exemplars, and cut scores. A broad cross-section of California's educators, assessment psychometricians, and policymakers have invested countless hours and expertise in developing performance standards for California's students. Districts do not need to start from scratch. A district could use the levels and descriptors developed by the state and focus its efforts on developing exemplars and uniform scoring criteria for locally developed benchmark assessment/assignments. The district's cut scores between performance levels could be parallel to or more rigorous than those of the state. Exemplars and uniform scoring criteria, with teachers evaluating student work, are essential for frequent and formative feedback.

Usually, performance standards are developed collegially. Under the leadership and guidance of a district, teachers of the same subject and at the same grade level work together to achieve reasonable consensus about the components of a performance standard system and the products to be developed. For instance, exemplars, by definition, are samples of student work that exemplify various ways to demonstrate performance. The student work collected for review and evaluation is not an odd assortment of assignments and assessments. The exemplars are specific to a uniform (standardized) assignment/assessment that is aligned to specific standards and given to all students of the same subject and grade level.

A common misconception is that performance standards must match content standards on a one-to-one basis. Because more than 200 content standards exist in the core subjects for each of the middle grades, standards-based education would soon be badly impaired if performance standards and scoring criteria had to be developed for all standards. Consequently, some schools are identifying *key* content standards and clustering other standards around them. This practice results in economy of time, and plentiful opportunities are provided for planning assignments that integrate a wider array of skills, concepts, and cross-curricular standards.

Through the collaborative process, content area teachers and the principal do the following:

1. Select the standards they want to assess (not too many at one time or the assessment becomes too long, unfocused, and difficult to evaluate).
2. Determine what evidence they need to collect from students that will demonstrate whether the students are gaining or have gained the necessary proficiency in the content standards.
3. Develop a question, prompt, or task that they think will elicit the evidence. (Assessment items usually go through a series of refinements based on actual student responses before they are perfected.) (See Chapter 3.)
4. Agree upon the way the assessment will be administered so that all students have

equal access to time and resources (exclusive of students who require documented special accommodations).

5. Develop an initial scoring guide (rubric-criteria) based on what is expected. Typically, scoring guides are based on four levels, five levels, or six levels, depending on the level of specific feedback desired for teachers and students (see Appendix 3-A for a four-point scoring guide for grade-seven writing).

6. Decide on a cut score that separates score points. (There is a cut score for each level, but the critical ones are those between the levels that will trigger targeted-accelerated assistance to those students just below proficiency (basic) and immediate interventions for those students who are below basic performance levels.)

7. Administer the assessment/assignment and reconvene with the student work to be evaluated. Read several papers, and based on initial scoring criteria, sort them into score-point categories.

8. Discuss student work samples.

   a. Were expected responses received?
   b. Do the scoring criteria need to be simplified, expanded, or refined to take into account that which was not expected?

9. Agree and defend why each of the student "exemplars" fits the finalized scoring criteria and score point received. (This "like mindedness" is referred to as calibration and gives a teacher the confidence to score anonymous papers with the same expertise and objectivity as colleague teachers across the district.)

These initial steps outline the time-intensive collaborative process teachers and principals go through to develop assessment assignments, scoring guides, exemplars, and cut points for a first-time performance task. The teachers score all papers, using the scoring guide and exemplars, also called anchor papers, as their references. The first time scoring a new assessment is always the most difficult and most time intensive. After the work is scored and recorded, the data can be used to inform subsequent instruction and make important decisions about interventions and resources.

The score a student receives on a formative assessment is often referred to as a performance indicator or benchmark score. The performance indicator may be one of several performance indicators (multiple measures) that determine the performance level. Figure 2-2 shows how a performance standard system is an integral part of curriculum, instruction, assessment, and accountability.

The benefits of developing a local performance standard system that is aligned with state performance levels are as powerful explicitly as they are implicitly. Explicitly, students benefit by having their work evaluated consistently and fairly by a like-minded audience (district evaluators and evaluators statewide). Teachers and parents can see how their students' work aligns with exemplars and know specifically what their students need to accomplish to get to the next level. Teachers with like perceptions of what constitutes proficiency know how to create additional classroom learning opportunities and how to

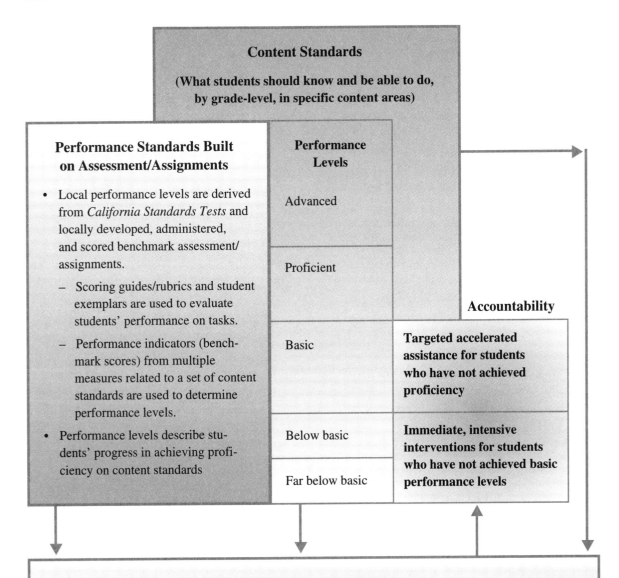

differentiate the instruction for students who are on the threshold of proficiency. Teachers and principals can identify those students who need supplemental classroom assistance and rally the necessary resources. The process is open and fair.

Implicitly, teachers and principals learn from one another and the process. They conduct high-level professional discussions about developing assessment strategies, the quality of student work, identification of exemplars, and scoring criteria that identify performance levels. Furthermore, the implicit value of this work builds a trusting relationship with colleagues and breaks down the isolation that classroom teachers often experience. Teachers reflect on how they can improve their lessons, and they begin to share best practices, a quantum step toward sharing and coaching one another to excellence. Teachers who participate on statewide assessment leadership teams (*Golden State Examinations* [*GSE*], *Assessments in Career Education* [*ACE*]) frequently remark that the process is one of the best, practical professional development experiences in their careers.

## Performance Standards and Grades

Not all students will achieve the same quality of work. In a standards-based system, the quality of student work is measured against established performance standards. Similar to grades, performance standards describe how well students perform relative to content and generally answer the question, How good is good enough?

Unlike traditional classroom grades, however, performance standards are specifically aligned to grade-level content standards and do not include subjective factors such as classroom values, weighting, curved scores, effort, behavior, promptness on assignments, and special accommodations. The distinction is important. It may be tempting to try to equate grades with performance standards, but it would be inadvisable to do so.

Performance standards are consensually developed, and they uniformly describe levels of performance related to content standards. When decisions are made about instruction, retention, promotion, intervention, remediation, or acceleration, the performance standards serve as objective, credible guides. Traditional grades are not consistent in a standards-based system (see also Appendix 2-D, "Grading in a Standards-Based System: Fundamental Questions," at the end of this chapter).

Serious confusion can occur when classroom teachers give letter grades that do not reflect the same criteria as performance-level expectations. Furthermore, in *Transforming Classroom Grading,*[3] Robert Marzano says, "A single letter grade or a percentage score is not a good way to report student achievement in any subject area because it simply cannot present the level of detailed feedback necessary for effective learning."

Letter grading is deeply ingrained in our culture. Parents expect letter grades. Teachers use them to motivate students, and grade point averages are used in determining college admission. The whole culture of grades is not one that can be or should be changed overnight.

However, in a system that bases accountability practices and high-stakes decisions on consistent, valid, and reliable data, traditional classroom grading practices are inadequate. A performance-level reporting system takes time to develop and implement. Districts may first want to develop a concurrent performance reporting system in addition to using traditional grades and then eventually work toward a single reporting system.

Assessment practices and the reporting of performance levels should provide a means by which students can accurately measure their progress toward achieving desired proficiency. Content and performance standards provide unmistakable evidence of what is expected to be learned and how well it should be learned. Those expectations are clear. With content and performance standards, student assessment data are credible, defensible, and, perhaps most important, understandable to students and their parents.

## Creation of a Standards-Based Performance Report

More than 200 content standards exist for each of the three middle grades (sixth, seventh, and eighth). It is improbable that a student performance report can be devised to include that much information. However, some software companies are getting close to that level of specificity. The prototype student performance report in Figure 2-3 identifies the major categories of content standards for English–language arts, mathematics, history–social science, and science and could be generated without sophisticated technology.

Figure 2-4 is an analysis of what a fictional student in grade seven achieved over the course of a year on a prototype performance report.

This prototype includes many of the elements that districts are currently using. It is informative, not prescriptive, for schools and districts. It assumes that schools will be providing ongoing multiple opportunities to help students become proficient (before-school and after-school activities, Saturday school, elective-replacement proficiency labs, intersessions, and summer school), that a performance standard system is being developed or is in place, and that the earned performance level of a student on the *California Standards Tests* will provide additional credible information for the district and school.

It also assumes that schools recognize that grade retention is a poor substitute educationally, psychologically, and financially for enhancing student achievement. Retention is the last intervention when all other options have failed (see Chapters 8, 9, 10, and 11 of this publication for more information).

The content standards for the visual and performing arts, health, and physical education are in development and are represented very simply on the prototype performance report. Exploratory and elective classes are organized differently at different school sites and are examples of what might be offered. Many of the study skills reflect the competencies asked for in the SCANS report (see Appendix 1-B).

Essential elements that should be on a standards-based performance report include a clear message to parents about:

- What their children should know and be able to do (content standards)
- How well their children are doing relative to the content standards (performance standards/levels)

Figure 2-3    Prototype Student Performance Report

## Standards-Based Education: Your School's Commitment to Excellence

*Standards-based education* represents a major commitment to academic excellence. It is very important for students and parents to understand how the process works:

- *Content standards* state what are the most important things for a student to know and/or to be able to do (i.e., new knowledge and skills to be learned in each subject and at each grade level).

- *Performance standards* represent the degree to which a student has achieved proficiency in mastering an overall set or subset of standards within a content area for a specific grade-level. Performance standards are expressed in **performance levels** and are derived from standardized, benchmark assessment/assignments *and other appropriate measures.*

- **Standardized benchmark assessments and assignments** are aligned to specific standards, uniformly administered and scored, and are used throughout the year to measure all students' progress. The results of these assessment/assignments are referred to as a benchmark score or performance indicator and become a part of the data used to determine a student's performance level.

  - Traditional assessments: Tests and quizzes that feature selected response items – true, false, multiple choice, fill in the blank, short written or constructed response. These assessments provide evidence of student knowledge, comprehension, and the skills necessary for application and analysis.

  - Performance assessments: Essays, complex problem solving, projects, presentations, or any other performance tasks that call for students to demonstrate their acquired knowledge and skills. These assessments provide evidence of a student's creative, analytical, organizational, and interpretive skills in using acquired knowledge.

  - *Rubrics/Scoring Guides* are used to evaluate the quality of student work on performance assessments.

### School Accountability

- All teachers focus their instruction on standards identified for their subject in each area of the core curriculum.
- All students are provided at the beginning of the school year with the standards for each subject in which they are enrolled.
- All students are provided with information about how their work will be evaluated and how their level of performance will be determined. There are to be no surprises.
- All teachers seek to modify instruction to meet a wide variety of learning styles and levels of ability.
- The school provides supplemental assistance and interventions for students who are not meeting performance standards. Parents will be invited to participate in decisions regarding supplemental programs.

## Your Town Middle School
### XYZ Unified School District

Prototype Student Performance Report
School Year 200x–0x

Grade 7

Student _____

Our school motto:
**Excellence is for everyone!**

Our school profile:

| Enrollment: Grades 6–8 | Our school | District average |
|---|---|---|
| Students | 461 | 504 |
| Teachers | 18 | 20 |
| Administrators | 2 | 2 |
| Classroom Support* | 4 | 4 |
| School Support** | 6 | 3 |

*Includes librarian and counselor.
**Includes office, clerical, cafeteria, and custodial support.

**Your Town Middle School is committed to academic excellence through standards-based education in all areas of the core curriculum.**

**Note: State Board–approved fifth performance level, "Far below basic," not included on prototype.**

## Parents' Guide to Performance Levels

**4 – Advanced** Uses major skills or processes with ease and confidence in completing required academic performance tasks and/or demonstrates a thorough understanding of important information and is able to use this knowledge to communicate complicated ideas and concepts skillfully

**3 – Proficient** Uses major skills or processes without significant error in completing required academic performance tasks but has some difficulty doing so at times and/or demonstrates a good understanding of important information and is generally able to use this knowledge to communicate difficult ideas effectively

**2 – Basic** Makes a number of errors when using major skills and processes required to complete academic performance tasks but usually accomplishes their basic purposes and/or demonstrates only partial understanding of important information, which limits ability to use required knowledge to communicate important ideas

**1 – Below basic** Makes many errors when using the processes and skills needed to complete academic performance tasks and seldom finishes work and/or demonstrates an incomplete understanding of important information, making impossible the use of required knowledge to communicate important ideas correctly (See note in column 2.)

### Parent Accountability

As a parent, you are responsible for:

- Keeping abreast of school news and activities.
  - 637-xxxxx, YT activity hotline
  - www.ytmiddleschool.ca.k12.us
  - Your Town weekly newsletter home (via student)
  - District monthly newsletter (via mail)

- Attending school functions (Back-to-School Night, Parent-Teacher Program evenings, Parent-teacher conferences, Student recognition assemblies, Open house)

- Keeping in touch frequently with teachers and counselors.
  - 637-xxxx Counseling Center
  - teachername@ytmiddleschool.ca.k12.us

- Letting your child know clearly that you support the school's rules and academic expectations.

- Ensuring daily school attendance—with no tardies.

- Expecting nightly homework and regularly monitoring the completion of homework assignments.

- Insisting on your child's attendance in and arranging for appropriate transportation for supplemental learning assistance programs (if performance levels are Basic, Below Basic, or Inc.)

# Your Town Middle School

Dear Parents,

There are several very important points to remember as you review your son's or daughter's student performance report:

1. Students must meet standards set by the district and state.
2. The complete list of standards is available in the school office. Please call or come by for a complete set of standards for each subject so that you can more carefully evaluate your child's progress. This is an abbreviated list of standards for this grade level.
3. Please read the "Parents' Guide to Performance Levels" on back panel.
4. District policy and California law may require grade retention for students who fail to meet standards. Please closely follow your child's progress and consult frequently with his or her teacher.

Principal

### O, S, I, U designations*

| Study Skills | 1st | 2nd | 3rd | 4th |
|---|---|---|---|---|
| • Listens carefully | | | | |
| • Is ready for class | | | | |
| • Works independently | | | | |
| • Work is done on time | | | | |
| • Uses time well | | | | |
| • Cooperates in groups | | | | |
| • Follows instructions | | | | |
| • Edits and refines work | | | | |
| • Keeps journal | | | | |
| • Does neat work | | | | |

### Emotional and Social Growth
- Respects authority
- Practices self-control
- Respects rights of others
- Is responsible for self
- Behaves responsibly

*Note:* If a "—" appears, standards in that category were not addressed during grading period.

If Inc. (incomplete) appears, student has not completed benchmark assessment/assignments required. Inc. are subject to same student accountability measures as receiving a (1) Below basic performance level. Student is required to complete work and replace the Inc. with an earned performance level of proficient or better.

## Core Academic Performance Levels (4, 3, 2, 1)

| Reporting periods | 1st | 2nd | 3rd | 4th | Final |
|---|---|---|---|---|---|

*English–language arts standards categories*
- Reading
- Listening and Speaking
- Writing
- Written and Oral Conventions

*Mathematics standards categories*
- Number Sense
- Algebra and Functions
- Measurement and Geometry
- Statistics, Data Analysis, and Probability
- Mathematical Reasoning

*History–social science standards categories*
- Analysis Skills
- Cultures and Social Structures of Medieval Civilizations
- Origins and Accomplishments of the Renaissance
- Historical Aspects of the Reformation
- The Scientific Revolution
- Age of Exploration
- Enlightenment
- Age of Reason

*Science standards categories*
- Cell Biology
- Genetics
- Evolution
- Earth and Life History
- Structure and Function in Living Systems
- Physical Principles in Living Systems
- Investigation and Experimentation

*O, S, I, U designations**
- Physical Education
- Exploratory Wheel *or*
- Elective I *or*
- Proficiency Lab

**O, S, I, U Designations**
(O) Outstanding (S) Satisfactory (I) Improvement needed (U) Unacceptable – parent-teacher conference necessary

## Student Accountability

- The performance standard achieved on the STAR California Standards Test combined with performance level data on appropriate assessments given by the district provide important information in determining the advancement of a student to the next grade or to a higher level of the same subject or retention in grade/subject.

- **Basic (2)** or **Below basic (1)** designations on performance levels determined by the district at anytime during the school year will necessitate student participation in appropriate accelerated-remediation programs (*before, after school tutorials, proficiency lab, intersession or Saturday school*). In addition, students will be required to complete any outstanding classroom assignments given by their teachers.

- **Basic (2)** or **Below basic (1)** performance level determined by the district at the end of the school year may require summer school attendance where students will have an opportunity to raise their performance levels. Students not "Basic" by the end of summer school are subject to continued interventions when school resumes in the fall and possibly retention in grade or subject to repeating a course of study.

- Content standards will remain the same for students with specific learning disabilities, but performance standards with modified performance levels may be prescribed.

**Based on performance levels a parent-teacher conference is required if circled. Please call 637-xxxx to make an appointment.**

Report period   1   2   3   4   Final

# Figure 2-4   Example and Analysis of a Standards-Based Performance Report for a Student in Grade Seven

| | Reporting periods | | | | |
|---|---|---|---|---|---|
| | *1st* | *2nd* | *3rd* | *4th* | *Final* |
| *English–language arts standards categories* | | | | | |
| • Reading | 2 | 2 | 2 | 2 | **2** |
| • Listening and Speaking | 2 | 3 | 2 | 3 | 3 |
| • Writing | 2 | 2 | 3 | 3 | 3 |
| • Written and Oral Conventions | 2 | 2 | 3 | 2 | **2** |
| *Mathematics standards categories* | | | | | |
| • Number Sense | 2 | 3 | 3 | 3 | 3 |
| • Algebra and Functions | — | 2 | 2 | 2 | **2** |
| • Measurement and Geometry | 2 | 3 | 3 | 3 | 3 |
| • Statistics, Data Analysis, and Probability | — | 3 | 2 | 2 | **2** |
| • Mathematical Reasoning | 2 | 3 | 2 | 3 | 3 |
| *History–social science standards categories* | | | | | |
| • Analysis Skills | 2 | 3 | 3 | 3 | 3 |
| • Cultures and Social Structures of Medieval Civilizations | 2 | Inc. | 3 | 3 | 3 |
| • Origins and Accomplishments of the Renaissance | — | — | 3 | 3 | 3 |
| • Historical Aspects of the Reformation | — | — | 3 | 3 | 3 |
| • The Scientific Revolution | — | — | — | 3 | 3 |
| • Age of Exploration | 2 | 3 | — | 3 | 3 |
| • Enlightenment | — | 3 | 2 | 2 | **2** |
| • Age of Reason | — | 2 | 3 | 2 | **2** |
| *Science standards categories* | | | | | |
| • Cell Biology | — | — | 3 | 3 | 3 |
| • Genetics | — | — | 3 | 3 | 3 |
| • Evolution | — | — | 3 | 3 | 3 |
| • Earth and Life History | Inc. | 3 | 2 | 3 | 3 |
| • Structure and Function in Living Systems | Inc. | 2 | 2 | 2 | **2** |
| • Physical Principles in Living Systems | Inc. | 3 | 2 | 2 | **2** |
| • Investigation and Experimentation | Inc. | 3 | 2 | 3 | 3 |
| *Physical Education* | S | S | O | O | O |
| *Exploratory Rotation Wheel* | | | | | |
| • 1ˢᵗ Computers | S | — | — | — | |
| • 2ⁿᵈ Drama/Art | — | — | — | — | |
| • 3ʳᵈ Spanish | — | — | — | — | |
| • 4ᵗʰ Health | — | — | — | S | |
| *or Elective I* | | | | | |
| • Band | NA | NA | NA | NA | |
| • Choir | NA | NA | NA | NA | |
| *or Proficiency Lab* | — | — | — | S | |

## Analysis of Prototype Standards-Based Performance Report for a Student in Grade Seven

**English–Language Arts**   This student also struggled all year with Reading and Writing standards. After-hours tutorial help enabled him to improve in two areas which seem to logically relate to his successful performance in most areas of history–social science. The primary language of this student is possibly other than English. His language difficulties contributed to lowering his overall academic performance, thus requiring him to enroll in a mandatory summer school or intersession remediation program.

**Mathematics**   This student struggled with mathematics standards related to Algebra and Functions and with Statistics, Data Analysis, and Probability. He was a candidate for his school's targeted proficiency lab in mathematics by the end of the first grading period. Although he showed growth in proficiency, his final performance level indicates that he must attend his district's mandatory remedial summer or intersession program to focus on those areas of the mathematics standards.

**History–Social Science**   The student was also a candidate for after-hours tutorial help in history–social science. He never managed to satisfy performance levels in two areas of the curriculum: the Enlightenment and the Age of Reason. Remedial summer or intersession school attendance is now required.

**Science**   Difficulty completing benchmark assessment/ assignments first grading period and  with the Structure and Function of Living Systems and Physical Problems in Living Systems again warranted after-hours tutorial assistance for this student and now requires that he attend mandatory summer or intersession school.

*Note*: If "—" appears, standards in that category were not addressed during the grading period.

If Inc. appears, student has not completed benchmark assessment/ assignments required. Inc. subjects student to same accountability measures as receiving a (1) Below Basic performance level. Student is required to complete work and replace the Inc. with an earned performance level.

Student has made progress in proficiency, however, the final performance  levels in highlighted areas indicates the need for additional targeted assistance before eighth grade.

- Separate areas for effort, skills, courses not subject to performance levels
- Definitions of terminology
- Descriptions of performance levels, assessments used, and scoring procedures
- Accountability of the school and teachers, parents, and students
- Assistance programs for students not performing at proficient levels
- Ways to be in touch with the school

Additionally, the report should be easy to interpret and fit on one sheet of paper. The information on the report will drive instructional decisions about students. It may not be at the same level of specificity as that kept by teachers to inform their daily practice, but it will be specific enough for parents to see the areas in which their child requires attention and improvement.

Complete sets of the content standards (district and/or state standards) should be available at schools and easily accessible by students, parents, teachers, and the community at large. State standards can also be obtained by accessing them on the California Department of Education's Web site *<http://www.cde.ca.gov>* and via the Department's CDE Press/Publications Division. Providing performance reports in the parents' first language greatly enhances parents' understanding and helps to include all parents in the school community.

Content and performance standards work together. The performance report card reflects the work of the student in a standards-based classroom and school. Students are clear about what is expected of them and the level of quality they need to achieve in the classroom. If there is consistent alignment of classroom expectations with state expectations, there should be no surprises on the *California Standards Tests* or from the results from that assessment. When expectations are high and clear at every level, the opportunity to close the achievement gap between groups of students and to raise the level of achievement for all students is within our reach (see also Appendix 2-E, "Classroom Checklist for Implementing Standards," at the end of this chapter).

## Professional Development

Professional development is at the heart of successful reform. Standards-based reform is a significant change in the way educators teach. While many teachers find an inherent comfort zone in standards-based education, significant numbers are hesitant or may be resistant to change (see Figure 2-5). All teachers, regardless of their inclinations or tenure, will need many opportunities for professional development and support in a standards-based system.

Professional development opportunities related to standards will include not only direct information and strategies for standards implementation but also collaborative work experience as a part of the process. Teachers coming from an elementary background may also need additional content training in the subject areas they teach so they have the depth of knowledge necessary to teach sophisticated subject matter. Professional development is discussed thoroughly in Chapter 14.

| Figure 2-5 | Concerns of Veteran Teachers About Standards-Based Education |

Teachers have genuine concerns about standards. It is one thing to prepare new teachers to work in a standards-based educational environment. It is quite another to retrain veteran educators who bring to their work beliefs and conventions that are deeply ingrained and may run counter to the basic tenets of the standards movement.

Many teachers, unconvinced that all students can demonstrate proficiency and meet high academic standards, often work in classes where students exhibit severe academic deficits or other kinds of learning handicaps. Other teachers struggle to help their students bridge the gap between street English and academic English as they assist the students in achieving at the level expected for their grade and subject.

For those and other teachers who may see themselves working in a day-to-day survival mode, the idea of standards makes little or no sense. Standards are only a distant vision that might someday be reached by others who follow in their footsteps. Perhaps even more telling is that many teachers in these or similar situations feel they do not have the ability to help students become proficient in the basic knowledge and skills the students did not master in the earlier grades. What can be done? Teachers need practical support groups at the school or district level. Such groups enable them to (1) discuss their situations openly and explore the potential meaning of standards for their specific teaching assignments; (2) gain at least partial answers to their most vexing instructional and classroom management problems; and (3) create the conditions in which they can take the first steps on the road to standards-based education in their classrooms.

## Conclusion

Effective middle-level educators know that they must uphold the basic right of all students to have equal access to the most valued curricular programs a school offers. Standards-based education can make that goal achievable The same high expectations apply to every student in the state. Districts, schools, and teachers are held accountable for teaching to the standards and guiding students to proficiency. Educational policymakers and others in public leadership roles, including members of the Legislature, are accountable for ensuring that the public schools receive the support they need to implement standards-based education.

Content standards allow teachers and principals to become more precise in providing clear statements of what subject matter is the most worthwhile in each area of the core curriculum. Performance standards define levels of accepted proficiency with concrete examples and provide parents, teachers, and students credible information regarding student progress. Local performance levels are derived from the STAR *California Standards Tests* and standardized multiple measures developed locally.

Traditional grades alone are not an adequate source of accurate measures of student progress. Neither are they adequate for providing specific feedback or making important decisions regarding retention, promotion, and targeted interventions. These are important areas of discussion for educators and parents. Students whose performance levels are not acceptable require varying degrees of immediate intervention and assistance. A standards-based performance report sent home at the end of each grading period keeps students and parents informed about student performance levels specific to subsets of content standards, the need for conferencing, and decisions regarding targeted interventions and instructional strategies.

Professional development for teachers is essential to standards-based education. The collaborative, professional work that needs to be done to implement standards and to maintain a responsive, formative system is a sophisticated and time-intensive process. Principals and superintendents are key to rallying public and parental support for the process within their districts and for aligning time and resources to this effort. The full capabilities of a district are needed to implement standards-based education successfully.

Implementation of standards-based education must be thought of as a long-range process. It may take five to ten years of sustained effort to move a district to the point where it is possible to say with credibility, we have a fully implemented standards-based education system. Once in place, the process of sustaining standards-based instruction is an ongoing dynamic process.

Standards in the middle grades take center stage and offer the promise of academic achievement for all students.

# Standards-Based Education

The success of a standards-based educational program, including the evaluation of the curriculum and the evaluation of the instructional program, is measured by whether or not all students are meeting the state's and district's goals for standards-based learning.

- **Ensuring equity and attaining excellence for all students are two over-riding goals of a standards-based education system.** What obstacles does your school and district face in these areas? Are there groups of students who may have been left behind and for whom your school and your district must make a concerted effort to bring to the level of the standards? How will your school work to ensure equity and excellence for students with specific learning disabilities or with limited proficiency in English? How can you help your school and your district to achieve these ends?

- **Implementing an effective standards-based education program can be a professional and personal "stretch" for both teachers and administrators.** In which areas do you feel the most comfortable? In which areas do you feel the least prepared? How ready is your school to fully implement an effective standards-based program for all students? What challenges do you personally face? How might you be supported to meet these challenges?

- **Content standards describe, by grade level, what students should know and be able to do.** Yet, when students enter the middle grades, they may not have experienced an educational program that fully covered the expected standards of earlier grades. This situation is sometimes called slippage. Does your school often encounter students who have suffered from slippage? What can your school do to accelerate the learning of its incoming students to ensure that all students have the levels of achievement they will need for success in the middle grades? What kinds of tightly targeted interventions does your school use to support its struggling students? How effective are these interventions? What can you do to make these interventions even more successful?

- **When they first calibrate their lessons to the standards, some middle grades teachers are pleasantly surprised to find that much of what they teach is already aligned.** Others are alarmed because there is only a minimal degree of alignment. When your school last calibrated its instructional program to the standards, how much of a match did it find? How many of the standards were fully covered in the current instructional program? Were some standards omitted altogether? How might your school increase the number of standards it covers through its daily instructional program? Are there activities that teachers are now doing that could be eliminated so that more emphasis could be placed on standards-aligned lessons? Do assessment results show that the students are learning the standards-based content in your curriculum?

## Standards-Based Education (Continued)

- **Appendix 2-E, "Classroom Checklist for Implementing Standards," contains practical suggestions for evaluating your professional response to standards-based education.** Score yourself. A score of 10 ranks you as proficient. A score of 12 or better qualifies you as having advanced proficiency in your efforts to bring classroom reality to standards-based education.

- **One key to an effective standards-based education system is to develop local assessments and class assignments that parallel the state's system.** A local assessment system could use the performance levels derived from the *California Standards Tests* in combination with locally developed, administered, and scored "benchmark" assessments and assignments. In this way, the school and district will be able to know students' progress in achieving standards. Review the progress of your school or district in developing local standards-based assessments and assignments. What is already in place, and what still needs to become operational? How ready are the teachers and administrators for a local standards-based assessment system? What kinds of professional development are needed to assist and support teachers and administrators?

- **Performance standards may become a replacement for grades.** Carefully review the standards-based report card that is included in this chapter. Compare it with the report cards currently in use at your school. What advantages does a standards-based report have over a traditional report with only letter grades? Are there any disadvantages? How could a standards-based report card be aligned to class assignments and the evaluation of students? How might parents be involved so they could come to understand the reasons for and to provide support for a standards-based report card? What could you do to make standards-based reporting a reality in your school and district?

- **Some schools are abandoning parts of the core curriculum and electives to focus all of their attention on reading, language arts, and mathematics.** Even though the *California Standards Tests* will eventually include more areas of the curriculum, it is currently assessing standards in only some content areas. How can a middle school continue to provide a high-quality, comprehensive curriculum (including areas like science, history–social science, visual and performing arts, foreign language, career awareness, service-learning, and adolescent skills) in a context of high-stakes assessment? How might elective or exploratory classes support or reinforce students' learning of the standards of the core curriculum? What steps does a school need to take to ensure that it offers a fully balanced and comprehensive curriculum for all its students? What kinds of professional development would help a middle school to ensure a high-quality program in all parts of the core curriculum? What could you do to make certain the curriculum continues to be broad and responds to student needs?

# Appendix 2-A

## The New California Curriculum Frameworks

The new California curriculum frameworks represent a rich source of information and guidance as teachers seek to teach to specific content standards and to assess student proficiency levels. Excerpts from the *Reading/Language Arts Framework for California Public Schools* are illustrative.[4] Using the seventh-grade Conventions Standard 1.3 as an example, the framework discusses "efficient and effective curricular and instructional guidelines," which is followed by suggestions for assessing student performance.

## Seventh Grade

## Curricular and Instructional Profile

### Conventions Standard 1.3

| DOMAIN | STRAND | SUBSTRAND | STANDARD |
|---|---|---|---|
| **Written and Oral English-Language Convention** | 1.0 Written and oral English-language conventions | | 1.3 Identify all parts of speech and types and structure of sentences. |

Prerequisite standard. **Sixth-Grade Written and Oral English-Language Conventions Standard 1.1:** Use simple, compound, and compound-complex sentences.

Corequisite standard. **Seventh-Grade Writing Strategies Standard 1.7:** Revise writing to improve organization and word choice.

### Curricular and Instructional Decisions

| Instructional Objective | Use sophisticated but appropriate sentence structures in oral and written discourse. |
|---|---|
| Instructional Design | At this level a challenge for students is to use sentence structures more sophisticated than simple kernel-sentence types but not excessively complex or convoluted. Instruction should, therefore, focus on options for combining kernel sentences in various ways and the rhetorical impact and appropriateness of those various combinations. |

To achieve a balance, instruction should address both sentence combining and decombining. A focus on sentence combining alone can easily, if inadvertently, create the impression that longer, more complex sentence structures are inherently or universally better than simpler sentence structures.

Ultimately, students should be expected to develop a sense of appropriate sentence structures well enough to apply that sense to revisions of their own drafts. Initially, however, students should work on combining (and decombining and recombining) contrived sentences, which can be selected judiciously to illustrate specific possibilities for improvement. (Sentences contrived for revision can be taken from student writing examples or created by decombining sentences from texts students will read.)

The advantages to teaching sentence structure initially in this way are as follows:

- When all students are looking at and working with the same set of examples, teachers can conduct efficient whole-class instruction based on those examples.
- Teachers can correct work or otherwise evaluate student work more easily and give feedback when all students work initially with the same set of examples.
- Teachers can ensure that they cover several important classes or categories of sentence combining when examples are chosen specifically to illustrate those classes or categories.
- The examples used during initial instruction give teachers and students a solid basis of reference as individual student work is being revised.

Consider, for instance, the following example of student writing:

> Cowboys in Uruguay and Argentina are called gauchos. The gauchos are found in the country. They live and work in grass-covered prairies. Some gauchos herd cattle in the pampas. They do not make much money. Gauchos wear colorful outfits. They carry large knives and they drink a beverage called maté. It's a type of tea.

Initially, teachers should demonstrate possible improvements in the writing sample while discussing with students the relative advantages or effects of each possibility. For example, students might compare the differences in emphasis between Example 1 and Example 2:

*Example 1.*　　Gauchos, who are the cowboys of Uruguay and Argentina, live throughout the countryside.

*Example 2.*　　Across the countryside in the pampas of Uruguay and Argentina, you find cowboys called gauchos.

**Instructional Design (Continued)**

Which choice is better suited to a paragraph about gauchos? Why? What other options for sentence combining are possible? Which options illustrate trying to put too much into a sentence? How would the sense of Example 1 change if the commas were removed?

In short, instruction should address the strategies that good writers use—consciously or otherwise—by making such strategies overt and clear for students. Instruction should demonstrate the techniques by which secondary ideas are subordinated to primary, important ideas in strong, active sentences. Most critically, instruction should emphasize the relationships among ideas in kernel and complex sentences to ensure that students appreciate that conventions (e.g., the use of commas in dependent clauses) support the communication of ideas.

**Instructional Delivery**

Teachers should direct initial instruction in strategies for developing complex sentence structures and for evaluating competing structures. For such instruction to be meaningful, it must center on active discourse between teachers and students. The challenge for many students at this level is not so much to combine sentences as such but to do so judiciously in relation to specific purposes of communication. Teacher demonstrations and evaluations of thinking critically out loud are indispensable to effective instruction.

**Assessment**

**Entry-Level Assessment**

**Monitoring Student Progress**

**Post-test Assessment**

1. *Entry-Level Assessment for Instructional Planning.* Brief in-class compositions on well-defined topics should give teachers a satisfactory overview of the relative sophistication with which students manipulate sentence structures.

2. *Monitoring Student Progress Toward the Instructional Objective.* All written and oral assignments provide opportunities for ongoing assessment of this standard. Students should be prompted to focus on good sentence structures in all assignments that follow the initial instruction on this topic.

3. *Post-test Assessment Toward the Standard.* The best type of summative evaluation comes from specifically evaluating sentence structures in conjunction with authentic assignments in writing and speaking that address the writing and speaking standards.

1. *Students with Reading Difficulties or Disabilities.* Students with reading difficulties or disabilities often use long strings of primitive kernel sentences in their writing. They may run a number of these sentences together without punctuation, splice them with commas, or join them with repeated use of conjunctions like *and* or *but*. In turn, many of the sentences are likely to overuse passive and intransitive verbs. When necessary, teachers should be prepared to begin instruction in sentence combining at the students' level. In addition, these students will probably take longer to make the transition from predominantly simple sentences to the wider use of longer, more appropriate complex sentences.

2. *Students Who Are Advanced Learners.* The highest-performing students are the ones most likely to be able to learn about language for its own sake and benefit from that learning. For instance, they can investigate in depth the relationships between grammatical dependency and nuances in meaning and be challenged; for example, to come up with contrasting sentence pairs, such as the following:

Teenagers, who don't drive well, should pay higher insurance rates.

Teenagers who don't drive well should pay higher insurance rates.

3. *Students Who Are English Learners.* Students with restricted proficiency in English will require intensive English-language instruction above and beyond that found in the regular language arts program. The type of explicit strategy instruction described previously for lower-performing students will help English learners as well. They might be exempted from some regular classroom work in sentence combining to provide more instructional time for intense work on well-formed grammatical kernel sentences.

Instructional materials should provide for a very wide range of student achievement levels in the seventh grade. Publishers will always be safe in providing *more* resources for a given set of standards—such as those for sentence combining and related conventions—than one might think sufficient for average students. (It is far easier for teachers to elect to not use some resources than to create them from scratch or to find them.) For instance, teachers should have the option of drawing from a rich variety of sample writing—examples of good and poor writing—to use as the basis for instruction in sentence combining.

# Appendix 2-B

# Face to Face with Content Standards: An Interview with a Teacher

*How is teaching different when you rely on standards to guide you?*

Standards reflect the thinking of a broad cross-section of people—educators, board members, representatives of institutions of higher education, parents, business persons, and other community people. Our standards represent what our community thinks is important for kids to learn. That may conflict with what a textbook publisher based in Texas or New York decides is significant. This happened to me before we had standards. I found myself rushing through this large, detailed textbook. But it didn't say what's most important to teach, and many teachers feel as I did. They have to cover it all or as much as they can. If I had had our content standards, I would have had a way to make some choices that would have helped me do a better job of managing the breadth of what I was teaching to my seventh graders. And it certainly would have added depth to the things I was trying to teach the kids. In short, the standards would have helped big time in deciding what's most important.

*Give an example of how teaching might have looked before and after standards.*

Before we had our content standards, it was always, "We're doing Greece" or "We're doing Egypt." There was always a map; there was always geography; there were all the bits and pieces about pharaohs and mummies and so forth. But the missing piece always was, What is most important for our students to learn from this study of ancient civilization? What's the bottom line? If I've finished with Egypt and the students can tell me that hieroglyphics was the Egyptian form of writing or if they can name the gods and goddesses, are those the important things kids should know? As a teacher without standards, I didn't know and still wouldn't

know. If you look at the test that the textbook publisher gives you, it focuses on little bits of knowledge like this. That's okay as far as it goes because you have to focus on bits of knowledge sometimes. But I think those little bits have to add up to something bigger—to a larger understanding of something. And that's where content standards come into play.

*Most of us memorized facts when we studied history in school. Are you saying that facts aren't as important in today's classroom?*

Facts are just as important as they ever were. You can't think without facts. I'm not saying do away with the facts. No one who really understands standards-based education would say this. But there are millions of facts. The question is how do you figure out which ones kids really need to know.

*Explain further.*

I used to give my seventh-grade kids mapping activities where they would have to memorize certain points on a map. I would give them a blank, and they would have to fill in certain cities or countries from memory. I was testing discrete bits of their geographical knowledge. But suppose I had been teaching with our social studies standard in mind that says, "Students will gain an understanding of the effects of climate and natural forces on the environment." If kids are wasting their time labeling a map and memorizing it for the test, I've squandered their time, cheated them—although I hate to admit it—because they could have spent the same time deepening their understanding about the location of cities and how their development and way of life are impacted by climatic conditions. This is heady stuff, and it's what standards are all about.

*Aren't teachers supposed to know what's important and unimportant?*

Teachers need help at this point. They are instructional experts, not curriculum designers. They should not have to spend time figuring out what are the most important concepts and skills that every student needs to learn. This is especially true for newer teachers. More experienced staff members probably do a better job, but even they can fall into the trivia trap. Having content standards has provided a huge breakthrough at this point.

*What's the hardest thing about trying to shift to standards-based teaching?*

It can be overwhelming for a teacher to be given a long list of standards for mathematics or science or history—any subject—and then told you're teaching to those standards and that you had better get busy and rethink the whole way you approach your school year and, really, your job. The message to get out is that teachers can teach to standards without rejecting everything they've ever done before. *But standards-based education means that we've got to learn new ways of doing things that can help kids get closer to where they need to be.*

*What do you mean? How does this work?*

For example, my principal asked teachers to reexamine all of their favorite classroom activities and to ask tough questions about them. Is drawing the Egyptian gods and goddesses on a poster and writing their names in hieroglyphics, which takes three days as a project, going to get the kids closer to one of the history standards? If it isn't, it either needs to be dropped or retooled.

One of the really hard things is accepting that when you're working with a lot of kids who are not at grade level or are not performing where they should be, every moment counts. You do not have the luxury of spending three days on something that makes the room look pretty but which fails to demonstrate that your students have learned something really important.

*Will standards-based education work? Is it going to pay off?*

Definitely. But it will take time. In fact, the challenge is time—finding the time to make shifts in thinking and to do the actual work of change. We need time to think, time to learn, and time to apply what we have learned. But it is going to pay off because we as teachers—and principals, too—are having to rethink how we help kids focus on the really big picture, the knowledge and skills that count most. A well-put-together set of standards in each subject for each grade will help get us there. It's doable. It's smart! And I think students, teachers, and parents want it to work. That's the big secret! They're tired of not knowing whether they are doing a good job!

# Appendix 2-C

# Curriculum Calibration, Lessons Learned
# from Underperforming Schools

Curriculum Calibration analysis of student work reveals that instructional materials used at underperforming schools are below grade-level as measured by the new California Content Standards.

At DataWorks Educational Research we evaluate student achievement for over 500 California schools each year using multiple measures. However, this year in a new role as External Evaluators, we became investigators searching out "barriers to student achievement" for several of California's II/USP schools. The Intermediate Intervention/Under Performing Schools Program (II/USP) requires schools identified by low SAT 9 scores to use an External Evaluator to initiate school-wide reform to improve student achievement.

As part of our investigation we performed an in-depth analysis of everything connected with student learning. We observed classroom instruction. We grilled the school's parents, teachers, students, paraprofessionals and administrators with bubble-in surveys, written comments and personal interviews. We disag-

gregated two years of SAT 9 results, reviewed two years of multiple measures data and dissected transcripts of student grades. For three months we reviewed this information with the II/USP schoolsite action team members as we worked together to prepare the school's final Action Plan for school improvement.

Even though we had reviewed extensive data, we thought something was missing. We wanted to go one step further but didn't quite know what to do. Suddenly, we decided to look at student work. We wanted to hold in our hands the actual pieces of work the students were doing – not exemplary work, not SAT 9 printouts – but real down to earth, day to day work. We faxed a direct request to the school principals: "Collect every single piece of paper that every student does for a solid week. Box it and ship it to us."

After several days, the incoming FedEx boxes grew to an astonishing accumulation of 6,318 examples of student work.

## Curriculum Calibration
## Grade-Levels of Instructional Material Being Presented to the Students

| Grade | Mathematics % on Grade Level | | | | | | Average Grade Level | Language Arts % on Grade Level | | | | | | Average Grade Level |
|---|---|---|---|---|---|---|---|---|---|---|---|---|---|---|
| | K | 1 | 2 | 3 | 4 | 5 | | K | 1 | 2 | 3 | 4 | 5 | |
| K | 100 | | | | | | K | 100 | | | | | | K |
| 1st | | 100 | | | | | 1.0 | | 100 | | | | | 1.0 |
| 2nd | | 23 | 77 | | | | 1.8 | | 20 | 80 | | | | 1.8 |
| 3rd | | | 45 | 55 | | | 2.6 | | 2 | 14 | 84 | | | 2.8 |
| 4th | | | 40 | 40 | 20 | | 2.8 | | 2 | 30 | 35 | 33 | | 3.0 |
| 5th | | 2 | 35 | 59 | 2 | 2 | 2.7 | | | 28 | 60 | 10 | 2 | 2.9 |

*Source: The DataWorks Assessment Newsletter,* Vol. II, No. 1 (February 2000). Fresno, Calif.: DataWorks Educational Research.

Armed with a dog-eared copy of the California Content Standards downloaded off the Internet we started working one-by-one through the entire 6,318 pieces of paper. We eventually hand coded the grade-level content standard covered on every single piece of student work.

When we finished tabulating the results we were surprised. As can be seen from the table, only kindergarten and first grade were being taught at grade level. Curriculum slippage begins at second grade where only 77% of the math material and 80% of the language arts material being presented to the students was on grade level. By the 5th grade only 2 percent of the work being given to the students was on grade-level. Keep in mind that we calibrated every assignment that the students were being asked to do. By the 5th grade, the student assignments were mostly second and third grade material. Instruction at this school was miscalibrated, often significantly below grade-level!

The Curriculum Calibration results were then presented to teachers, principals, school board members and superintendents. Each presentation produced similar results. The room was in a state of shock. Mouths were open. People looked at each other in a combination of denial, disbelief, hurt and anger.

*"Our instruction is below grade-level? Are we teaching below grade-level?"*

*"I never realized this!"*

*"I have been teaching what I always did."*

*"I've got a three inch binder of the standards somewhere, but really didn't know what to do with them."*

## So, What Are the Standards?

The California Content Standards are a progressing, expanding, non-repeating curriculum of increasing complexity, depth, and breadth for all students. According to the California Mathematics Standards, for example, students in kindergarten count to 30; first grade to 100; second grade to 1,000; third grade to 10,000 and fourth grade to millions. In Language Arts kindergartners write words and brief sentences; first-graders write a paragraph. By sixth grade students should be writing multiple paragraph compositions of 500 to 700 words (word-processed!).

## What to Do ASAP

- Immediately adopt a new school vision, a mission statement:

  ALL INSTRUCTION AND ASSESSMENT AT THIS SCHOOL WILL BE AT GRADE-LEVEL ACCORDING TO THE CALIFORNIA STANDARDS

- Perform a Curriculum Calibration to see where you stand.

- Order sufficient rubber stamps to print "GLS K," "GLS 1," "GLS 2" etc. to calibrate every ditto, handout and worksheet floating around the school.

- Redirect training and resources to concentrate on teaching at grade-level.

## Schoolwide Instructional Recalibration

Teaching to the rigorous California standards requires a major instructional recalibration. Start teaching from the first day of school at grade level. In the fourth grade, for example, teach multiple paragraph compositions right from the start as opposed to teaching students where they are, i.e., repeating single sentences or single paragraphs.

Curriculum Calibration provides a real missing link to explain student achievement.

We have all looked at SAT9 scores, grades and multiple measure results and said, "OK, now what?" Well, now we have a quantifiable piece of hard data to connect what goes on in the classroom to what the assessments are showing.

The Curriculum Calibration results can provide a simple, easy-to-understand unifying focal point for school-wide reform to improve student achievement: *All Instruction on Grade-Level.* As one principal summed it up:

*"In my entire career, the Curriculum Calibration is the best school evaluation I have ever seen!"*

# Grading in a Standards-Based System: Fundamental Questions

by Susan A. Colby

As districts and states continue the move toward standards-based education, questions arise around best practices for implementation. One concern is the teacher's quandary: how to evaluate, record, and communicate student progress in a standards-based system. In many ways this is a practical problem confronting individual teachers at the classroom level. But by working together to address specific grading problems, they can more fully make the transition to a standards-based system. Before developing a standards-based grading system, educators need to ask three questions. The first question (or set of questions) focuses on the written standards:

- *Do the standards embody the skills and knowledge that we would like our students to have? Are they written with a focus on what the learner will do? Are they measurable? Do they provide equal access to educational opportunities for all students?*

If districts, teachers, and schools are required to use standards that they do not believe are of high quality or if the implementation of standards does not address issues of equitable access for all, then perhaps these educators have more important concerns to address before developing a standards-based grading system. The . . .

[next] question focuses on how well classroom instruction relates to the standards:

- *Are teachers consistently using standards to guide classroom instruction?*

If teachers are not teaching to the standards or if classroom instruction is driven by textbooks, units, themes, and tests, then teachers must first learn how to use standards to guide instruction. A . . . [final] question focuses on how well assessment relates to the standards:

- *Are assessments purposefully aligned with standards and instruction?*

Until assessments correspond to specific standards, the transition to a standards-based grading system will be difficult. A teacher must plan for assessing all students on each standard for a standards-based grading system to be useful. A related issue is whether teachers must report on how well each student has done in relation to each standard. When high-quality standards drive instructional and assessment decisions and when teachers report on how well each student progresses according to standard, then a standards-based grading system is essential.

From *Educational Leadership,* Vol. 56 (March 1999). Reprinted with permission from the Association for Supervision and Curriculum Development.

# Appendix 2-E

# Classroom Checklist for Implementing Standards

| Professional practice | Checkoff | Self-assessment remarks |
|---|---|---|
| 1. The standards are highly visible in the classroom. They are expressed in language understandable to students and parents. | | |
| 2. Examples of exemplary student work are evident throughout the classroom. | | |
| 3. Students can explain spontaneously what is needed for each assignment to be considered proficient. | | |
| 4. For every assignment, project, or test, the teacher provides in advance explicit expectations for proficient work. | | |
| 5. Student evaluation is always done according to the standards, *never* on a curve. | | |
| 6. The teacher can explain to any parent or other stakeholder the specific expectations for each student for the year. | | |
| 7. The teacher may vary the length and quantity of the curriculum content daily to ensure that students spend more time on the most critical content standards. | | |
| 8. Commonly used standards, such as those used for written expression, are reinforced in every subject area. For example, spelling always counts in mathematics, science, music, physical education, and every other discipline. | | |
| 9. The teacher has created at least one standards-based performance assessment in the past month. | | |
| 10. The teacher exchanges student work with a colleague for independent review at least once every two weeks. | | |
| 11. The teacher provides feedback to students and parents about the quality of student work compared with the standards, not with the work of other students. | | |
| 12. The teacher helps to build a community consensus about the importance of standards and high academic expectations for all students. | | |
| 13. The teacher uses a mix of assessment techniques, including extended written responses in all disciplines. | | |
| 14. Other standards-based professional practices are used that are appropriate to the teacher's classroom. | | |

From *Making Standards Work,* by Douglas B. Reeves. Denver: Center for Performance Assessment, 1998. Used with permission.

*"The important thing for you is not how much you know but the quality of what you know."*

—Desiderius Erasmus

# Assessment Takes Center Stage

I n a standards-based education system, assessment takes center stage, sharing a lead role with standards and accountability. Its function is to measure the progress of students and to provide reliable data to teachers, administrators, policymakers, and the public.

Evaluation of student work and the provision of specific feedback to the student have always been integral and important parts of instruction. Together, they are the basis for growth and improvement not only by the student but by the teacher as well. Increasingly, evaluation of student work has extended beyond the classroom and has become the basis for other stakeholders to make decisions about students and groups of students, programs, and the effectiveness of teachers and administrators.

Policymakers and taxpayers want assurance that tax dollars are consistently producing a well-educated populace. Educators need reliable data to formulate decisions and drive instruction. As a result, evaluation of student

work has become a sophisticated process that has evolved into a system of assessment that serves many legitimate and sometimes competing needs.

In 1994, reauthorization of the Elementary and Secondary Education Act (ESEA), Title I, provided impetus to state assessment reform efforts. The reauthorization required tests that measured performance against standards, rather than those that compared students' performance with that of other students. In addition, the law explicitly mandated several assessment components.[1]

- Use of multiple, up-to-date measures of student performance
- Use of assessments that are valid and reliable for clearly identified purposes
- Administration of assessments at least three times, once between grades three and five and again between grades six and nine and ten and twelve
- Disaggregated achievement data that indicate the performance of students by gender, race, income, and other categories
- A minimum of three performance levels (two showing levels of proficiency and one for lack of proficiency)

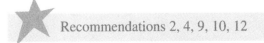

Recommendations 2, 4, 9, 10, 12

- Determination of what constitutes "adequately yearly progress" and accountability of districts and schools for meeting such targets

As a result, the number of assessments administered and the time required to administer them have grown in California and across the nation. Since these assessments are given during classroom time, many, if not most, teachers question their value and the reorganization of their instructional time for assessments that may serve only the needs of other stakeholders. This is a legitimate concern that dominates discussion by stakeholders.

As California's assessment program evolves, solutions are being sought to mitigate the effect of decreased instructional time. There is, however, no simple solution to the problem. It would be so much easier if one short, all-purpose test could be developed, but unfortunately, no single measure can adequately serve all needs. Nor would we want it to. Multiple measures throughout the school year provide perspectives from which to evaluate student work and to determine whether students are truly performing "up to standard" in all areas.

## California's Statewide Assessment System: An Overview of a Dynamic and Evolving System

California's statewide assessment system is composed of several instruments that range from kindergarten through grade twelve (see also Appendix 3-A, "California Assessment System Chart," at the end of this chapter). It is a system that continues to evolve and be refined.

California's current mandatory assessment program is called STAR—the acronym for Statewide Testing and Reporting. Legislation for the STAR Program was enacted in 1997. Its evolution and future plans can easily be traced in Appendix 3-B, "California's Statewide Assessment-Implementation Timeline," (at the end of this chapter). The following discussion highlights those assessments that have implications for middle grades students.

The *Stanford Achievement Test, Ninth Edition, Form T (SAT 9)* was selected by the State Board of Education as the norm-referenced assessment instrument to be used in STAR. The *SAT 9* is administered annually to all California public school students in grades two through eleven.

The *California Standards Tests,* aligned to the state's content standards, are administered in the second through eleventh grades. The subject areas assessed are language arts and mathematics in grades two through eleven and history–social science and science in grades nine through eleven. *California Standards Tests* are criterion-referenced assessments of students' achievement of California's content standards. Writing samples at grades four and seven were added for the 2001 annual assessment. As the *California Standards Tests* are developed to include performance assessment components, they will incorporate items that assess higher-order thinking skills, and results will be reported, by performance levels, for individual students.

In addition to the tests in English, limited-English-proficient students who have been enrolled in California public schools for fewer than 12 months must also take a test in their primary language, if one is available. Primary language testing is a district option for students who have been enrolled more than 12 months prior to testing. For testing of students whose primary language is Spanish, the State Board designated the *Spanish Assessment of Basic Education, Second Edition (SABE/2),* published by CTB/McGraw-Hill. Spanish is the only language for which a primary language test for limited-English-proficient students was submitted for State Board consideration.

In the winter of 1999-2000, the State Board of Education adopted English-language development standards that focus on English learners' proficiency in listening, speaking, reading, and writing in English. The instrument used to assess those students' progress is the *California English Language Development Test (CELDT).*

Senate Bill 2X of 1998 authorized the development of the *High School Exit Examination.* Beginning with the graduating class of 2004, California public school students must pass this test to receive a high school diploma. The purpose of the *HSEE* is to help ensure that students who graduate have demonstrated competency in the content standards adopted by the State Board of Education in reading, writing, and mathematics. Students must be afforded multiple opportunities to satisfy the *HSEE* requirement for a high school diploma and receive appropriate instruction on the standards covered by the test.

It is imperative that students receive instruction in the state content standards for English–language arts and mathematics, and *the middle grades are a critical time for them to acquire the knowledge and skills necessary to pass the HSEE*. Preparation for the exit examination begins in kindergarten; however, if students reach the middle grades without the requisite proficiency in earlier standards, learning in the middle grades takes on added importance.

The responsibility for providing students with the standards-aligned instruction necessary to pass the *HSEE* does not rest on the high schools alone. The *HSEE* legislation requires middle schools to identify students at risk of not passing the test and to provide those students with the instructional assistance they will need to be successful on the examination. As early as the ninth grade, students may begin to take the *HSEE,* although the results for students taking the test at that grade level will only be diagnostic results. All students in grade ten, however, will be required to take the *HSEE* beginning in the 2001-2002 school year. They may take each subsequent administration of the examination until they have passed each section of the test.

## Multiple Measures of Assessment

Employing multiple measures of standards-based achievement is an important part of an educational accountability system that adequately measures the depth and breadth of what students are actually learning. In addition to providing a more complete and accurate representation of student achievement over time, multiple measures serve to ensure that instruction does not focus on a single test.

All teachers know that a single assessment does not measure the many dimensions of student learning. As stated in *Multiple Measures: Accurate Ways to Assess Student Achievement,*[2] "In order to capture a complete and accurate picture of student achievement, schools must utilize a variety of measures when determining the effectiveness of educational interventions and educational programs."

However, using multiple measures in a standards-based education system is not without its challenges. Since large-scale, statewide assessments cannot provide the level of specificity or formative, ongoing feedback needed by local educators to effectively enhance the learning of individual students, responsibility for this purpose rests with districts and schools.

Consequently, local educators must acquire the sophisticated skills necessary to select or develop assessments that are technically sound and that authentically reflect each student's learning based on California's standards and performance-level expectations. Administrators and teachers must learn how to use the data from these multiple assessments to effectively enhance instructional practice with targeted precision.

Ideally, in a standards-based system, a variety of assessment instruments, both formal and informal, are used throughout the school year at all grade levels. Different assessments are used for different purposes, and the results should be evaluated based on those purposes. Understanding this concept will assist educators in developing purposeful and useful assessments.

## Purposes of Assessments and Basic Assessment Terminology

Although assessments can serve a variety of purposes, this discussion will focus on the four purposes outlined by Richard Stiggins in *Classroom Assessment for Student Success.*[3] Included

are definitions in context of frequently used assessment vocabulary.

### Assessment for Public Accountability

This type of assessment is usually a large-scale, standardized assessment and is often nationally normed. The results of this type of a norm-referenced assessment provide policymakers and taxpayers information about the overall condition of education in the state compared to that in other states and countries.

**Norm-referenced** tests typically are used to evaluate how well individual students and groups of students perform compared to all other students in the same grade taking the same test nationwide. These assessments are commonly given at the end of a school year and are designed to rank students with one another. The *SAT 9,* used as part of California's Statewide Testing and Reporting System (STAR) Program is an example of a norm-referenced test.

The *SAT 9* is a commercially developed test, based on a general set of expectations from across the nation. It is not specifically aligned to California's content standards. Results from norm-referenced tests are reported in terms of percentiles, which rank from 1 to 99. So, for example, a student receiving a percentile score of 73 in reading has scored as well as 73 percent of the student population that took the test. *It does not mean that the student got 73 percent of the questions right.* The average score is the 50th percentile; therefore, in a norm-referenced test, 50 percent of the students taking the test will typically score below average.

### Assessment for Program Planning

The second instrument in the STAR program, the *California Standards Tests,* was initially referred to as the STAR augmentation. These are not norm-referenced tests; they are criterion-referenced tests of the California content standards and serve more than one purpose. In addition to being used for accountability in meeting standards and program planning by policymakers, they will be primarily beneficial for school and district program planning. The results from this assessment will guide educators in making decisions about instructional practices, targeted professional development, and allocation of time and resources. Information can be disaggregated by class, school, district, and demographic subgroups so that programs can be designed to close achievement gaps between subgroups as well as to raise overall student achievement.

Students' individual results on this assessment will be reported as student performance levels. These performance levels will identify students who are and who are not proficient on grade-level standards. The *California Standards Tests'* performance levels will provide districts with important information they can use to make decisions affecting individual students as well as programs.

**Criterion-referenced** tests are used to determine how well students have acquired a specified set of learning outcomes (such as knowledge about certain topics covered in a particular subject area or proficiency in specific standards). Scores from criterion-referenced tests rank students in relation to identified levels of performance. Therefore, unlike a norm-referenced test, in which 50 percent of the students taking the test will typically score below average, all students taking a criterion-referenced test can pass the test and meet the standard if they know the material. This

important distinction provides an insightful basis for shaping instructional practice and holding students accountable to absolute rather than relative performance.

### Assessment for Decision Making

When decisions, particularly high-stakes decisions such as promotion, retention, graduation, remediation, recognition, and certification, need to be made on behalf of a student, it is essential that the assessment used for this purpose be valid, reliable, and fair. The STAR *California Standards Tests* and the *High School Exit Examination (HSEE)* are examples of state tests used for decision making, program planning, and public accountability. Students below basic proficiency on the *California Standards Tests* may be subject to grade retention. Students not passing the *HSEE* will not receive a high school diploma until they pass that examination. Statewide assessments are usually administered at the end of a course or grade (summative).

Local assessments used for decision making are given more frequently during the course of a school year to verify student achievement and to guide targeted assistance and program delivery to struggling students.

**Validity** means that an assessment measures what it is supposed to measure. If an assessment purports to cover certain content standards, it should be carefully reviewed by those who are going to use the assessment and its results to see that it does. For instance, if the assessment stretches beyond or falls below the expectations of grade-level standards or if the assessment reflects only a portion of the standards, the results will not provide a valid basis on which to make decisions. The lack of validity renders any inferences or actions based on test scores inappropriate. An acceptable level of validity must be demonstrated before test results are used to make decisions.

**Reliability** means consistency in measuring what the assessment is designed to measure. Reliability is the extent to which a test result accurately or consistently measures "true" achievement of an individual or group. This is a statistical term that defines the extent to which errors of measurement are absent from a measurement instrument. Does the assessment provide accurate, reliable information each time and under different circumstances? If a sixth-grade student took an examination on one day in one school and the same examination again a month later in another school (hypothetically assuming he or she didn't remember taking the first test and had acquired no other knowledge or skills in the interim that would affect the outcome), would the student score the same? Or if the student took a different form of the assessment, would the scores be consistent?

Reliable scores are more easily obtained from selected response assessments where there is only one correct answer and the test can be scored uniformly by machine. Reliable scores from performance assessments are not as easily obtained, because the scores depend on human judgment, and there are multiple ways of a students' achieving proficiency. Therefore, those who score performance assessments are trained for consistency, and their rate of reliability is carefully monitored.

If test instruments provide consistent results, then the difference between the results on a pretest and the results on a post-test provides a reliable source of information about student learning over time. If policymakers and the public receive reliable scores, they can be confident in making decisions about rewards and consequences.

**Fairness** means that the assessment should be fair and free of bias for all students. No group of students should be advantaged or disadvantaged because of bias based on gender, culture, socioeconomics, background knowledge, or access to resources. For instance, an assessment based on a historical television documentary that all eighth grade students were to watch at home and critique in class the following day would be an example of an unfair assessment. Not all students may have had access to a television or the authority within their family to select the program. Some students may have had other obligations. Some variables can have powerful and unfair influence on the test scores, thus providing an inaccurate picture of student achievement.

It would also be unfair to assess students on material they had not had the opportunity to learn in their classrooms. The California *High School Exit Examination* is aligned to State Board–approved content standards from seventh through tenth grade in English–language arts and mathematics, including algebra. Students *may* take the examination in ninth grade and *must* take the examination in tenth grade. It would have been unfair to mandate a test of twelfth grade standards for a tenth grade population. The tenth grade students would not have had the opportunity to learn the material on which they would be tested. It is expected that students in the tenth grade will have had the opportunity to learn the material if their teachers in grades seven through ten have been consistently teaching to their grade-level standards.

## Assessment as Part of Instruction

This assessment purpose is probably the most important and powerful tool the classroom teacher has because it engages students and the teacher in a process that enhances learning. This type of assessment is generally formative, frequent, and ongoing.

**Formative assessments.** Formative assessments are diagnostic and given before and during the teaching process. They are an integral part of learning. Students are able to reflect critically on what they know, what they have misconceptions about, and what they need to do to reach proficiency on the selected standards. The results of formative assessments provide the basis for students and teachers to refine and reshape their work.

Students may even contribute to the development of the assessment and scoring criteria, which serves to clarify expectations and to demystify the assessment. Middle grades students are generally enthusiastic participants in this process because it shifts evaluation of their learning to themselves. Because formative assessments are frequent and related directly to the curriculum that is being taught, these particular assessments are usually *unique to the classroom and teacher.*

**Benchmark assessments.** Some formative assessments are *collegially adopted or developed* within a district or school. In a standards-based system, benchmark assessments provide a uniform basis for measuring student progress on standards at specific intervals during the course of the year. These benchmark assessments are the basis for a local performance standards system. The student score is a school and district's performance indicator and becomes part of the data used in establishing a performance level for the student.

To minimize the effect of the time that assessment administration requires in the classroom, state assessments are designed to serve more than one purpose. However, it is not possible to construct an assessment that will satisfy all needs for information about student achievement. For instance, *SAT 9*'s primary purpose is for public accountability. It is less useful for program planning or to drive instruction because it is norm-referenced, is not aligned to California's standards, and is given only once at the end of the school year. It does, however, provide trend data about general performance that can guide programs in the absence of other, better-suited assessments. It is helpful in making decisions about students in some federally funded programs because it ranks and compares students with a national sample.

*SAT 9* is not intended to guide instruction, but many teachers are not clear about its intended purpose and may be focusing too much class time on test preparation to raise their students' test scores and school *API* rankings rather than on meaningful instruction. "In some cases, schools resort to inappropriate practices, such as teaching specific tests items, or items like test items, in order to raise scores. These practices do little to improve student learning."[4]

Both the State Board of Education and the State Superintendent of Public Instruction acknowledge the pressure administrators and teachers feel to increase student test scores and *API* rankings, but:

> "Changing instructional practices to obtain higher test scores—at the expense of learning—is not an appropriate response. . . . As educators,

we have the responsibility to develop an instructional approach to maximize the achievement of each student. We feel confident that a focus on student learning will also result in higher test scores and student learning."[5]

In 2000, the State Board of Education adopted policy guidelines regarding the appropriateness and inappropriateness of certain test preparation practices (see also Appendix 3-C, "The State Board of Education's Policy on Preparation for State Tests and the Standardized Testing and Reporting [STAR] Program," at the end of this chapter). According to the guidelines, districts and schools wanting to improve student learning should focus time and instruction on teaching to the standards, not to the test. Performance scores on norm-

referenced and criterion-referenced assessments will then reflect true achievement in learning.

Classroom formative assessments can improve student learning. These assessments are useful to students and their teachers because they are criterion aligned and provide timely feedback, but their unique characteristics and limited scope are not appropriate for high stakes decisions, overall program planning, or public accountability (see Figure 3-1).

The discussion and Figure 3-1 outline the need to administer different types of assessment based on their intended purposes. Classroom assessments and local benchmark assessments have the most impact on student learning when they are used as part of standards-based instruction. With assessments aligned to the California

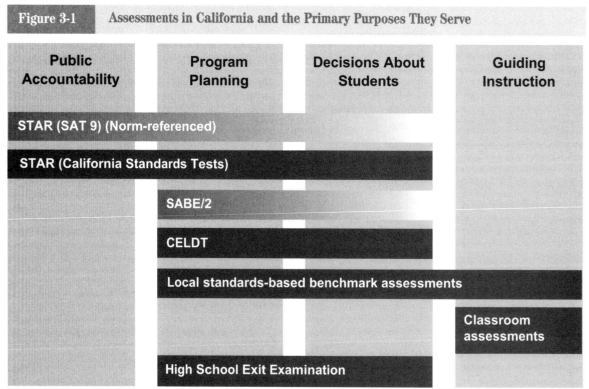

**Figure 3-1**    Assessments in California and the Primary Purposes They Serve

| Public Accountability | Program Planning | Decisions About Students | Guiding Instruction |
|---|---|---|---|

STAR (SAT 9) (Norm-referenced)

STAR (California Standards Tests)

SABE/2

CELDT

Local standards-based benchmark assessments

Classroom assessments

High School Exit Examination

(Note: Solid color bars represent assessments based on California's content standards and English language development [ELD] standards.)

standards (content and performance), classroom assessments, local benchmark assessments, and the *California Standards Tests* become inherently consistent. The old questions of Why don't we test what we teach? and Why don't we teach what we test? are resolved if teaching focuses on the standards.

## Local Assessments

Statewide assessments have their strengths, but they also have their weaknesses. Local assessments are necessary companions because they fill a role that statewide assessments cannot. Generally, statewide tests assess only those standards that can be measured through paper-and-pencil format in a limited amount of time. For example, it is not possible for a statewide test to measure certain skills identified in the standards for listening, speaking, and multimedia presentations. Nor would a statewide test necessarily address district-defined standards and outcomes. The absence of certain standards on developed statewide tests does not mean they are not essential and should be ignored or de-emphasized. It does mean all standards cannot be measured fully or adequately in a selected-response format. Local assessments should fill this gap.

While reliable scores can be produced from constructed-response prompts and scoring rubrics, doing so is costly and time consuming on a large-scale assessment. Consequently, most large-scale assessments use a multiple-choice format. Students select what they believe to be correct from among several responses and fill in the appropriate bubble for that response on an answer form that will be machine scored. Score reliability is high, and these assessments are not as expensive or time-

intensive as those that allow students to construct their own responses and that depend on trained scorers to evaluate student performance.

Unfortunately, selected-response questions rarely access the upper levels of cognitive thinking. Effective constructed-response assessments encourage creativity; higher levels of thinking, including creative problem solving; and the deeper, more complex dimensions of student learning. The STAR *California Standards Tests'* writing assessments in grades four and seven and the writing portion of the *High School Exit Examination* attempt to "bridge" from selected-response into more constructed-response items that allow students to authentically demonstrate their writing ability. A great need exists at the local level for assessments employing performance tasks. The "doing" of the content standards, applying skills and knowledge, engages young minds and attaches relevance to their learning.

Figure 3-2 aligns Benjamin Bloom's cognitive taxonomy, familiar to most veteran teachers, to the continuum of assessment formats (selected-response to constructed-response and other performance tasks). Constant use of assignments and assessments that are worksheet oriented or in the selected-response format deprives students of opportunities to use the higher-level thinking identified in the California standards and to develop the creative problem-solving skills needed in today's global economy (see also Appendix 3-D, "Developing, Using, and Communicating Complex Reasoning," at the end of this chapter).

Large-scale assessments are generally formal, standardized tests. Assessments at the local level do not necessarily have the same characteristics as those of a formal test. The line between informal classroom assessments and

| Bloom's Taxonomy | Assessment Continuum |
| --- | --- |

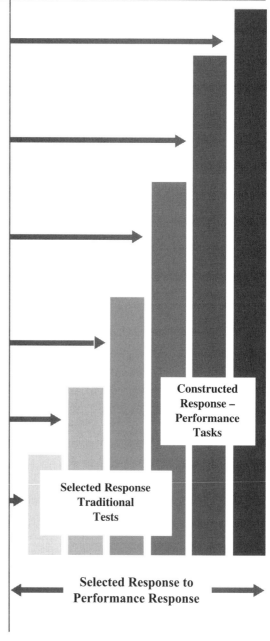

**Evaluation: Highest mental process**
Students judge the merit of an idea, a solution to a problem, aesthetic work, or their own work based on experience, learning, and expectations. There may be many correct ways of responding.

**Synthesis: Higher mental process**
Students employ original and creative thinking, drawing on experience and previous learning to produce an original work, make predictions, and solve problems in which a variety of creative answers may be acceptable.

**Analysis: High mental process**
Students think critically and in depth to identify motive, reasons, or causes for a specific occurrence; analyze available information to reach a conclusion, inference, or generalization; or analyze a conclusion, inference, or generalization to find evidence to support or refute it.

**Application: Medium mental process**
Students apply previously learned information, a rule, or process to a problem and thereby determine a single right answer to that problem.

**Comprehension: Basic mental process**
Students demonstrate that they have sufficient understanding to organize and arrange material mentally and can rephrase and sequence that information.

**Knowledge: Initial and lowest of mental processes**
Students recognize or recall information.

Constructed
Response –
Performance
Tasks

Selected Response
Traditional
Tests

Selected Response to
Performance Response

*Source:* Adapted from *Taxonomy of Educational Objectives, Handbook I, Cognitive Domain.* Edited by Benjamin Bloom. New York: David McKay, 1956.

assignments may become blurred, particularly if the assessment/assignment is extended over time and out of the direct control of the teacher. Many research reports, projects, journals, multi-media presentations may be worked on outside the classroom. However, this lack of uniformity compromises the classroom's assessment/assignments' ability to be used for reliable, high-stakes decision making. There is not a middle grades teacher who has not received an out-of-class project and wondered about the extent of parental involvement, external assistance, or advantaged resources involved in it.

Informal, standards-based assessment/ assignments at the classroom level are essential to learning and informing individual instruction, particularly if the student has multiple opportunities to redo and refine the original assessment/assignment until it demonstrates proficiency or better. However, assessment characteristics of validity, reliability, and fairness, which are critical to high-stakes decisions and targeted program planning, are generally not found in informal classroom assessments/assignments.

An alternative or supplement to the classroom assessment that provides standardization is the school or districtwide benchmark assessment. This assessment may also call for performance tasks, but it is more formal and has a standardized on-site administration and scoring procedure that helps maintain the validity, reliability, and fairness of the assessment. These assessments are collegially developed or adopted and scored. Benchmark assessments are generally given to all students in the same course and grade level in the district at prescribed intervals. They measure proficiency on subsets of standards and might include writing samples, literary responses, oral reports, demonstrations showing understanding of how-to-manuals, dramatizations, open-ended mathematics problems, memory maps, laboratory investigations, keyboarding or typing tests, and projects using specialized software in the school's computer lab.

Through these uniform benchmark assessments, teachers can really evaluate how their students are doing relative to the selected standards in not only their classrooms but also other grade-level classrooms in their district. These benchmark assessments become sophisticated means of providing valuable information for not only classroom practice but also school and districtwide decision making. They should not be thought of as another test, but a powerful extension of the learning process.

## Assessment and Curriculum Development

In a standards-based system, assessment development and lesson planning follow a different process and sequence than in the traditional textbook-driven system. Figure 3-3 compares the differences.

Before a lesson is taught, an assessment of intended student learning is already developed or in development. When planning standards-based assessments, ask the question, What evidence must be collected from students that will demonstrate their knowledge and proficiency on this (these) standard(s)? Once this question has been answered, the assessment is designed, and the scoring criteria are developed. The teacher is then ready to plan the curriculum and scaffold the learning activities until students are prepared to demonstrate their learning through the assessment. This process

**Figure 3-3**    Instruction and Assessment

## A Comparison of Traditional Practice vs. a Standards-Based Education System

| *Traditional Practice* | *Standards-Based Education System* |
| --- | --- |
| Select a topic from the curriculum. | Select and then analyze the standard(s) to be met. |
| Design instructional activities. | Design or select an assessment through which students can demonstrate mastery of the standard(s); determine the required performance level, if it is not already given. |
| Deliver a lesson. | Identify what students must know and be able to do in order to perform well on the assessment. |
| Design and administer an assessment. | Plan and deliver instructional activities that include direct instruction and teacher-student interaction. This process helps all students gain the knowledge and skill(s) identified in the standards. |
| Give a grade or feedback. | Provide all students with adequate opportunities to learn and practice the necessary skills and knowledge. |
| Move on to a new topic. | Assess students and examine their results to plan further instruction or individual support, if needed. If appropriate, give a grade or other feedback. |

*Source:* Adapted from (a) Kate Jamentz, *Standards: From Document to Dialogue.* San Francisco: Western Assessment Collaborative, 1998; and (b) Douglas Reeves, *Making Standards Work.* Denver: Center for Performance Assessment, 1997.

is referred to as "backwards planning" and is a worthy topic for professional development.[6]

Developing or selecting technically sound assessments requires a level of training that most teachers may not have had. Prior to collegial assessment development, professional training is essential. Educators should know how to write and evaluate good multiple-choice and selected-response questions that stretch into the analytical levels of a cognitive taxonomy. High-quality multiple-choice questions can provide reliable data and are easy to score, but they are difficult to write.

Constructed-response and written-response assessments are even a greater challenge to write (see also Appendix 3-E, "Item Development Guidelines for Teacher Teams," at the end of this chapter). Their language needs to be concise and grade-level appropriate. The task must be interesting and doable for the students but novel enough that the students must use higher-level cognitive thinking.

In addition to the standards-based assessment, teachers must anticipate the variety of student responses and design or adopt a general scoring guide that will assist them in evaluating student work. The scoring guide also clarifies in advance the content standards to be covered and the levels of performance expected to demonstrate proficiency or better. Appendixes

3-F, "Four-Point Scoring Guide for Writing Tasks for Grade Seven," and 3-G, "Four-Point Scoring Guide for Writing Tasks for Grades Nine and Ten" at the end of this chapter are examples of four-point general scoring guides for written response items. Examples for both grades seven and nine and ten are included so that readers can see the relationship to corresponding grade-level standards and the degree of growth expected between grades seven and ten when students are presented with the *High School Exit Examination*'s writing tasks.

## Conclusions

Assessments are developed for different purposes. No single assessment can effectively provide data for all purposes. Multiple measures statewide and locally are necessary to cover the range of purposes of policymakers, taxpayers, and educators. Classroom and benchmark assessments are essential to learning and assessing the highest levels of the cognitive taxonomy as identified in California's standards.

Recommendations on performance assessments from the National Research Council in their 1999 report *Testing, Teaching, and Learning: A Guide for States and School Districts*,[7] mirror many of the premises of this chapter:

- Teachers should administer assessments frequently and regularly in classrooms for the purpose of monitoring individual students' performance and adapting instruction to improve their performance.
- Assessment should involve a range of strategies appropriate for inferences relevant to individual students, classrooms, schools, districts, and states.

- Standards-based assessments should be sensitive to effective instruction. Districts, schools, and teachers should use the results of these assessments to revise their practices and thereby help improve student performance.
- Standardized norm-referenced tests of content knowledge should be used as general indicators of comparative performance but should not be the focus of instruction.
- Multiple measures should be combined to enable individuals and schools to demonstrate competency in a variety of ways. Such measures should work together to support the coherence of instruction and students' achievement of all dimensions of the standards.

Standards-based assessment and related instruction follow a different sequence of planning for which teachers may need professional development. Teachers may also need specific training in the development of sound assessments. The development of benchmark assessments is a collegial process requiring district support of time and resources.

Results from a standards-based system of statewide, district, and classroom assessments can be the most important information available to help increase student achievement. Sound assessment practice is an essential component of a standards-based system and joins hands with standards and accountability at center stage for not only middle grades students but all students in kindergarten through grade twelve. Middle grades teachers and students take center stage in that continuum and are no longer caught in the middle.

# Assessment

- **California has made a major commitment to student assessment. There are also multiple elements of this structure that are a part of recent legislation.** Ask your principal to devote a faculty meeting to this subject. Use the chart in Appendix 1-B as a starting point. Especially review the degree to which aspects of student assessment are understood by you and your colleagues. Are there areas of understanding that should be strengthened? How aware are parents about these issues? What things might your school do to ensure that students, parents, and the professional staff fully benefit from the provisions of California's assessment system?

- **Organizations that represent the academic disciplines generally agree that nearly all students are capable of achieving a high standard of performance in a rigorous curriculum.** As your school moves toward performance-based assessments, are you finding increased numbers of students rising to the academic challenge? In what way are you seeing this occur? If this is not occurring, do you have ideas about probable causes? Is there a deliberate schoolwide effort to focus on this challenge? What is your personal role?

- **Content and performance standards, curriculum and instruction, and assessments of student performance need to be aligned.** Ask your principal to help organize faculty forums that meet regularly to address alignment issues and related tasks.

- **Design and implementation of performance assessments includes planning assessments and assignments that allow students to demonstrate what they know relative to the content standards, developing functional scoring criteria or using generic rubrics, applying those criteria to student work, and ultimately determining individual student performance.** Consider each of these variables and assess how well you and your colleagues who teach the same grade and subject are doing in your efforts to develop and implement these components. Are there ways to improve your consensus-building process? Could teachers of other subjects and grades benefit by these efforts? How might you develop a cross-discipline assessment with teachers from another subject area? Invite them to participate with you.

- **If you are a principal, how would you evaluate your professional ability to provide direct assistance to teachers who need help in developing performance assessments?** Do you regularly provide such assistance? If not, do you broker assistance by others? What kind of professional assistance would benefit you as you seek to support your staff? With whom will you share your need?

# Appendix 3-A

# California Assessment System Chart

| | STAR Program | | | | | | | | |
|---|---|---|---|---|---|---|---|---|---|
| | **Stanford 9** | **California Standards Tests** | **Primary Language SABE/2** | **California English Language Development Test** | **High School Exit Examination** | **Golden State Examinations\* / Assessments in Career Education\*** | **Physical Fitness** | **NAEP** | **CHSPE\* / GED\*** |
| Type | Norm-referenced | Standards-based | Norm-referenced | Standards-based | Standards-based | GSE – Standards-based; ACE – Criterion-referenced | Criterion-referenced | Criterion-referenced | Criterion-referenced |
| Grades | Grades 2–11 | Grades 2–11 | Grades 2–11 | Grades K–12 | Grades 9–12 | Grades 7–12 | Grades 5, 7, 9 | Grades 4, 8, 12 | CHSPE – Age 16 and up; GED – Age 18 and up |
| Content | **Grades 2–8**: Reading, Spelling, Written Expression, Mathematics, History–Social Science, Science. **Grades 9–11**: Reading, Writing, Mathematics, History–Social Science, Science | English–language arts, Mathematics. **Grades 9–11**: History–Social Science, Science. **Grades 4, 7**: Written Composition | Reading, Spelling, Language arts, Mathematics | Listening, Speaking, Reading, Writing | Language arts, Mathematics. **2000–01 Grade 9** Optional; **2001–02 Grade 10** Required; **Grade 9** Optional | **GSE**: Reading/literature, Written composition, First-year algebra, Geometry, High school mathematics, U.S. history, Government/civics, Economics, Biology, Chemistry, Second-year coordinated science, Physics, Spanish. **ACE**: Agricultural care, Computer science and information systems, Food service and hospitality, Health care, Level 1, Technology care | Aerobic capacity, Body composition, Abdominal strength and endurance, Trunk extensor strength and flexibility, Flexibility | **2001 Grades 4, 8, 12**: U.S. history, Geography. **2002 Grades 4, 8, 12**: Reading, Writing | **CHSPE**: Reading, Writing, Mathematics. **GED**: Literature/language arts, Writing, Mathematics, Science, Social science |
| **Results** | Individual, School, District, County, State | Individual, School, District, County, State | Individual, School, District, County, State | Individual | Individual | Individual | Individual, School, District, County, State | National, State | Individual |

*Voluntary for students.

Prepared by the California Department of Education • Standards and Assessment Division   August 2000

# Appendix 3-B

# California's Statewide Assessment-Implementation Timeline

| | | |
|---|---|---|
| Fall 1997 | | Standardized Testing and Reporting (STAR) Program legislation enacted |
| Spring 1998 | | First administration of the test for the STAR Program |
| | SAT 9 | Stanford Achievement Test, Ninth Edition, Form T to all students in grades 2–11 |
| Spring 1999 | | Second administration of the tests for the STAR Program |
| | SAT 9 | Stanford Achievement Test, Ninth Edition, Form T to all students in grades 2–11 |
| | SABE/2 | SABE/2 for LEP Spanish-speaking students enrolled in a California school for less than 12 months |
| | California Standards Tests/ELA & Math | First administration of California Standards Tests in language arts and mathematics for grades 2–11 (These tests align with the adopted California academic content standards.) |
| Spring 2000 | | Third administration of the tests for the STAR Program |
| | SAT 9 | Stanford Achievement Test, Ninth Edition, Form T to all students in grades 2–11 |
| | SABE/2 | SABE/2 for LEP Spanish-speaking students enrolled in a California school for less than 12 months |
| | California Standards Tests/ELA & Math | Second administration of the California Standards Tests in language arts and mathematics for grades 2–11. |
| Spring 2001 | | Fourth administration of the tests for the STAR Program |
| | SAT 9 | Fourth administration of the Stanford Achievement Test, Ninth Edition, Form T to all students in grades 2–11. |
| | SABE/2 | Third administration of the SABE/2 for LEP Spanish-speaking students enrolled in a California school for less than 12 months |
| | California Standards Tests/ELA & Math | Third administration of the California Standards Tests in language arts and mathematics for grades 2–11, including writing samples for grades 4 and 7; performance-level setting completed in ELA (Results are expected to be available for use in California's accountability system.) |
| | California Standards Tests/H-SS & Sci. | First administration of the California Standards Tests in history–social science and science for grades 9–11. |
| | CELDT | First administration of the California English Language Development Test (not part of STAR) |
| | HSEE | First administration of the High School Exit Examination to be administered to grade nine students who <u>choose</u> to take the test (not part of STAR) |
| Spring 2002 | | Fifth administration of the tests for the STAR Program |
| | SAT 9 | Fifth administration of the Stanford Achievement Test, Ninth Edition, Form T to all students in grades 2–11 |
| | SABE/2 | Fourth administration of the SABE/2 for LEP Spanish-speaking students enrolled in a California school for less than 12 months |
| | California Standards Tests/ELA & Math | Fourth administration of the California Standards Tests in language arts and mathematics for grades 2–11 (Both ELA and mathematics results are expected to be available for use in California's accountability system.) |
| | California Standards Tests/H-SS & Sci. | Second administration of the California Standards Tests in history–social science and science for grades 9–11 (Anticipated initial availability for use in California's accountability system.) |
| | CELDT | Second administration of the California English Language Development Test (not part of STAR) |
| | HSEE | First administration of the High School Exit Examination to be administered to grade ten students who are <u>required</u> to take the test (not part of STAR) |

# Appendix 3-C

# The State Board of Education's Policy on Preparation for State Tests and the Standardized Testing and Reporting (STAR) Program

## Introduction

In general, the best preparation for state tests, including the STAR tests, is good instruction. This can be broadly defined as instruction in the content specified in California's content standards, employing the instructional principles and practices set forth in the content-area frameworks. It is the standards and the frameworks, therefore, that should guide instructional programs. The instructional program should be designed to ensure that students master the standards at their own and earlier grade levels, since the standards at particular grades are based on content introduced at earlier grades. The instructional program should ensure that students are able to demonstrate mastery of the content standards in multiple formats—e.g., multiple choice, short answer, and essay. The instructional program should include practice assignments that are timed, and test reports for individual students and groups of students should be used to identify skill areas that may require emphasis.

A simple way to determine whether a contemplated test preparation procedure is permissible is to ask, "If the specific test for which I am preparing students were discontinued and a different test of the same type or of a different format were substituted, would my test preparation procedure remain the same or would it change?" If it would remain the same, then it probably is permissible because it is most likely generic preparation for any test or test format rather than for one specific test or format. On the other hand, if that test preparation would change, then it probably is not

permissible because it is most likely intended to improve achievement on a particular test rather than to teach general test-taking skills.

## Background

As stated in Section 60611 of the California *Education Code,* "No city, county, city and county, or district superintendent of schools or principal or teacher of any elementary or secondary school shall carry on any program of specific preparation for the statewide pupil assessment program or a particular test used therein." Further, as set forth in *Title 5, California Code of Regulations,* Section 854, also in reference to the statewide testing program, "No program or materials shall be used by any school district or employee of a school district that are specifically formulated or intended to prepare pupils for the designated achievement tests." *Title 5* regulations, however, do permit the use of "materials specifically included within the designated achievement test," including "practice tests provided by the publisher as part of the designated achievement test" (*Title 5, California Code of Regulations,* Section 854).

*The Standards for Educational and Psychological Testing* state that "the integrity of test results should be maintained by eliminating practices designed to raise scores without improving performance on the construct or domain being tested." They comment that practices such as "teaching test items in advance, modifying test administration procedures, and discouraging or excluding certain test takers from taking the test can lead to

*Source:* California Department of Education, Standards and Assessment Division.

spuriously high scores that do not reflect performance on the underlying construct or domain of interest" (Standard 15.9). These standards also note that "the appropriateness of test preparation activities can be evaluated . . . by determining the extent to which test scores are artificially raised without actually increasing students' level of achievement" (Standard 13.11).

### Statement of Policy

The following test preparation policy was adopted by the State Board of Education on September 7, 2000:

> No city, county, city and county, or district superintendent of schools or principal or teacher is to use any test preparation materials or strategies developed for a specific test. This includes but is not limited to published materials, materials available on the Internet, and materials developed by schools, district or county offices of education, and/or outside consultants.

### STAR Test Preparation Examples

The STAR program consists of three tests; The *Stanford Achievement Test, Ninth Edition, Form T (Stanford 9)*; the *Spanish Assessment of Basic Education, Second Edition (SABE/2)*; and the *California Standards Tests*. The *Stanford 9* and *SABE/2* are norm-referenced achievement tests; the *California Standards Tests* are criterion-referenced tests. All are multiple-choice tests designed to verify breadth of learning. The *California Standards Tests* at grades four and seven also require students to produce a writing sample. The information below provides examples of test preparation practices that are and are not appropriate for the *Stanford 9, SABE/2, California Standards*

*Tests*, and standards-test writing assessments at grades four and seven. The practices identified here as appropriate and inappropriate represent specific applications of the statute and regulations.

### STAR Multiple-choice Tests: *Stanford 9, SABE/2*, and *California Standards Tests*

**Appropriate Test Preparation:**

- Use practice tests provided by the test publisher as part of the state testing program.
- Prepare students with test-taking strategies designed to make them better at taking any type of test rather than to prepare them specifically for taking the *Stanford 9, SABE/2*, or *California Standards Tests*. This practice may, in fact, make the test more valid by reducing the influence of factors such as previous testing experience. Examples of appropriate strategies might include:
  – using time efficiently
  – understanding directions
  – placing answers correctly on answer sheets
  – checking answers
  – using the problem-solving tactics of educated guessing, estimating, and working problems backward
  – exposing students to various test formats, including questions that contain "none of the above," "all of above," "not here," negative wording, and true-false statements

The suggestions noted above apply to materials produced by test-preparation companies as well as those prepared by individual teachers, schools, districts, and county offices of education.

**Inappropriate Test Preparation:***

- Conducting reviews or drills that use actual test items or identical format items of the *Stanford 9, SABE/2,* or *California Standards Tests.*
- Conducting a test preparation program designed specifically to prepare students to perform well on the *Stanford 9, SABE/2,* or *California Standards Tests* as opposed to a program designed to teach general test-taking strategies. In regard to the norm-referenced *Stanford 9* and *SABE/2,* the norm groups to which California students are being compared received no specific preparation for these tests so that the scores of students who do prepare for these specific tests may be invalid.
- Preparing students in ways that improve scores without improving underlying achievement.
- Using sample items to prepare practice items in the same format.
- Using alternate forms of the test. Practice with alternate forms affects the accuracy of generalizations that might be made about a student's mastery of the content domain the test is designed to sample.
- Using copies of tests from previous years.
- Reviewing the test to be administered and then reviewing the test-specific curriculum content with students before administering the test.

*This section is not intended to cover all inappropriate test preparation practices.

## California Standards Writing Tests at Grades Four and Seven

**Appropriate Test Preparation:**

- Have students write regularly in all content domains. The *Reading/Language Arts Framework* contains standards that describe writing strategies, applications and conventions for these grade levels as well as teaching strategies for implementing these standards effectively.
- Have students edit their own work and the work of other students.
- Share scoring rubrics and sample papers with students and help them use these materials to evaluate their own writing.
- Provide written directions for writing prompts throughout the school year and teach students to identify key words in them.
- Teach students to reread directions for written assignments and then read their responses to verify that they have fulfilled all requirements.

**Inappropriate Test Preparations:***

- Having worksheets that only ask students to edit for mechanics, conventions, and the like. While not prohibited, these types of worksheets generally are not effective in helping students learn to write well.
- Focusing on one type of writing in the expectation that it will be tested during a specific year.

## Consequences of Inappropriate Test Preparation

Confirmed instances of inappropriate test preparation involving city, county, district, or school personnel may result in a number of negative consequences for the parties involved. These may include, but would not necessarily be limited to, the following:

- Notice of STAR testing irregularities may be posted on the STAR Internet site for the school involved.
- Schools may become ineligible for awards such as those available through the Governor's performance award programs.

- Personnel may be subject to district sanctions as outlined in district policies or teacher contracts.
- Students may become ineligible for scholarships and awards such as those provided through the Governor's Scholars Program.

# Appendix 3-D

# Developing, Using, and Communicating Complex Reasoning

Middle grades students should have frequent opportunities to develop and demonstrate complex reasoning and to use written and oral communication to convey their thought processes. Content and performance standards in core subjects should reflect curriculum and instruction that prepare students to engage in progressively more demanding cognitive tasks, including those that require them to:

- *Participate in oral discussions* of solutions to mathematical problems; outcomes of scientific experiments; or the formulation and testing of hypotheses in science, social studies, and other subjects.
- *Use knowledge of facts, procedures, and operations to solve problems,* arrive at conclusions, or propose novel solutions based on original thinking.
- *Prepare papers, essays, or other appropriate written materials which describe the steps followed in conducting research, analyzing data, and using other complex reasoning in studying social, political, economic, and scientific problems and issues.* This work should reflect proficient writing skills and appropriate use of numbers, symbols, graphs, photos, charts, and other visual materials. Written work should be shared with other students, who are encouraged to ask questions, offer suggestions, provide alternative problem-solving logic, and otherwise interact creatively.
- *Engage in history–social science, mathematics, and science projects that call for a high level of abstractive thought before solutions can be found—sometimes re-ferred to as "power problems."* These projects should require extended reasoning, which takes the student beyond conventional facts and rules. Assignments of this type might be given once a semester and typically require highly focused homework. Parents should be apprised of "power problems" and invited to work with their child, if appropriate; but in all cases their role is to make certain that the assignment is completed.
- *Provide detailed descriptions of how answers are determined for selected test items in history–social science, mathematics, and science.* Items should require students to process, analyze, compare, contrast, generalize, or use other types of abstract thought. Students' responses should reflect the application of new knowledge and skills introduced during classroom instruction or learned through related assignments.
- *Use graphs, pictographs, charts, and other similar representation of statistical data to communicate complex ideas.* Use real or hypothetical data and demonstrate the ability to choose the most appropriate type of graphic representation.
- *Use computer software applications,* which develop abilities to use spreadsheets and graphing calculators, to process information, or to otherwise perform calculations, solve problems, or analyze data.
- *Complete assignments on the Internet* to locate data, including original source materials, and to provide web site addresses in bibliographic material.

# Appendix 3-E

# Item Development Guidelines
# for Teacher Teams

## General Item-Writing Guidelines

1. Use the standards to guide item-writing efforts. This will help ensure that all items are linked to targeted standards.

2. Make sure that items:

   - Focus on high-level thinking, reasoning, and problem-solving skills as much as possible.
   - Use simple, concise language to clearly articulate the tasks to be completed.
   - Include only information that is relevant and necessary for answering the items or completing the tasks.
   - Are within the appropriate range of difficulty for the intended student population.
   - Use the lowest readability level possible (e.g., grade-appropriate vocabulary and simple, concise sentences).
   - Use graphics (when applicable) that are clear and easy to understand.
   - Do not use language or content that could be offensive or inappropriate for a population or subgroup.
   - Do not include or implicitly support negative stereotypes.

3. Develop two to three times the number of items actually needed for the final assessment. This will make it possible to drop ineffective items following classroom tryouts and analysis of test results.

4. Allow ample time for editing and proofreading of items. Check for clarity, as well as for errors in spelling, grammar, and punctuation.

*Source:* WestEd. Printed with permission.

## Multiple-Choice Item-Writing Guidelines (specific)

- Present a clearly formulated, concise problem in the item's stem. The best stems focus on a single aspect of content (e.g., a concept or principle) and one type of cognitive performance (e.g., recall of knowledge or application of knowledge).
- State the item stem in positive terms whenever possible. Students, especially second-language learners, often have difficulty understanding questions that are phrased in negative terms (e.g., "Which is *not* an example of . . . "). They often overlook the word "not," and, therefore, misinterpret the question. If it is necessary to phrase a question using negative terms (e.g., "not," "except"), make sure to capitalize or bold-face the negative terms so that they stand out to students.
- Avoid the use of unnecessary or irrelevant details in the item stem and answer choices.
- Use answer choices that are brief and parallel (e.g., if one answer choice begins with a verb, make sure all answer choices begin with verbs).
- Use answer choices that are grammatically consistent with the stem of the item. Grammatical inconsistencies can provide clues that help uninformed students correctly guess the appropriate answer.
- Include distracters that are plausible and attractive to uninformed students. For example:
  - Use common or likely misconceptions or errors of students as distracters.

- Make distracters similar to the correct answer in both length and complexity of wording.
- Use scientific- and technical-sounding words to help make distracters enticing.

- Do not give clues that might enable students to guess the correct answer or to easily eliminate incorrect alternatives. For example:
  - Avoid using similar wording in the item stem and correct answer choice.
  - Avoid writing the correct answer in a style that is distinctly different from the distracters.
  - Avoid stating the correct answer in greater detail or length than the distracters.
  - Avoid including absolute terms (e.g., "always," "never," "all," "none," "only") in distracters.

- Make sure each item has a correct answer that is unquestionably correct or clearly best.

## Written-Response Item-Writing Guidelines (specific)

### For all written-response items:

- Present a clearly formulated problem or situation (in paragraph form) in the item's prompt. Make sure that the described problem or situation is novel but not entirely unfamiliar to students. The context or details in the prompt should not be beyond the ability of students to imagine.

- Provide specific instructions that tell students everything they need to do when responding to the prompt. Be sure, however, not to provide excessive information which might remove the challenge for students.

- Present the instructions in the form of statements rather than questions whenever possible (e.g., "Explain three reasons . . ." rather than "What are three reasons . . .").

- Avoid unnecessary detail in both the prompt and instructions. Ask yourself, "Is this essential information?" If the answer is "no," eliminate it.

### For long written-response items:

- Clearly state the evaluation criteria (i.e., what students must demonstrate to receive a satisfactory rating). Providing this information helps students understand what is expected. (See Appendix 3-F.)

- Make sure that the information presented in the prompt, instructions, and evaluation criteria is consistent. For example, concepts included in the evaluation criteria should reiterate or support information given in the instructions and the prompt.

# Four-Point Scoring Guide for Writing Tasks
# for Grade Seven

*(Based on California's English–language arts
content standards for grade seven)*

## 4

The writing—

- *clearly* addresses all parts of the writing task.
- demonstrates a *clear* understanding of purpose and audience.
- maintains a *consistent* point of view, focus, and organizational structure, including the *effective* use of transitions.
- includes a *clearly presented* central idea with *relevant* facts, details, and/or explanations.
- includes a *variety* of sentence types.
- contains *few, if any, errors* in the conventions of the English language (grammar, punctuation, capitalization, spelling). These errors do *not* interfere with the reader's understanding of the writing.

### Fictional or autobiographical narrative writing—

- provides *a thoroughly developed* plotline, including major and minor characters and a *definite* setting.
- includes *appropriate* strategies (e.g., dialogue, suspense, narrative action).

### Response to literature writing—

- develops interpretations that demonstrate a *thoughtful,* comprehensive grasp of the text.
- organizes *accurate and coherent* interpretations around *clear* ideas, premises, or images from the literary work.
- provides *specific* textual examples and details to support the interpretations.

### Persuasive writing—

- *authoritatively* defends a position with precise and relevant evidence and *convincingly* addresses the reader's concerns, biases, and expectations.

### Summary writing—

- is characterized by paraphrasing of the main idea(s) and *significant* details.

## 3

The writing—

- addresses all parts of the writing task.
- demonstrates a *general* understanding of purpose and audience.
- maintains a *mostly consistent* point of view, focus, and organizational structure, including the *effective* use of *some* transitions.
- presents a central idea with *mostly relevant* facts, details, and/or explanations.
- includes a *variety* of sentence types.
- contains s*ome errors* in the conventions of the English language (grammar, punctuation, capitalization, spelling). These errors do *not* interfere with the reader's understanding of the writing.

### Fictional or autobiographical narrative writing—

- provides an *adequately developed* plotline, including major and minor characters and a *definite* setting.
- includes *appropriate* strategies (e.g., dialogue, suspense, narrative action).

*Source:* Standards and Assessment Division, California Department of Education.

*Response to literature writing—*

- develops interpretations that demonstrate a comprehensive grasp of the text.
- organizes accurate and *reasonably* coherent interpretations around *clear* ideas, premises, or images from the literary work.
- provides textual examples and details to support the interpretations.

*Persuasive writing—*

- *generally* defends a position with relevant evidence and addresses the reader's concerns, biases, and expectations.

*Summary writing—*

- is characterized by paraphrasing of the main idea(s) and *significant* details.

## 2

The writing—

- addresses *only parts* of the writing task.
- demonstrates *little* understanding of purpose and audience.
- maintains an *inconsistent* point of view, focus, and/or organizational structure, which may include *ineffective or awkward* transitions that do not unify important ideas.
- *suggests* a central idea with *limited* facts, details, and/or explanations.
- includes *little* variety in sentence types.
- contains *several errors* in the conventions of the English language (grammar, punctuation, capitalization, spelling). These errors *may* interfere with the reader's understanding of the writing.

*Fictional or autobiographical narrative writing—*

- provides a *minimally developed* plotline, including characters and a setting.
- *attempts* to use strategies but with *minimal* effectiveness (e.g., dialogue, suspense, narrative action).

*Response to literature writing—*

- develops interpretations that demonstrate a *limited* grasp of the text.
- includes interpretations that *lack* accuracy or coherence as related to ideas, premises, or images from the literary work.
- provides *few, if any,* textual examples and details to support the interpretations.

*Persuasive writing—*

- defends a position with *little, if any,* evidence and *may* address the reader's concerns, biases, and expectations.

*Summary writing—*

- is characterized by *substantial* copying of key phrases and *minimal* paraphrasing.

## 1

The writing—

- addresses *only one part* of the writing task.
- demonstrates *no* understanding of purpose and audience.
- *lacks* a point of view, focus, organizational structure, and transitions that unify important ideas.

- *lacks* a central idea but may contain *marginally related* facts, details, and/or explanations.
- includes *no* sentence variety.
- contains s*erious errors* in the conventions of the English language (grammar, punctuation, capitalization, spelling). These errors interfere with the reader's understanding of the writing.

### Fictional or autobiographical narrative writing—

- *lacks* a developed plotline.
- *fails* to use strategies (e.g., dialogue, suspense, narrative action).

### Response to literature writing—

- demonstrates *little* grasp of the text.
- *lacks* an interpretation or *may* be a simple retelling of the passage.
- *lacks* textual examples and details.

### Persuasive writing—

- *fails* to defend a position with *any* evidence and *fails* to address the reader's concerns, biases, and expectations.

### Summary writing—

- is characterized by substantial copying of *indiscriminately selected* phrases or sentences.

# Appendix 3-G

## Four-Point Scoring Guide for Writing Tasks for Grades Nine and Ten

*(Based on California's English–language arts content standards for grades nine and ten)*

### Response to Writing Prompt

#### 4

The essay –

- *clearly* addresses all parts of the writing task.
- provides a *meaningful* thesis and maintains a consistent tone and focus and *purposefully* illustrates a control of organization.
- *thoughtfully* supports the thesis and main ideas with *specific* details and examples.
- provides a *variety* of sentence types and uses *precise, descriptive* language.
- demonstrates a *clear* sense of audience.
- contains *few, if any errors* in the conventions of the English language. (Errors are generally first-draft in nature.)

*Persuasive compositions:*

- *authoritatively* defends a position with precise and relevant evidence and *convincingly* addresses the reader's concerns, biases, and expectations.

#### 3

The essay–

- addresses all parts of the writing task.
- provides a thesis and maintains a consistent tone and focus and illustrates a control of organization.
- supports the thesis and main ideas with details and examples.

- provides a *variety* of sentence types and uses *some descriptive* language.
- demonstrates a *general* sense of audience.
- contains some errors in the conventions of the English language. (Errors do *not* interfere with the reader's understanding of the essay.)

*Persuasive compositions:*

- *generally* defends a position with relevant evidence and addresses the reader's concerns, biases, and expectations.

#### 2

The essay–

- addresses *only parts* of the writing task.
- *may* provide a thesis and maintains an *inconsistent* tone and focus and illustrates *little, if any* control of organization.
- *may* support the thesis and main ideas with *limited, if any,* details and/or examples.
- provides *few, if any,* types of sentences, and uses *basic, predictable* language.
- demonstrates *little* or *no* sense of audience,
- contains *several errors* in the conventions of the English language. (Errors *may* interfere with the reader's understanding of the essay.)

*Persuasive compositions:*

- defends a position with *little, if any,* evidence and *may* address the reader's concerns, biases, and expectations.

*Source:* Standards and Assessment Division, California Department of Education.

## 1

The essay may be too short to evaluate or–

- addresses *only* one part of the writing task.
- *may* provide a *weak, if any* thesis; *fails to maintain* a focus, and illustrates *little,* or *no* control of organization.
- *fails* to support ideas with details and/or examples.
- provides *no* sentence variety and uses *limited* vocabulary.
- demonstrates *no* sense of audience.
- contains *serious errors* in the conventions of the English language. (Errors interfere with the reader's understanding of the essay.)

### Persuasive compositions:

- *fails* to defend a position with *any* evidence and fails to address the reader's concerns, biases, and expectations.

## Response to Literacy/Expository Text

## 4

The response–

- demonstrates a *thorough* and *thoughtful,* comprehensive grasp of the test.
- accurately and coherently provides *specific* textual details and examples to support the thesis and main ideas.
- demonstrates a *clear* understanding of the ambiguities, nuances, and complexities of the text.
- provides a variety of sentence types and uses *precise, descriptive* language.

- contains *few, if any,* errors in the conventions of the English language. (Errors are generally first-draft in nature.)

### Response to informational passages:

- *thoughtfully* anticipates and addresses the reader's potential misunderstandings, biases, and expectations.

### Response to literary passages:

- clearly demonstrates an awareness of the author's use of literary and/or stylistic devices.

## 3

The response–

- demonstrates a comprehensive grasp of the text.
- accurately and coherently provides general textual details and examples to support the thesis and main ideas.
- demonstrates a *general* understanding of the ambiguities, nuances, and complexities of the text.
- provides a variety of sentence types and uses *some descriptive* language.
- contains *some errors* in the conventions of the English language. (Errors do not interfere with the reader's understanding of the essay.)

### Response to informational passages:

- anticipates and addresses the reader's potential misunderstandings, biases, and expectations.

### Response to literary passages:

- demonstrates an awareness of the author's use of literary and/or stylistic devices.

| 2 | 1 |
|---|---|
| **The response–** | **The response–** |

The response–

- demonstrates a *limited* comprehensive grasp of the text.
- provides *few, if any,* textual details and examples to support the thesis and main ideas.
- demonstrates a *limited,* or *no,* understanding of the ambiguities, nuances, and complexities of the text.
- provides *few, if any,* types of sentences and uses *basic, predictable* language.
- contains *several errors* in the conventions of the English language. (Errors may interfere with the reader's understanding of the essay.)

*Response to informational passages:*

- *may* address the reader's potential misunderstandings, biases, and expectations, but in a limited manner.

*Response to literary passages:*

- *may* demonstrate an awareness of the author's use of literary and/or stylistic devices.

The response–

- demonstrates *little, if any,* comprehensive grasp of the text.
- provides *no* textual details and examples to support the thesis and main ideas.
- demonstrates *no* understanding of the ambiguities, nuances, and complexities of the text.
- provides *no* sentence variety and uses *limited* vocabulary.
- contains *serious errors* in the conventions of the English language. (Errors interfere with the reader's understanding of the essay.)

*Response to informational passages:*

- does *not* address the reader's potential misunderstandings, biases, and expectations.

*Response to literary passages:*

- does *not* demonstrate any awareness of the author's use of literary and/or stylistic devices.

# 4

*"Quality is never an accident; it is always the result of high intention, sincere effort, intelligent direction, and skillful execution; it represents a wise choice of many alternatives."*

—Willa A. Foster

# Accountability Takes
# Center Stage

Most middle-level educators have a deep sense of commitment to the students they serve. They know the challenges presented by this young adolescent population, and they know the joys of being part of this pivotal period in students' lives. It is a difficult job even in the best of circumstances, yet teachers' personal and professional sense of caring and responsibility helps them "stay the course." Responsibility is notched up to accountability when one is answerable not only to self but to others.

Being accountable is about being answerable for our actions and the results that are produced and then refining our actions to produce the best results. Educators hold themselves accountable for many different dimensions of a student-centered school. Professionally reflecting on daily work, evaluating and revising instructional methods based on the success or failure of students to grasp the

 Recommendations 8, 9, 10, 11

material, and guiding students to make wise choices are just a small sample of personal and professional accountability.

In a standards-based system, accountability takes center stage beyond personal and professional accountability. Thus a standards-based education becomes a system of accountability. This system of accountability stretches beyond individual efforts, to the collective efforts of the school and district. Systemwide accountability holds all stakeholders (students, parents, teachers, principals, district administrators, policymakers, and state officials) accountable for expected standards-based outcomes of student learning.

The state's accountability system focuses on student achievement as it relates to norm-referenced and criterion-referenced (standards-based) assessments. These assessments also serve the needs of districts and schools for program planning and decisions about students (see Chapter 3). They are not, however, frequent or formative enough to hold students accountable for progressive attainment of content and skills. Nor do they offer the variety of perfor-

82

mance tasks that measure higher levels of student thinking and creative problem solving. Consequently, while the accountability systems of districts and schools are aligned to the state's system, local entities must have additional measures to meet their own specific needs. This chapter will look at accountability in general and from both the state and local perspectives.

## A Standards, Assessment, and Accountability Model

States across the nation have been remarkably swift in embracing the broad features of standards-based education. Forty-nine states now have statewide academic standards for what students should know and be able to do in at least some subjects; 50 states test how well their students are learning; and 27 hold schools accountable for results, either by rating the performance of all their schools or identifying low-performing ones.[1]

Each state has its own plan for standards-based reform and incorporates one or more of the three components of a standards-based system. Figure 4-1 shows how standards, assessment, and accountability theoretically work together to produce higher levels of student learning. This model relies on information and responsibility and the premise that every stakeholder "knows what is expected, what they will be measured on, and what the results imply for what they should do next."[2]

California employs all three components of this standards-based reform model and is currently in the process of implementing a new statewide accountability system. Prior to establishment of the statewide system of accountability, many districts in California were in the process of developing local standards-based accountability systems with multiple measures and reporting these measures to the state. The Public Schools Accountability Act (PSAA) of 1999[3] established the statewide system of accountability and relieved districts from the responsibility of reporting local multiple measures. The PSAA statewide system has not replaced local standards-based accountability systems; rather, it is the umbrella component that provides a coherent and uniform look at student achievement through a common statewide perspective.

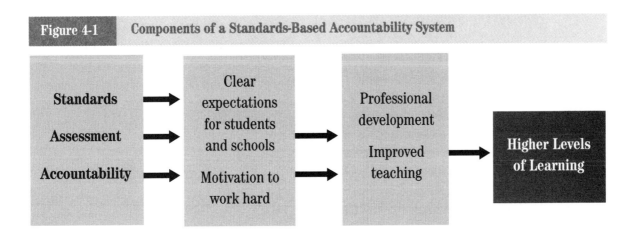

**Figure 4-1**     **Components of a Standards-Based Accountability System**

## An Overview of California's Accountability System

Like most other states, California has invested enormous energy and political capital over the last decade in improving education. At center stage in California's standards-based reform efforts are three interwoven elements:

- (1) Academic content standards across the curricular areas of language arts, mathematics, science, and history–social science that clearly define what students must know and be able to do as a result of instruction in these areas; and (2) evolving performance standards (see Chapter 2)
- An assessment and reporting system consisting of a norm-referenced test for national comparison purposes and a criterion-referenced test based on the state's content standards (see Chapter 3)
- An accountability system that will employ multiple measures of assessment to inform schools how successfully students are meeting standards and that includes corresponding awards and incentives to teachers and schools that are meeting and exceeding target goals, technical assistance to low-performing schools, and sanctions for schools that consistently fail to meet their target goals

Among the requirements of the Public Schools Accountability Act is the creation of an *Academic Performance Index (API)* for each school. The *API* consists of a variety of indicators that are used to measure the overall performance of schools. The *API* draws from components of the assessment system that have been determined to be valid and reliable by the State Board of Education.

Initially, the *Academic Performance Index* was based solely on results from the *Stanford Achievement Test, Ninth Edition, Form T (SAT 9)*. However, to provide a more complete and accurate picture of student achievement with regard to the state's content standards, additional components are being phased in over time (see Figure 4-2 for a tentative timeline of proposed expansion). As additional components are added to the *API*, California's statewide accountability system will comprise multiple measures of standards-aligned student achievement.

While the statewide accountability system is evolving, it still will not be complete for several more years. Accountability indicators, such as annual test results, growth targets, school rankings, rewards, assistance, and sanctions—each important factors in the accountability schema—have attracted prominent media attention since the 1999-2000 school year. With this spotlight comes the motivation to perform well and to be accountable for student success across the state.

## Awards and Incentives for High-Achieving Schools

When a job is done well, those who have worked hard deserve recognition. California's PSAA contains provisions for rewarding schools that demonstrate high levels of student achievement. Through the Governor's Performance Award Program, monetary and nonmonetary awards are earmarked for schools that meet or exceed *API* performance growth targets. Under the Certificated Staff Performance Incentive Act, certificated staff members can receive cash incentives. The School-Site

Figure 4-2

**Tentative Timeline for the Proposed Phase-in of Indicators in the *API***

| | 1998 | 1999 | 2000 | 2001 | 2002 | 2003 | 2004 |
|---|---|---|---|---|---|---|---|
| **SAT 9** | X | X | X | X | X | X | X |
| **CA Standards Tests** | | | | | | | |
| ELA (grades 2–11) | | | | X | X | X | X |
| Math (grades 2–11) | | | | | X | X | X |
| History–social science (grades 9–11) | | | | | X | X | X |
| Science (grades 9–11) | | | | | X | X | X |
| **Attendance**[1] (Staff and pupil) | | | | | X | X | X |
| **Graduation Rates**[1] | | | | | X | X | X |
| **High School Exit Examination** | | | | | | | X |

[1]These components are required by legislation once they are determined to be valid, reliable, and available.
Note: All items beyond 2001 are tentative until approved by the State Board of Education.

Employee Performance Bonus program provides rewards for all staff at a school site (see also Appendix 4-A, "State Monetary Award Programs Based on the *Academic Performance Index (API)*," at the end of this chapter).

Nonmonetary awards to high-achieving schools include, but are not limited to, classification as a distinguished school, listing on a published public school honor roll, and public commendations by the Governor and the Legislature.

## Assistance for Low-Performing Schools

A good accountability program also provides assistance to schools that are still performing below the statewide average. The PSAA stipulates that schools failing to meet their *API* growth targets *and* that have an *API* below the 50th percentile relative to all other public elementary, middle, or high schools will be invited to participate in the Immediate Intervention/Underperforming Schools Program (II/USP).

Through the leadership and collaboration of a state-approved external evaluator, the broad-based school site and community team conducts an extensive review, makes recommendations, and develops an action plan to raise the academic achievement of students in the II/USP school. Short-term academic objectives are set for a two-year period to allow the school to make adequate progress toward established growth targets. The school action plan is multi-faceted and focuses on:

- Improving student academic performance

- Improving the involvement of parents and guardians
- Improving the effectiveness and efficiency of the allocation of resources and management of the school
- Identifying and developing solutions that take into account the underlying causes for low student performance

## Sanctions

Under the provisions of the PSAA, schools that consistently fail to meet their target growth are subject to sanctions. If an II/USP school fails to meet its short-term growth target after the first 12 months of implementing its action plan, the local governing board must hold a public hearing to ensure that members of the school community are aware of the lack of progress. The local board then must choose from a range of interventions for the school to use to continue implementing its action plan and make progress toward meeting its growth targets (*Education Code* Section 52055).

If a school has not met its performance goals 24 months after receiving implementation funding, either of the following can occur:

1. The school can continue to participate in the program for an additional year, assuming it demonstrated significant growth.
2. Failing to demonstrate significant growth, the school is deemed a low-performing school, and the State Superintendent of Public Instruction assumes the legal rights, duties and powers of the governing board with respect to the school. The State Superintendent, in consultation with the State Board of

Education and the governing board of the school district, can reassign the principal of that school and take other actions provided in law, including reorganizing or closing the school (*Education Code* Section 52055.5).

## State and Local Accountability Systems

A purposeful system of accountability not only gives the public and policymakers a public accounting of how well schools and groups of students are doing but also provides data that shape instructional improvement. It is the latter part of the accountability system that is most meaningful to schools and teachers because instructional improvement is the foundation on which real school improvement is built. Neither state nor local accountability systems work in a vacuum. They must work together to provide the continuous flow of data in both directions and to develop corresponding and appropriate responses to those data.

Figure 4-3 shows a model of data types (left), data sources and frequency of data collection and dissemination (center), and data-driven decisions (right). The prime data source is from the classroom and the data emanate upward. Student work reflects what is being taught and learned by depth and breadth through multiple measures. The need for specificity and frequency of individual student data declines as the data move upward. Teachers need specific frequent, feedback for students and groups of students. Schools and districts need broader feedback for making programmatic decisions and specific valid and reliable feedback for high-stakes decisions

Figure 4-3 Model of Data Types and Sources, Data Collection and Dissemination, and Data-Driven Decisions

| Examples of Standards-Based Data Types | Source<br>Collection & Dissemination Frequency | Examples of Data-Driven Decisions and Programs |
|---|---|---|
| Percent of students in performance levels for all core academic subjects based on valid and reliable state accountability systems | **Federal**<br><br>*1+ years (varies)* | • Title I compliance<br>• Funding<br>• Federal legislation<br>• Policy decisions |
| Number and percent of students in performance levels for all core academic subjects based on STAR and local accountability reporting as required (API) | **State**<br><br>*Annually* | • API awards, assistance, and sanctions<br>• State Initiatives<br>• Legislation<br>• Policy decisions<br>• Programs to build district capacity |
| Number and percent of all students in performance levels for all core academic subjects and strands based on valid and reliable measures. Data disaggregated by schools and subgroups | **District**<br><br>*Grading periods/quarterly* | • Districtwide planning/policy<br>• Allocation of resources<br>  – Time<br>  – Materials<br>  – Staffing<br>• Professional development |
| Number and percent of all students in performance levels for core academic subjects and strands based on valid and reliable measures. Data disaggregated by teachers and subgroups | **School**<br><br>*Grading periods/quarterly* | • Schoolwide planning<br>• Professional development<br>• Interventions<br>• Resource allocation |
| Scores and performance levels relative to subject-matter strands and standards from benchmark assessments, by teacher and student subgroups | **Grade-Level/Department/ Teaching Teams**<br><br>*Monthly or biweekly evidence of student progress* | • Grade-level, team planning<br>• Student interventions<br>• Peer coaching<br>• Development of benchmark assignment/assessment |
| Scores and performance levels relative to specific standards (derived from assignments and assessments) | **Teacher/Classroom Students**<br><br>*Daily and weekly evidence gathered toward student attainment of standards* | • Formative feedback<br>• Revised work<br>• Teaching strategies<br>• Classroom interventions<br>• Lesson planning<br>• Professional reflections |

about individuals. Disaggregated data are needed for all groups so that achievement gaps between subgroups can be systematically closed.

The need for good data is undeniable and the need to take targeted action based on the data is even greater. In the past, decisions were based on some data, some anecdotal information, some trends, program indicators, and gut feelings. Today, technology assists us in gathering data and disaggregating data in ways that were never before possible. Because we now have the capability to gather, track, sort, and act on results at every level, we must do so. "Results goad, guide, and motivate groups and individuals. . . . In this sense, all results—good or bad—are ultimately good, because they provide feedback that can guide us, telling us what to do next and how to do better."[4]

## Local Accountability System

In a local accountability system, no single entity shoulders all the responsibility. Policymakers, district administrators, principals, teachers, parents, and the students themselves play critical roles. Students are accountable to their teachers and their parents. Teachers are accountable to the principal. The principal is accountable to the superintendent. The superintendent is accountable to the school board, which represents parents and the broader community. And the entire district is accountable to the state. That is bottom-up (deliver-up) accountability in which each stakeholder is accountable for delivering an expected outcome.

Top-down (provide-down) accountability involves the reverse order. Each stakeholder is responsible for providing the appropriate resources and support to those who are being held accountable. The system is reciprocal. Together, all stakeholders share the common goal of student success and high achievement and the responsibility for attaining that goal. Figure 4-4 is a model of a reciprocal, standards-based accountability system in the middle grades. Obviously many more locally defined inputs and outcomes exist that stakeholders are expected to provide down and deliver up, but this system focuses primarily on standards-based achievement.

## Middle Grades Accountability Support

Middle grades educators work with a unique population of young adolescents. It is not enough for stakeholders to know only about standards, assessment, accountability, and the use of data. They must also know and understand that middle-level students have very different needs from those of young children or those of postpuberty teenagers. Standards for middle grades students take a jump in rigor. These young adolescents are expected to write more, read more, experiment more, and think more than they ever had to do in elementary school. All of this comes at a time when many adolescents are not interested in academic rigor or in what adults expect of them.

Consequently, middle grades teachers may also need unique support to do their jobs. Some may need additional content training, some may need coaching on differentiated instruction that engages the adolescent mind and learning style, some may need specialized training in accelerated-remediation strategies for students who have severe learning deficits, and some

## STATE

| PROVIDES | DELIVER(S) |
|---|---|
| • Support for initiatives<br>• Assistance<br>• Guidance<br>• Incentives/sanctions<br>• Data | • Completed assessments<br>• Accurate and timely reports<br>• Reliable, valid data |

## DISTRICT/SCHOOL BOARD/PARENTS

| | |
|---|---|
| • Understanding and support for initiatives<br>• Policy formulation based on data<br>• Targeted allocation of resources based on data and middle grades needs | • District leadership in implementing data-driven improvements, resulting in higher levels of student achievement |

## SUPERINTENDENT

| | |
|---|---|
| • Policy support<br>• Collection, analysis, and dissemination of data<br>• Understanding of middle grades needs<br>• Data-driven allocation of resources for curriculum, personnel, and training | • Middle school leadership in implementing data-driven improvements, resulting in higher levels of student achievement |

## MIDDLE GRADES PRINCIPAL

| | |
|---|---|
| • Support for standards-based reforms in a middle grades environment<br>• Targeted assistance<br>• Data sharing/analysis<br>• Professional development | • Higher levels of student achievement through effective, standards-based practice and targeted student assistance |

## MIDDLE GRADES TEACHER

| | |
|---|---|
| Student-centered, standards-based:<br>• Planning<br>• Differentiated instruction<br>• Assessment<br>• Evaluation<br>• Feedback to students<br>• Multiple opportunities to learn and perform | • Attainment of grade-level standards by completing standards-based assignments and assessments<br>• Participation in multiple learning opportunities |

## MIDDLE GRADES STUDENT

**Note: Middle grades needs refer to the unique needs of young adolescents supported by a student-centered, middle school philosophy.**

may need classroom management training to effectively channel the energy and emotions of their students. Outside their classrooms, middle grades teachers need counseling support for students, immediate intervention opportunities for students with below-basic performance levels, specialized support for students with disabilities, and time-out support for students with behavior problems.

All teachers, at all grade-levels, need non-student-contact time and support to implement standards-based systems, but the teachers of middle grades students may need even more time and more support to successfully deliver what they are accountable for. Unlike elementary and grade nine English classes, middle grades classes in California have not had the advantage of class-size reduction. Unlike teachers in self-contained elementary classes, middle grades teachers may have 60 to 180 students whose grade-level standards go beyond writing single sentences and multiple paragraphs. These students are expected to produce multipage compositions, essays, journals, and research reports.

Many successful strategies involve students reviewing each other's work, but peer review does not provide the sophisticated evaluation and targeted feedback needed for accelerated student improvement. Nor is it adequate for benchmark performance assignments and assessments. The sheer volume of work for effective middle grades teachers is often staggering and can lead to burnout. Targeted professional development, outside classroom support systems, collaborative professional work and planning time, class-size reduction, and assistance with scoring written performance tasks are important discussion topics for stakeholders who are providing support and

resources to middle grades teachers. Other interested stakeholders in this discussion would include personnel at destination high schools, who also have an accountable interest in the preparation of entering students.

Unified school districts include both a bottom-up and a top-down accountability system that includes elementary, middle, and high schools. In nonunified districts, accountability is not systemic. In fact, little or no articulation may exist between schools and teachers. In a standards-based accountability system, this lack of articulation is worrisome to many high schools and high school teachers who fear that they will be held accountable for students who were not adequately prepared in middle school.

In the proposed schema of the *API* (Figure 4-1), the results from the *High School Exit Examination* and the *California Standards Tests* in history–social science (grades nine through eleven) and science (nine through eleven) will affect only high schools. Prior to grade nine, schools and teachers are not being held accountable on a statewide basis for attainment of the standards in history–social science and science. Eventually they may be, but until they are, local accountability systems will not want to ignore or devalue the importance of teaching to all the content standards and holding teachers and students accountable for teaching and learning them. Students must be prepared for all academic subject areas when they exit middle school.

Understanding the special needs of middle grades students and teachers is essential to the support and resources provided down to the classroom from the district level. The next level of provide-down accountability is that of the school principal.

## Middle Grades Principals

School-site administrators, as well as those in district and county offices of education, are pivotal in making an accountability system work at the local level. Keeping local needs and considerations in mind, administrators:

- Build capacity by working to provide teachers with standards-based materials and training.
- Work with local school boards, feeder elementary and destination high schools, staff, and the community to make decisions that ultimately and positively shape student learning and achievement.
- Make important decisions regarding planning, funding, and other resources (such as those used for instructional materials, professional development, and staffing needs) that serve to make standards-based instruction available and accessible for all students.
- Evaluate local achievement results to determine the effectiveness of teachers, local procedures and plans, programs, materials, professional development, and so forth.
- Report local achievement results to parents, the public, and the media, helping these audiences to understand what the data reveal about students and the effectiveness of the school/district.
- Build on successes and strengths but are willing to make necessary changes when weaknesses or areas of concern surface.

## Middle Grades Teachers

Teachers in the middle grades are responsible for providing relevant and appropriate standards-aligned instruction to their young-adolescent students. They are responsible for:

- Providing information about the standards to students and parents to ensure understanding and agreement about what students will be expected to know and be able to do by the end of each school year
- Working closely with parents and enlisting parental participation and support in students' schooling
- Working with colleagues to develop common grade-level, standards-based assignments and benchmark assessments with corresponding scoring guides
- Planning engaging, student-centered, standards-based lessons that build toward a relevant assessment
- Using the results of a variety of relevant assessment and diagnostic measures to inform instructional planning and practices, to report, and explain progress to students and parents
- Differentiating classroom instruction and strategies to meet the varying needs of their students (English-language learners, advanced students, or students with special needs)
- Providing appropriate assistance and brokering interventions for students in need of additional help in meeting instructional goals
- Employing effective classroom management techniques that are appropriate for the middle grades

- Engaging in dialogue with colleagues and administrators to discuss successes, challenges, and areas in which professional development is needed.

To assist teachers in meeting their responsibilities, the state is developing a comprehensive system of teacher support. Beginning teachers are supported through programs like the Beginning Teacher Support and Assessment program (BTSA). Experienced teachers who may be struggling to carry out some of their responsibilities are supported through local Peer Assistance and Review (PAR) programs. Local PAR programs assist participating teachers in acquiring the professional strategies necessary to provide a high-quality, standards-based education to all students.

Genuinely outstanding teachers are now provided financial incentives to become *board certified* by the National Board for Professional Teaching Standards. Board-certified teachers are available to assist other teachers to increase their classroom effectiveness.

Teachers needing assistance in content areas have available to them a series of intensive and in-depth summer institutes focused on strengthening content-area expertise. These institutes are coordinated through the University of California and California State University system. Information about these institutes can be accessed through the Department's Web site: *<http://www.cde.ca.gov>*.

Each stakeholder has specific support responsibilities for which they are accountable (see Figure 4-4). The one area that is not outlined in the figure is the dual role of parents, who are represented at the district policy level because they are taxpayers, but who have a personal interest as well.

# Parents of Middle Grades Students

Parents have always played an important role in the education of their children. Among other things, parents are personally responsible for developing their children's early language skills; transmitting values to their children; disciplining their children; and feeding, clothing, and providing shelter and medical care for them. Parenting encompasses many forms and is not consistent. Children come from a variety of advantaged, disadvantaged, and culturally diverse backgrounds.

Parents are held accountable for the attendance of their children in a public school or recognized educational alternative (e.g., private school, independent study program). On a personal accountability level, parents are requested to support their children and the efforts of their teachers by:

- Demonstrating that they value education and the professional expertise of the teacher
- Getting their children to school on time and to bed early on the nights before school
- Talking regularly to them about what is going on in school
- Keeping in close contact and staying actively involved with their school (even if their children beg them not to)
- Making every effort to understand the learning expectations for their children
- Supporting their children's instruction and learning in every way possible
- Asking routinely about their homework and helping to ensure that they complete all assignments

- Talking to teachers and administrators about any special needs or concerns regarding their children
- Insisting that their children take advantage of multiple learning opportunities, particularly if they are below basic performance levels.

## Middle Grades Students

With cumulative top-down and parental support, middle grades students are accountable for attainment of grade-level standards by:

- Coming to school prepared to learn
- Taking responsibility for their own learning
- Staying informed and understanding what is expected of them
- Asking for clarification, assistance, or extra help whenever they need it
- Completing all classroom and homework assignments on time
- Putting forth their best efforts in their learning experiences and assessments
- Taking printed information from school home to parents

## Support Stakeholders

There are other stakeholders in a standards-based system whose assistance and support are crucial. They may not be in the direct line of accountability shown in Figure 4-4, but they are nevertheless valuable partners and should hold themselves accountable for providing support to community schools. County offices of education, teacher associations and unions, youth and service organizations, businesses, postsecondary schools, municipal services, and recreational districts

all play a role in providing support. Districts and schools that actively seek and use the assistance and resources from other stakeholders enrich the whole school program.

## Development of a Local Accountability System

The development of local accountability systems varies across the state. Progress is incremental. Some of the steps in developing a consensually built local accountability system may be to:

- Begin with a self-assessment of where the district and school are in the process (see also Appendix 4-B, "Self-Scoring Guide for Assessment and Accountability," at the end of this chapter).
- Inventory the accountability tools currently in use and the data that these tools produce.
- Analyze the quality of the data for making relevant and targeted decisions.
- Collegially plan what is needed to fill in the gaps.
- Clarify provide-down input and deliver-up outcomes of each group. (How will these be measured and evaluated?)
- Determine what the incentives and consequences will be for stakeholders.
- Develop a framework and timeline for accomplishing the work.
- Develop new accountability tools in accordance with the framework.
- Analyze the quality of the new data for making relevant and targeted decisions.
- Make appropriate and targeted data-driven decisions to improve student achievement and monitor change.

- Keep stakeholders involved and informed.
- Assess the effectiveness of the system by evaluating student achievement data.

Accountability systems at the state and local levels play an important role in supporting and motivating those who are accountable for delivering results. Being accountable beyond the intrinsic personal and professional levels enables a systematic and consistent approach to gathering data, sorting them, analyzing them, and using them to drive instructional decisions. A results-oriented accountability system depends on not only data but also the profes-sionals who know what the data imply and how to use them to shape educational improvement. Building a system with the involvement of all stakeholders clarifies roles and expected support and outcomes.

Instructional decisions at the middle grades are based on not only the data but also the developmental needs of the young adolescent. Standards, assessment, and accountability take center stage compatibly with the middle grades philosophy. Together, systems and student-centered education promise greater levels of achievement for all students.

# Accountability

- **A system of accountability ultimately means that each and every stakeholder assumes both a personal and a collective responsibility**. What are you accountable for as an individual? What are you accountable for as a member of your team, grade level, department, school? To deliver higher levels of student achievement, what support and resources do you need from the stakeholders above you? How well do the district-adopted instructional materials in language arts, mathematics, science, and history–social science (including technology) support instruction that will enable students to meet state and local standards? Do the stakeholders who provide you support and resources understand the special needs of a young adolescent population? Do they understand what standards, assessment, and accountability systems require? What can you do to facilitate this understanding? To deliver higher levels of student achievement, what do you need and what do you need to do?

- **The statewide *Academic Performance Index (API)* continues to incorporate the results of standards-based measures. Based on *API* rankings, schools may receive rewards, assistance, or sanctions**. Are the *API* targets of your school and district being met? If not, what plans are under way to meet them? In what ways are STAR results used to determine how well students are meeting standards? How can these results be used to identify and prepare students at risk of not passing the *High School Exit Examination?* What is your school or district doing locally to motivate teachers and students to work hard and to recognize achievement? What is your school or district doing when individuals or groups fall short?

- **Local accountability systems vary by district across the state.** How does your school and district monitor its progress? Using the rubric in Appendix 4-B, evaluate your system. Discuss your evaluation with your colleagues. Where are your school and district in developing and implementing their own accountability system? Are all stakeholders part of the process? What is your next step? How are you monitoring your progress in areas not yet covered by the *API*—science and history–social science?

- **Standards and assessments are integral parts of an accountability system.** Reflect on your standards, both content and performance (Chapter 2). Reflect on your assessments (Chapter 3). How do they fit together? How do the results from these assessments drive your instruction and assist you in moving toward higher levels of student achievement?

- **Results are measurable. They are not anecdotal or isolated instances of success or failure.** How does your school monitor its progress toward attaining its goals? What are its sources of data? Are the data consistent, reliable, and valid? Are you

## Accountability (Continued)

and your colleagues sufficiently trained in administering assessment instruments and evaluating results? What criteria constitute the basis for intervention? What do the data imply if a few students do not show any gain? What do the data imply if students show less gain or more gain than your colleagues' students? What are your responsibilities in either case? What do the data imply if minimal gain is made in your grade level, team, or department? Can you target improvements based on the data? Do you know how to use the data to shape instruction and refine your practices?

# Appendix 4-A

# State Monetary Award Programs Based
## on the *Academic Performance Index (API)*

| | *Governor's Performance Award (GPA)* *(SB1X, Chapter 3 of 1999)* | *School-Site Employee Performance Bonus* *(SB 1667, Chapter 71 of 2000)* | *Certificated Staff Performance Incentive Act* *(AB 1114, Chapter 52 of 1999)* |
|---|---|---|---|
| ***Amount of Funds Appropriated*** | $227 million | $350 million | $100 million |
| ***Group Receiving Awards*** | School for schoolwide use | All staff at school site <br> School for schoolwide use | School certificated staff (all site positions requiring certificated staff) |
| ***Eligibility*** | Open to all schools with *APIs* | Open to all schools with *APIs* | Open to all schools with *APIs* in deciles 1–5 in 1999 |
| ***Conditions*** | ✓ 2000 *API* must meet or exceed 5% growth target. <br> ✓ All subgroups must make 80% of school target. <br> ✓ Elementary and middle schools must have 95% *Stanford 9* participation rate; high schools must have 90% *Stanford 9* participation rate. <br> ✓ Schools at 800+ must gain at least one point. | ✓ Eligibility for GPA program will determine eligibility for the performance bonus. | ✓ 1998-99 *Stanford 9* growth must be demonstrated. <br> ✓ 2000 *API* must show at least two times annual growth target. <br> ✓ All subgroups must make 80% of two times the school's target. <br> ✓ Elementary and middle schools must have 95% *Stanford 9* participation rate; high schools must have 90% *Stanford 9* participation rate. |
| ***Distribution Setup*** | ✓ Funded at $63 per student. | ✓ All site staff (on FTE basis) will receive bonus. <br> ✓ An equal amount of money will be given to the school for schoolwide use. | ✓ Largest gains receive the largest awards, based on growth (number of *API* points increased over two times the school's target). <br> • 1,000 certificated staff (on FTE basis) in schools with largest growth get $25,000 each. <br> • 3,750 certificated staff (on FTE basis get $10,000 each. <br> • 7,500 certificated staff (on FTE basis) get $5,000 each. |
| ***Distribution Decision*** | Use of funds at school decided by existing site governance team/schoolwide council representing major stakeholders; ratified by local board. | | Inclusion of certificated personnel receiving funds decided by district in negotiation with teachers' union. |
| ***Continuation Status*** | Ongoing | One-time bonus | Ongoing |

# Appendix 4-B

# Self-Scoring Guide for Assessment and Accountability

**Assessment and Accountability:** The school, district, and community regularly review student progress toward accomplishing the expected schoolwide learning results. This assessment process is integrated into the teaching/learning process and encourages students and teachers to make connections between what they are teaching and learning and achievement of the expected schoolwide learning results. Assessment results are the basis for reevaluation and redesign of the curriculum, instructional practices, and students' personal learning plans.

| 4 | 3 | 2 | 1 |
|---|---|---|---|
| The school regards assessment as integral to the educational process. The district and school establish levels of accomplishment for the expected schoolwide learning results and create a system to continually assess student process through a comprehensive assessment program that emphasizes student knowledge, performance, and depth of understanding. All staff members are involved in the continual evaluation system and feedback loop linked to authentic assessment of expected schoolwide learning results. | The school regards assessment as providing important feedback information and has regular formal assessment procedures in place that focus on systematic improvement in student performance relative to established norms or benchmarks. Many teachers make efforts to embed performance assessment tasks into instruction in order to assess students' learning processes and ability to use knowledge, critical thinking skills, and communication skills. | Data about student achievement are collected sporadically and unevenly, often in response to external demands. Although these data are viewed as a means for improving instruction and documenting successful strategies or weaknesses in the program, there is a lack of expertise in assessment and an absence of a systematic process that makes improvement or meaningful change difficult. Thus, little real attention is paid to preventing student failure, and few changes in classroom instruction result from the assessment process. | Data about student achievement are collected as needed and generally on an individual basis. The school's instructional strategies are uniform and unchanging. Students' backgrounds (e.g., private or deprivation) are viewed as reasons for poor performance, over-riding school factors. |
| Formal and informal data on student achievement, including analysis of student products, are routinely gathered. These data are analyzed to evaluate student performance and identify appropriate strategies and activities for instruction and assessment. Teachers and administrators use these data to inform instruction and as the subject for discussions and collegial feedback (including feedback from students). Teachers incorporate assessment tasks into instruction in order to stimulate thinking, including students' ability to analyze, organize, interpret, explain, synthesize, evaluate, and communicate important experiences or ideas. | Student achievement data and documented improvements in student morale, attendance, and behavior are analyzed periodically to evaluate student performance levels and reflect on the effectiveness of instruction as well as to determine grades and plan subsequent instruction. Modifications in curriculum and instruction are made as a result of these analyses. | Assessment of student performance is based on tasks designed to measure what students have learned and, in some classes, how well they can communicate their knowledge to others. These assessments are used by teachers to give students feedback and determine grades. Staff members have a superficial understanding of what should be involved in meaningful performance-based accountability and assessment. | Assessment of student performance is viewed as separate from instruction, usually taking the form of end-of-unit or end-of-semester tests that measure what students have learned. These assessments are used to judge student performance and determine grades. |
| Self- and external assessments lead to sustained achievement and excellence and provide a basis for evaluation and modifications of students' personal learning plans. | Students are encouraged to consider their assessment results in relation to their personal learning plans. | | |

*Source:* WestEd. Local Accountability Improvement Project: Technical Proposal. Submitted to California Department of Education's Local Accountability Assistance Unit, May 26, 2000. Elizabeth Cooley, project director. Printed with permission.

*"Never dare to tell me again anything about 'green grass.' Tell me how the lawn was flecked with shadows. I know perfectly well that grass is green. . . . Make me see what it is that made your garden distinct from a thousand others."*
—Robert Louis Stevenson

# Middle School Philosophy Takes Center Stage: Defining and Affirming Authentic Middle Schools

California's commitment to middle grades education during the 1990s was a bold and exciting adventure. From a relatively few schools that bore the name middle school at the beginning of the decade, approximately 1,400 California middle schools now do so. But more than the name has changed. A major philosophic change has accompanied the move toward schools that address the educational needs of young adolescents. These schools provide affirmative responses to the rapid and profound developmental changes occurring during the middle years. And they do so with no-nonsense expectations for high academic achievement. With standards, assessment, and accountability, middle school philosphy takes center stage.

## Characteristics of Successful Middle Schools

The National Middle School Association (NMSA) has published a set of characteristics of successful middle schools that produce the kind of student identified in *Caught in the Middle* and *Turning Points*.[1] *This We Believe,* an NMSA publication, notes that exemplary middle-level schools address the distinctiveness of early adolescence with a variety of instructional and organizational features. Further, developmentally responsive middle schools have:

- A shared vision
- Educators committed to young adolescents
- A positive school climate
- An adult advocate for every student
- Family and community partnerships
- High expectations for all students

The NMSA publication also states that schools embodying those characteristics provide:

- A challenging, integrative, and exploratory curriculum
- Varied teaching and learning approaches
- Assessment and evaluation that promote learning
- Flexible organizational structures

 Recommendations 1, 2, 3

99

- Programs and policies that foster health, safety, and wellness
- Comprehensive guidance and support services.[2]

Another publication identifies key components of successful middle schools. Based on empirical data and conventional wisdom and including substantial documentation by research scholars, the components are summarized as follows:

- *Interdisciplinary teaming* refers to an organizational structure in which a core of teachers is assigned to the same group of students. Various configurations ranging from two to five team members in two, three, and four subject areas have been successful. Teaming provides support for two essential aspects of middle-level education: (1) a positive psychosocial environment that allows flexibility, variety, and heterogeneous grouping of students; and (2) a structure to plan and deliver a curriculum that balances cognitive and affective factors. Because teachers share the same students and, ideally, have a common planning period, they can respond more quickly to the needs of individual students by collaborating, meeting jointly with parents, and designing thematic units.
- *Advisory programs* consist of a small group of students (usually 20 or fewer) assigned to a teacher, administrator, or other staff member for regularly scheduled meetings to discuss topics of concern to students. The programs are designed to develop close, trusting relationships between students and adults, increase student engagement with learning, develop students' study skills, and nurture feelings of self-

esteem and belonging. Social and academic support includes discussing problems with individual students, providing career information and guidance, developing students' self-confidence and leadership, and discussing academic issues or personal problems involving social relationships, peer groups, moral or ethical issues, and health concerns. Teacher-led advisory programs also help create a more positive school climate, develop students' self-esteem, and prevent dropouts.
- *Varied instruction* includes integrating learning experiences, addressing students' own questions, and focusing on real-life issues; actively engaging students in problem solving; accommodating individual differences; emphasizing collaboration, cooperation, and community; and seeking to develop good people who care for others and demonstrate democratic values and moral sensitivity. Some of the more common programs include multiage grouping over longer periods of time, cross-age tutoring, cooperative learning, hands-on and student-centered activities; and the use of block time and flexible scheduling. Learning tasks are developmentally appropriate and are adapted to individual differences.
- *Exploratory programs* capitalize on the innate curiosity of young adolescents, exposing them to a range of academic, vocational, and recreational subjects for career options, community service, enrichment, and enjoyment. Exploratory topics include foreign languages, intramural sports, health, clubs, student government, home economics, technological arts, independent study projects, music, art, speech,

drama, careers, consumer education, and creative writing.

- *Transition programs* focus on creating a smooth change of schools for young adolescents. Eighty-eight percent of public school students begin the middle grades in a new school. This transition may overwhelm the coping skills of some students and harm their psychological adjustment, self-esteem, and motivation to learn if planning for transition is lacking. Frequently, elementary school students visit the middle-level school they will be attending. There the middle school counselors can familiarize the visiting students with the setting and the programs offered and are often able to provide the visitors with older buddies to accompany them. These efforts help the students make smooth transitions from elementary school to middle school and from middle school to high school.[3]

Pronouncements on middle schools made by the California Department of Education, the Carnegie Council on Adolescent Development, and the National Middle School Association parallel one another in significant ways. The characteristics of middle school programs and structures described in this publication can be found in a broad cross section of official position papers, books, articles, and research reports produced by those organizations during the 1990s. The question must now be asked, What difference does it all make? The answer can be found in the most comprehensive middle school research project of the decade, conducted by Robert Felner and others and underwritten by the Carnegie Corporation. It concludes that high-quality middle-level schooling based on the key themes of middle

school reform pays off in statistically significant ways. According to the research, middle schools reap major positive benefits when they provide:

- Small communities of learners, including interdisciplinary teaching teams and advisory programs
- A strong core academic program, including an emphasis on literacy
- Elimination of tracking in favor of inclusive classrooms
- Creative participation by teachers in school governance
- Teachers who are academically competent and knowledgeable about young adolescents
- Schoolwide assurances of students' personal health and safety
- Extensive involvement of families in the schooling of their children
- School-community partnerships in such areas as service-learning and health and social services

The findings show that the higher the level of implementation of middle school philosophy and practice, the more dramatic is the positive impact on student achievement and behavior as well as other variables. The research, first reported nationally in the *Kappan,* is summarized in Appendix 5-A, "The Impact of School Reform for the Middle Years," located at the end of this chapter.

## Empowering Middle Grades Students

Findings on the developmental characteristics of young adolescents made educators painfully aware that a new, demanding learning environment was crucial for students to achieve at their highest potential. Gone was the assumption that young adolescents were unprepared to engage in more complex thinking skills needed in problem solving, investigating, experimenting, and creating. Although acquisition of basic knowledge and skills was to remain a priority, young adolescents would be given assignments calling for rigorous intellectual pursuits. Maximum intellectual growth and high levels of academic achievement are best realized within a school culture that celebrates every dimension of adolescent growth and development.

(See also Appendix 5-B, "Acceptance of Young Adolescent Priorities Leads to Reciprocal Identification with Academic Values," at the end of this chapter.)

## Affirming and Sustaining the Middle School Vision

Initially, creative breakthroughs in any field are fragile. The idealized vision of middle schools is no exception. Insights, practices, and policies linked to the reform of middle-level education have become institutionalized in many instances—not only in California but nationally, a praiseworthy and desirable trend. The fundamental principles of middle-level education addressed earlier in this chapter are thereby validated and should become part of expected professional practice. However, if educators conclude that implementing programs and practices from a checklist will result in a successful middle school, they will be disappointed.

The California Department of Education, the Carnegie Council on Adolescent Development, and the National Middle School Associa-

tion are careful to say that the identified characteristics are present in effective middle schools. But they do not say that the mere possession of those characteristics will guarantee an effective middle school. Realistically, the program elements may be in place but lack the necessary substance. Challenges that middle-level staff may face in striving to become effective are the following:

- Turnover among teachers and administrators is high in many middle schools. Therefore, a need exists for continual internal dialogue about philosophy, policy, and practice if the middle school vision is to be sustained. Whenever a new teacher or principal arrives or staff members leave, the dynamics of a faculty are altered. When the number of personnel changes is multiplied, the impact may be exponential. The original level of staff cohesion and collegiality must be renewed through new levels of understanding, commitment, and team building.
- An authentic middle school vision communicates clearly the commonly agreed-upon simple yet powerful definitions to those who have responsibility for translating the vision into reality, leading to a common understanding and acceptance among professional staff members.
- The middle school vision must also be capable of being clearly and concisely communicated to students, parents, and the general public. New or revised policies and practices must be shared in ways that are understandable. Logical answers to questions about why changes are necessary must be provided.

- Standards-based middle schools must clearly and repeatedly share expectations about achievement with all students and their parents. They must also describe what the school will do to help all students succeed. Parents must share in affirming content standards and should be helped to understand performance levels fully, including their relationship to the mastery of subject matter.
- The middle school vision, although linked to basic convictions about the nature of early adolescence, must be flexible. Each generation of young adolescents brings new challenges, priorities, and expectations in keeping with ever-changing shifts in values associated with its peer culture.

Figure 5-1 summarizes many of the most common characteristics of middle schools as they move to incorporate standards-based education into their current structures.

## Standards-Based Middle Schools for the Twenty-First Century

Most observers agree that standards-based education can take a powerful model for schooling young adolescents and make it even more dynamic and effective. Conclusions and recommendations that will help to ensure the effectiveness of middle schools are listed as follows:

- Middle schools evolve as they adapt to the demands of a new century. Those that continue to emphasize inclusive classrooms, interdisciplinary team teaching, academically competent and caring teachers, and an emotionally and physically safe learning environment will find that standards-based education fits well with those professional priorities.
- Middle schools communicate their responsiveness to a wide range of developmental differences among students. Research shows that young adolescent students belong in classrooms with caring teachers and peers who encourage one another to do well. Expectations that all students participating in standards-based education will succeed in response to the same content standards require strong professional concern for students at all levels of ability, a high level of knowledge of content on the part of the teachers, and the most creative kinds of academic support services.
- There is no single right way to organize a middle school. However, some ways are more effective then others. Because the implementation of the essential characteristics of effective middle schools does not ensure excellence, each program element in place should be examined and its qualitative level assessed. Quality assurances as to flexible scheduling, interdisciplinary team teaching, advisory programs, parent involvement, engagement with the community, and academically competent and caring faculty members are potent indicators of how successful standards-based education will be in a particular school.
- The primary goals of academic integrity and strong emotional connections with students may be pursued in many different ways. What counts most is a passion on the part of teachers and principals for academic excellence and a deep commitment to engage young adolescents in their most formative stages.
- A broad repertoire of instructional strategies is essential, including continuing

Figure 5-1

**Common Characteristics of Standards-Based Middle Schools**

► **Expanded intellectual abilities, including development of complex thinking skills**

► **High levels of academic proficiency in the core curriculum**

► **Increased physical, social, and emotional maturity**

A comprehensive, coherent, and dynamic school mission statement exists. It is **student centered,** incorporates essential program characteristics, and helps to determine all major educational decisions at the school site.

## Common Characteristics

**Core curriculum clearly defined by sets of content and performance standards for each subject**

High academic expectations set for all students, with multiple programs for support

Principals and teachers who are bold, caring, committed leaders in education

School viewed as a community of learners made up of students, parents, and *all* staff

Student evaluation based on multiple measures

Many instructional strategies used by teachers to respond to varied learning styles

Self-understanding and academic values developed through counseling programs

Parents involved in wide variety of programs and support services

Activities and athletic programs consistent with development of young adolescents efforts to engage students in learning activities requiring the development of complex thought processes.

- Middle schools are dynamic institutions with a clear sense of mission. Any middle school faculty that has not yet defined its purposes should give that task its highest priority. Mission statements should reflect changes within the larger society and the local community.

- Many middle schools periodically revise their existing mission statements to include commitments to standards-based education, mainly to allow subsequent educational decisions to be tested against the propositions embedded in the school's purposes. If the fit does not exist or is questionable, the decision is modified, or the mission statement is refined. The relationship between standards-based education and the mission should be featured prominently.

- Standards-based education offers significantly increased expectations of achievement for *all* students because it is focused, involves thorough and credible assessment practices, and provides regular, direct feedback to students and teachers. Various sources of data are gathered that reflect the effectiveness of the instruction directed to meeting the content standards. Decisions are based on those data. Teachers may need to be taught how to use the feedback to determine the effectiveness of their instruction and make adjustments when indicated.

- Students and their parents need to know what their school is doing differently to help ensure that the word *all* is a meaningful commitment as to access to the most valued and rigorous curricula. Successful standards-based middle schools are earnest about that goal. They are prepared to take bold steps and try new and sometimes risky ideas. Further, they request extensive involvement and commitment from parents and community members, including participation in building consensual understanding of the various elements of standards-based education and volunteering to support learning through such activities as tutoring and mentoring.

- Principals are not expected to be expert in every level of curriculum and instruction. However, their role in a standards-based middle school is refocused to that of an instructional leader. Along with the teachers, principals learn the complexities and challenges of developing and implementing a performance standard system, the benchmark assessments, and scoring criteria. The principal's leadership extends beyond the concerns of one content area, one classroom, or one team. The instructional leader folds the concerns together, brings consistency to every level, and provides direct support to teachers through coaching, training, and appropriate resources.

- Middle schools ensure an effective dialogue and full cooperation between themselves and their companion elementary and secondary schools. Programs that provide academic support across all age and grade levels require significantly greater cooperation among all levels of schooling.

(See also Appendix 5-C, "Digital Literacy in Twenty-First Century Middle Schools: A Scenario," at the end of this chapter.)

# Authentic Middle Schools

- **Exemplary middle schools have common characteristics that have been recommended or recognized in *Turning Points, Turning Points 2000,* and the National Middle School Association.** How many of these characteristics does your school embody? Do you have a master plan and timeline for incorporating these characteristics? How have these characteristics enhanced student achievement? How does the middle grades philosophy provide a solid foundation for standards-based reform?

- **Is your middle school student centered?** Do the students feel that yours is a caring faculty? Do the teachers and other staff members make a deliberate attempt to develop strong, positive relationships with students, leading to higher levels of achievement? Is improvement needed? What can your faculty do? What can you do?

- **Among the common characteristics of standards-based middle schools identified in Figure 5-1, which, if any, require increased attention by your school?** What specific suggestions do you have for accomplishing this task? Are any components missing from the illustration that you believe are essential? What are they?

- **Consider your own school.** Are instructional practices and support programs related to a comprehensive plan in which the pieces fit together logically? Are there changes you would like to make? Are there others on the staff who may feel the same way? What can you do about it? Will you?

- **Are there instructional strategies you would like to use but do not because you feel that you are unprepared?** Do they require others to participate who are unwilling to do so? If so, consider your priorities. Do you know how to use performance data to evaluate your instructional strategies? Would you like to discuss them with someone? Do you have colleagues who share your thinking? Are you willing to discuss your concerns with them? With your principal? If not, what prevents you? How can you resolve your concerns?

- **Observers frequently remark that too little communication exists between the several levels of schooling: elementary, middle, and secondary.** Is that criticism valid in your own circumstances? If so, why does the problem continue to exist? Who is accountable for improving the situation? How has the need for better articulation been magnified because of content standards, grade-level performance standards, the *High School Exit Examination,* promotion and retention policies? What part of the problem is your responsibility? What actions do you think would help most to ensure that education becomes a seamless process in your school district?

- **Instructional leadership is often shared among teachers, and the principal is at the periphery (because of many other demands).** If the principal takes an active role in curriculum, standards-based instruction, and assessment, what are the benefits to teachers and students? What types of support and training does the principal need to make that happen?

# Appendix 5-A

# The Impact of School Reform for the Middle Years

by Robert Felner, Anthony W. Jackson, Deborah Kasak, Peter Mulhall,
Steven Brand, and Nancy Flowers

*The authors discuss research findings that strongly support the view that high-quality schooling, well implemented, can make profound contributions to the achievement, mental health, and social-behavioral functioning of students who are often left behind and for whom there is frequently a sense that school cannot make a difference in their lives.*

The Illinois Middle Grades Network (IMGN), in partnership with the Project on High Performance Learning Communities, has intensively studied what is now a network of more than 97 schools as they undergo the process of restructuring from a more traditional organization toward the type of school envisioned in the Carnegie Council on Adolescent Development report *Turning Points: Preparing American Youth for the 21st Century.*

The IMGN ultimately became an intensive subset of schools within the broader network of schools supported through Carnegie Corporation's Middle Grade School State Policy Initiative (MGSSPI). The recommendations in *Turning Points* are summarized here:

- Create small communities for learning where stable, close, mutually respectful relationships with adults and peers are considered fundamental for intellectual development and personal growth. The key elements of these communities are schools-within-schools or houses, students and teachers grouped together as teams, and small-group advisories that ensure that every student is known well by at least one adult.
- Teach a core academic program that results in students who are literate, including in the sciences, and who know how to think critically, lead a healthy life, behave ethically, and assume the responsibilities of citizenship in a pluralistic society. Youth service to promote values for citizenship is an essential part of the core academic program.

- Ensure success for all students through elimination of tracking by achievement level and promotion of cooperative learning, flexibility in arranging instructional time, and adequate resources (time, space, equipment, and materials) for teachers.
- Empower teachers and administrators to make decisions about the experiences of middle grade students through creative control by teachers over the instructional program linked to greater responsibilities for students' performance, governance committees that assist the principal in designing and coordinating schoolwide programs, and autonomy and leadership within subschools or houses to create environments tailored to enhance the intellectual and emotional development of all youth.
- Staff middle grade schools with teachers who are expert at teaching young adolescents and who have been specially prepared for assignment to the middle grades.
- Improve academic performance through fostering the health and fitness of young adolescents by providing a health care coordinator in every middle grade school, access to health care and counseling services, and a health-promoting school environment.
- Reengage families in the education of young adolescents by giving families meaningful roles in school governance, communicating with families about the school program and students' progress, and offering family opportunities to support the learning process at home and at the school.

From *Kappan,* Vol. 78 (March 1997). Used with permission.

• Connect schools with communities, which together share responsibility for each middle grade student's success, through identifying service opportunities in the community, establishing partnerships and collaborations to ensure students' access to health and social services, and using community resources to enrich the instructional program and [provide] opportunities for constructive after-school activities.

The Project on High Performance Learning Communities is built on the premise that, despite the strong appeal of the principles of *Turning Points* and the state-level plans that have resulted from MGSSPI efforts, the degree to which implementation of these recommendations—or of any other current restructuring and reform prescriptions—will produce the desired results is not clear. . . . There is a dearth of empirical research (especially intensive longitudinal evaluation studies) on school restructuring that focuses directly on its impact or informs its design and implementation.

In this article we describe the evolution and current status of one effort to evaluate a comprehensive, integrated set of recommendations for transforming the education of young adolescents. Specifically, we sought to assess and evaluate the process of implementation of the recommendations of *Turning Points* for middle grade reform, as defined above, as well as their impact on students' academic achievement, socioemotional development, and behavioral adjustment. We particularly wished to explore the association between the levels of implementation of the reforms—highest level of implementation (LOI), middle LOI, and lowest LOI—that participating schools attained and relevant

outcomes for students. The overall evaluation research focuses on several core issues:

1. As participating schools move from more traditional structures, norms, and instructional practices to increasing levels of fidelity in their implementation of *Turning Points* recommendations, are there parallel changes in critical areas, including levels of health, well-being, and socioemotional functioning and academic achievement and progress? . . .

2. One of our central concerns has been the ways in which racial and ethnic minority children, children from economically disadvantaged families, and those experiencing other conditions which place them at risk are affected by the *Turning Points* recommendations.

3. Implementation of the recommendations of *Turning Points* may have differing levels and patterns of impact as a function of differences in school settings and community contexts. It is crucial to consider these contextual interactions when interpreting relationships between school changes and student outcomes.

Before we turn to further discussion of findings, . . . we ask readers to consider our results as preliminary, for a number of reasons. The results discussed here are based on data that were collected through our third year of large-scale data collection. [However], our more recent results are highly congruent with those reported here and add weight to the current findings.

In [the three groups] of schools, there are more than 15,000 students and nearly 900 teachers. (Once again, schools were grouped

Student Achievement Test Scores, by the School's Level of Implementation of *Turning Points* Recommendations

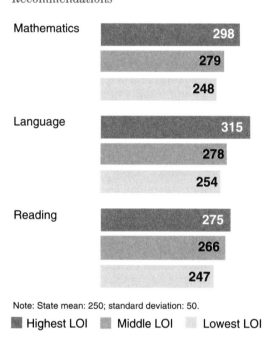

Mathematics
298
279
248

Language
315
278
254

Reading
275
266
247

Note: State mean: 250; standard deviation: 50.

■ Highest LOI  ■ Middle LOI  □ Lowest LOI

according to levels of implementation of *Turning Points* recommendations: highest LOI, middle LOI, and lowest LOI.) The data show that, across subject areas, adolescents in highly implemented schools achieved at much higher levels than those in nonimplemented schools and substantially better than those in partially implemented schools.

We also examined different domains of student outcomes as they related to the level of implementation that schools had obtained. These included teachers' ratings of student behaviors as well as students' self-reports of depression, fear, worry, anxiety, and self-esteem. . . . In the most fully implemented schools, teachers reported far lower levels of student behavior problems than do teachers

in less implemented and nonimplemented schools. . . . Similarly, students in the more fully implemented schools are less fearful of being victimized, are less worried about something bad happening at school and about the future, and have higher levels of self-esteem.

Preliminary findings are extremely encouraging and show the kind of impact the implementation of *Turning Points* recommendations could have on adolescents' achievement and adjustment. . . . Assuming that these patterns hold over time, our findings should encourage policymakers to move forward rather than to stop or move away from restructuring [middle grade education]. . . .

Our findings to date strongly support the view that high-quality schooling, well implemented, can make profound contributions to the achievement, mental health, and socio-behavioral functioning of students who are often left behind and for whom there is often a sense that school cannot make a difference in their lives. These data also argue for resources to be used effectively in schools with high concentrations of at-risk students and, in some instances, for resources to be increased significantly in order to create the necessary conditions for all students to be successful.

Teacher Ratings of Student Behavioral Problems, by the School's Level of Implementation of *Turning Points* Recommendations

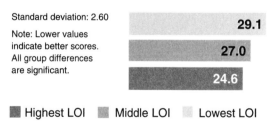

Standard deviation: 2.60

Note: Lower values indicate better scores. All group differences are significant.

29.1
27.0
24.6

■ Highest LOI  ■ Middle LOI  □ Lowest LOI

# Appendix 5-B

# Acceptance of Young Adolescent Priorities
# Leads to Reciprocal Identification
# with Academic Values

The complex physical and emotional changes taking place in the lives of students during grades six through eight introduce multiple agendas that compete with academic goals. As a result the intellectual priorities of teachers and parents may be temporarily set aside in favor of more demanding considerations, at least from the standpoint of the students.

Teachers, principals, and parents need to accept the legitimacy of the nonacademic preoccupations of middle grades students, even if they seem on the surface to be trivial. It may be surprising to everyone but the students themselves that subject matter is not always their most basic concern.

Research indicates that physical appearance, peer popularity, and athletic activities represent areas of intense concern among young adolescents and that their friends are their single most significant personal preoccupation. Again, this should not be surprising because the socializing functions of schools are very important to the eventual development of mature young adults.

When teachers, counselors, and principals accept the priorities of young adolescents, they can become more tolerant and more intelligent about ways to nurture and strengthen the school's academic expectations. The emphasis should be on *acceptance,* and not necessarily on *approval.*

It is axiomatic that there will be tensions between teachers and students regarding relative priorities, but these need not and should not lead to disabled relationships. Students do not ask for approval. But they have the right to ask for acceptance of legitimate aspects of their growing-up experiences. The weight of a significant volume of research in the social and behavioral sciences is on their side.

School should indeed be a major intellectual experience, but it is also a significant socializing experience. There is an interesting twist to this discussion that is understood by many educators and parents. When students experience acceptance by the significant adults in their lives, the consequence often leads to a much closer identification with the academic goals that those adults value.

The potential also exists for a schoolwide domino effect. Even a few students who develop a clear sense of academic values prized by their teachers and parents can positively influence large numbers of other students in their own classroom and throughout their school.

In essence there is no necessarily unresolvable conflict between the priorities of adolescents related to their growing, maturing bodies and emotions and the parallel concerns of adults for the growth and development of their minds. When each of these discrete yet integrally related agendas is understood and accepted as valid by teachers and parents, everyone's life becomes more enjoyable, and the likelihood of academic success takes a quantum leap forward.

Teachers and principals who strive to understand what makes young adolescents tick and who respond with sensitivity and acceptance will find themselves being rewarded by students who increasingly identify as their own the adult values that relate to intellectual growth and academic achievement. This agenda lies at the heart of successful standards-based middle schools.

From *The Middle School Years,* by James J. Fenwick. San Diego: Fenwick Associates, 1993.

# Appendix 5-C

# Digital Literacy in Twenty-First Century Middle Schools: A Scenario

*Middle schools of the new century must increasingly provide the means by which students and teachers may develop and make use of digital technology in order to enhance both teaching and learning. This scenario provides a glimpse of the possibilities inherent in the advanced use of digital technology in the middle grades. A few schools have already achieved this level of sophistication. All are challenged to pursue the goal.*

Information technology continues to explode, and there is no end in sight. As a case in point, library science continues to experience a massive technological transition from conventional shelves, stacks, and three-by-five cards to the use of technology based on horizontal bandwidths, CD-ROMS, ISPs, and interactive networks—to name only a few of the present rapidly unfolding scientific marvels that are continually revolutionizing the field.

Electronic school libraries and media centers now make it possible to integrate conventional print and media collections with data sources via the Internet as well as through regional networking capabilities dedicated to linking together kindergarten through grade twelve schools, institutions of higher education, research labs, and other types of informational sources across the world. The possibilities appear limitless. What will this mean for a twenty-first century middle school? Consider this scenario:

A group of middle school students descends on the computers in their school's electronic library. These students are working on a project that requires them to demonstrate learning of knowledge and skills embedded in the content standards of the curriculum they are studying. It also requires digital literacy, the ability to access electronically mediated information sources, including CD-ROMs and the Internet, and to evaluate and validate the quality and credibility of the data that they find through their electronic searches.

Their teacher believes in activity-based instruction. This has led to an assignment that emphasizes collaborative, interdisciplinary learning—a mirror of the way adults in the real world of business, industry, and the professions tackle the search for answers to basic questions or strive for synergy in creating collective solutions to community problems, world issues, or corporate challenges.

The group navigates carefully through the electronic database that brings the library collection to their fingertips almost instantaneously. The Internet is then accessed, and students debate which search engine is the most appropriate to use for their project. They decide to use at least three different search engines and to compare the results. A laser printer stands ready to provide hard copies of information. Other devices allow downloading of audio-voice clips, other types of sound bytes, videos, photographs, and film.

Some of this information already has been integrated via multimedia technology and is available in this format for downloading.

Hypertext links, or successor technology, enable students to return to their original data sources on the Internet or to refer to new sites housed in cyberspace, allowing them to connect with sites halfway around the world. Students also use hypertext links to check on the credibility and integrity of their data sources by electronic cross-referencing. This provides them with information about the authors of their data. It also reveals evidence of either well-substantiated information or raises questions about the integrity of what they have found through their use of various Internet search engines.

Final determination is made about information that will be used in completing the project. The students have been well taught about the concept of intellectual property rights and copyright laws and are careful to document all of their sources, including Internet addresses.

The data search process, qualitative assessments of information, and final choices of material to be used in completing their project are then followed by group-learning activities designed around the use of complex reasoning skills. These may involve analysis and synthesis, generation and testing of hypotheses, or other types of higher-order thinking.

Student work is compiled in a format designed to show evidence of meaningful connections between their new knowledge and prior experience. Students next prepare project reports, using multimedia technology that allows them to integrate content in ways that reflect a growing understanding of interdisciplinary learning.

The entire project has also pushed them to demonstrate and further develop their academic literacy and digital literacy skills and knowledge. Their work is saved on a CD-ROM for presentation to their teacher and fellow students. The CD-ROM becomes a part of the students' personal portfolios after their work has been assessed in order to determine proficiency levels related to the knowledge and skills addressed in the content standards that prompted the original assignment.

The scenario presented here is far more than a visionary glint in the eyes of technologists. Many features of the electronic library are already available or are being placed in service in growing numbers of schools, universities, and other public institutions around the country.

Perhaps of greatest interest to teachers is that the emerging electronic library and its corollary of digital literacy will make a major contribution to the goals of powerful teaching and learning that require quick and selective access to massive amounts of information. This capability is essential to the development of enhanced academic proficiency by students in standards-based middle schools.

*"Do not let what you cannot do interfere with what you can do."*

—John Wooden

# Creating a School Culture to Sustain Standards-Based Education

Middle schools are being challenged to expand their mission to incorporate the principles of standards-based education. This task involves building on the heritage fostered by *Caught in the Middle* and *Turning Points,* which called on educators to provide young adolescents with a caring transition between elementary school and high school and focus on intellectual development and academic achievement. Consequently, middle schools are establishing more challenging norms for student performance, ensuring that all teachers consistently apply common expectations for what students should learn and how well they should learn it and holding educators accountable for high student performance.

Addressing this challenge requires a focus on the physical-emotional and curricular-instructional dimensions of middle schools to enhance teaching and learning. California's middle schools understand the need for a physically attractive learning environment and caring teachers who seek to identify closely with the intellectual, physical, social, and emotional development of their students. Although few if any schools have achieved these goals completely, many are creating learning environments in which students are treated respectfully, strong student-teacher relationships are formed, physical and emotional security is present, and students and teachers enjoy spending some of the most important years of their lives. Researchers have developed a framework for examining ways in which schools can become "invitational"—that is, places fundamentally attractive to those who teach and study there. That research can serve as the prelude to a more intense consideration of those aspects of school culture focusing on the development of standards-based education.[1]

## Personality of Place

Almost all schools can develop their own identity and build student, faculty, and community pride. Questions to be addressed by schools attempting to distinguish themselves include the following:

- Are places available for students to sit, relax, and enjoy the school, including

Recommendations 3, 5, 6, 15

---

John Wooden, retired UCLA basketball coach

places other than the cafeteria? Are there open interior spaces equipped with casual furniture and art? Are outside courtyards and foyers maintained as attractive places for student interaction? Are there well-maintained plantings and attractive landscaping? Does the ambience say, Education is important, and you are important?

- Are the interior walls painted in attractive colors with schemes students have helped to devise? Are they scrupulously maintained? Are they free of graffiti?
- Are the rest rooms clean, free of odor, and safe? Are all the fixtures in working order?
- Are the windows clean inside and out? Are broken windows fixed? Are burned-out light bulbs replaced? Is other maintenance attended to promptly?
- Is the evidence of students' achievements prominently displayed in classrooms, corridors, offices, and other highly visible places? Is the work changed frequently to maximize the number of students recognized?
- Have opportunities been seized to develop special facilities not a part of the original school design (e.g., celestial observatory, amphitheater, greenhouse, computer labs)?
- Are there areas on campus where the students have access to current technology for conducting experiments, doing research, or creating presentations?
- Do student government meetings take place in a formal environment that tells student leaders that what they are doing is important (e.g., a carpeted floor and a formal conference table)?
- Are efforts made to ensure that students and visitors approach the entrance to the school with feelings of pride because of neat,

well-cared-for premises regardless of the school's age?

These questions address just a few of the issues that students, faculty, parents, and the general public care about deeply. The answers to the questions provide the context for assumptions about the importance of education in any school that go far beyond a simple preoccupation with aesthetics. Rather, the answers have to do with the degree to which education is truly honored in a community. This assumption is just as true for schools as it is for corporations. Outward appearances speak volumes about the core values of both private and public institutions.

## Positive Rules and Policies

Schools should establish rules and policies that encourage and permit rather than restrict or direct. Positive rules govern quality, service, creativity, and innovation and focus on building and expanding rather than restraining, controlling, limiting, and inhibiting. Students, teachers, counselors, and principals should understand that rules and policies should be used to reinforce positive traits and restrict negative behavior. Sanctions should be explicit as to antisocial behavior. Rules and policies governing negative behavior should be enforceable because otherwise the integrity of school discipline would be threatened. All rules and policies must be clearly stated and widely communicated, and punishment for infractions of rules governing negative behavior should be administered equitably.

Although rules and policies are essential, they should be subject to continuing review for appropriateness and should not remain merely because of tradition. Schools whose rules and policies may be skewed to controlling and restricting students should look for ways to expand rewards for positive behavior.

## Importance of Caring Relationships

The challenge to middle schools to provide a caring adult relationship for all students remains a high priority and must be continually reinforced through deliberate planning. Expressed in many ways, caring is an essential ingredient in the development of positive educational values. However, research on students' attitudes toward school concludes that many students still suffer from what can be described as a "caring disability." *Turning Points* states that:

> Caring is crucial to the development of young adolescents into healthy adults. Young adolescents need to see themselves as valued members of a group that offers mutual support and caring relationships. They need to be able to succeed at something and to be praised and rewarded for that success. They need to become socially competent individuals who have the skills to cope successfully with the exigencies of everyday life. They need to believe that they have a promising future, and they need the competence to take advantage of real opportunities in a society in which they have a stake.[2]

## Examples of Caring Behavior

Caring relationships within the school setting are expressed in multiple ways. The following suggestions represent only a partial list of possibilities. Caring is evident when students:

- Are affirmed as worthy individuals and assigned responsibilities that match their maturing levels of ability and independence. They are allowed to make decisions that fit their age, needs, and interests.
- Are helped to fully participate in their classes—to achieve a sense of belonging—through learning experiences that emphasize opportunities for recognition based on academic achievement and citizenship.
- Understand that their teachers are committed to helping them achieve academic success and that individual help is available for each student.
- Are provided full information about standards and academic performance levels and the ways in which their work will be evaluated. They are partners in their education and are able to monitor their own progress.
- Have access to a mentorship experience with at least one teacher or other significant adult. These experiences are long term, preferably during the entire time students are enrolled in their present school. Mentoring experiences are never forced and can be altered as appropriate.
- Are corrected or disciplined without being shamed, abused, or confused. They know that adults will make reasonable allowances for mistakes without personal condemnation. They also know that teachers will concentrate more on what is done well than to dwell on past failures.
- Are given ways to help themselves by helping others, taking on such service-learning roles as teacher assistants, cross-age tutors, and community volunteers (see Chapter 12).

- Can express what they feel, believe, and value. They can talk things out with their teachers and peers without being ignored, afraid, or ashamed. They learn essential interpersonal communication skills that emphasize respect for the feelings and beliefs of others.
- Are helped to learn that caring relationships are a two-way process and that caring for others often leads to being cared for in return.
- Are contacted in person by a teacher or counselor when absences occur. They are made to feel that their presence in school is important and that their success is something that the entire faculty cares about.
- Experience early identification and help when their grades decline. They receive sympathetic assistance and encouragement in working out personal problems. Academic "bungee cords" are readily available to help them in times of crisis, and they know how to access them.
- Have something to believe in and work for because adults live their ideals before them.

Caring relationships in the school provide the groundwork for successful implementation of systemic school reforms.[3]

## Participation, Cooperation, and Collaboration

Teacher-student relationships in middle schools should possess many of the essential qualities found in professional-client interaction rather than under authoritarian control. School should be perceived as a place characterized by cooperation rather than coercion and conflict.

Principal-teacher relationships should model cooperative behavior and provide the affirmation necessary to allow deeper, more humane interaction between teachers and students. Dynamic middle schools are action oriented. A willingness exists to address difficult challenges and reward those who succeed—whether they are students or faculty members. Risk taking occurs more frequently. The endless recycling of creative ideas through committees and administrative layers is avoided where flexibility is possible. Students and teachers are encouraged, even expected, to explore the cutting edge of change. For those who dream dreams, the answer is still Why not? rather than Why?

Ethnic and linguistic differences among students are consistently honored in supportive schools. Students are encouraged to share their personal commitments and find ways to grow morally and ethically through the knowledge and respect gained from their encounters with other students. Students with disabilities find an environment that offers genuinely positive acceptance of differences. All students are empowered to learn and develop as closely as possible to their full potential, and the contributions of all students are recognized and valued.

## A Middle School Culture Supporting Standards-Based Education

Anne Wheelock identifies examples of "norms, beliefs, practices, and routines" that incorporate assumptions and beliefs necessary for a middle school culture to sustain standards-based education reforms. She draws on the earlier work of Martin Haberman in identifying factors that provide evidence of what she describes as "good student work" and "rich pedagogy." The work of the two authors forms the basis of the discussion that appears in the following pages. Teachers and principals searching to build a school culture that promotes academic excellence and rich pedagogy within a standards-based teaching and learning environment will give a high priority to ensuring that the following norms, beliefs, practices, and routines are in place. Accordingly, students:

- *Are involved with issues they regard as important and that have meaning in their own lives.* When the importance of specific learning tasks is not immediately evident, time should be allowed in class to discuss relevance and meaning. Knowledge and skills do not exist in an intellectual or experiential vacuum. Middle grades students are helped to understand that content standards represent the efforts of specialists and scholars to identify the most important things that students should know and be able to do.
- *Engage in exploring human differences.* Ideally, learning should take place within a rich, heterogeneous context of ethnic, linguistic, and cultural variables. Middle grades students need to understand as much as possible about the deeper meaning of such learning experiences and recognize that human diversity can contribute to enriched understanding of nearly any learning activity.
- *Participate in planning many of their learning experiences.* Participation, cooperation, and collaboration are essential elements of

a rich middle school culture. Consequently, students should participate in the implementation and continued development of standards-based education. For example, they should be involved in helping to develop performance tasks used to evaluate their academic performance levels and become thoroughly knowledgeable about the scoring criteria developed for that purpose.

- *Can apply such ideals as fairness, equity, and justice to their school and classroom relationships and to the larger world about them.* Many middle grades students may be confronting complex issues outside their immediate school environment for the first time as they explore local, state, national, and global challenges—whether economic, social, or political. The ideals of fairness, equity, and justice cut across all areas of the curriculum and content standards and lie at the heart of efforts to inculcate honor, civility, and service.
- *Are actively involved in their learning.* They may conduct an experiment, act in a play, construct a model, write an essay, or otherwise creatively and productively engage in various active learning assignments and assessments. The activities provide evidence of the connection between knowing and doing. Bringing critical elements of the curriculum together, active learning often produces a powerful synergistic effect. For example, students move from knowing musical notes to playing an instrument; from identifying a problem to solving it; from developing a hypothesis to testing it; from using color theory to painting a canvas; or from using knowledge of specialized software to designing a building

or retrieving original documents for a social studies project.

- *Are involved in real-life situations that bring them into direct contact with adults in many different walks of life.* In the minds of some critics, standards-based education has acquired a reputation for intellectual sterility—a by-the-numbers approach to curriculum and instruction. To the contrary, standards-based education helps teachers to make relevant connections and to engage students in diverse, real-life, field-based learning that helps students develop academic proficiency.

- *Are actively involved in inclusive classrooms that value divergent questioning strategies, multiple assignments in the same class, tiered instruction, and activities that allow for alternative responses and solutions.* Heterogeneous grouping remains a hallmark of middle grades education. Standards-based education recognizes that students learn in many different ways and at different rates of speed and promotes flexiblity in adapting to those expectations. Strategies include effective, purposeful, differentiated instruction and fluid grouping of special needs students at both extremes of the learning continuum (e.g., GATE students and students needing remediation). (An extensive discussion of learning styles and differentiated instruction can be found in Chapter 8 of this publication.)

- *Are urged to consider ideas together with reasoning that includes the ability to compare, contrast, analyze, synthesize, evaluate, and generalize.* Middle school students typically experience major developmental breakthroughs in their ability to engage in

tasks that require complex reasoning. Teachers should, therefore, provide ample opportunities for the students to demonstrate their expanding ability and develop assignments that require students to use demanding intellectual processes.

- *Redo, polish, or otherwise strive to perfect their work.* Evidence of good student work and rich pedagogy lies at the heart of developing and implementing standards. The knowledge and skills students possess must be refined so that they can reach the elusive goal of excellence. Prime examples of practicing until perfect include participating in sports, solving problems, playing a musical instrument, composing a work of art, using effective oral and written expression. Only through repeated efforts to refine the quality of significant assignments can students improve their level of academic performance.

- *Know how to access and use information.* Good work and rich pedagogy include the ability to locate and use sources of information (e.g., the library, CD-ROMs, DVDs, the Internet) needed to complete assignments. Gaining access to information also includes the ability to know what questions to ask, to determine the integrity of sources of information, and to distinguish between documented and undocumented data.

- *Engage in reflective thought.* Middle grades students need to understand the processes involved in using their developing intellectual abilities effectively. They can do so by reflecting on their own experiences, thereby gaining an understanding of others. Standards-based education pays specific attention to the knowledge and skills and the core values on which a democratic society must depend, including tolerance, honesty, and respect for others.[4]

(See also Appendix 6-A, "Major Characteristics of a Middle School Culture Capable of Implementing and Sustaining Standards-Based Education," and Appendix 6-B, "Learning to Manage Information in Twenty-First Century Middle Schools," at the end of this chapter.)

## Nurturing Motivation, Effort, and Investment in Schoolwork

Wheelock's formula for a school culture that sustains standards-based education also involves the role of teachers in shaping their relationships with and among students in ways that nurture motivation, effort, and investment in schoolwork. She notes that:

> Establishing a motivational climate in which every student feels safe to work with diligence, tackle new learning, learn from mistakes, and do work that meets standards—the essence of being smart—begins with individual teachers who care enough about students' success that they repeatedly probe for clues that will help them understand how to best help each student to meet standards. Making student investment in school a norm schoolwide means taking individual teachers' practices and beliefs about learning and structuring them into the daily life of all classrooms to create a "press for achievement" and a climate that motivates every student to learn.[5]

Experiencing these qualities depends on many important factors within a school's culture that are reflected by its values, belief systems, and organizational priorities. In addition to those factors addressed earlier, Wheelock's discussion of motivation, effort, and investment provides the context for identifying additional elements of a middle school culture capable of sustaining standards-based education:

- *Effort, care, and quality are the primary bases of success in school.* By their very definition, content and performance standards signal that it is more important to do work that reflects effort, care, and quality than it is to cover the textbook. Completing work quickly is no longer an adequate indication of a successful learner. Students who once depended on passing grades by subscribing to school norms that rewarded memory and right answers need to be helped to adapt to the classroom world of standards that requires much different learning behaviors.

- *Beliefs about intelligence and learning affect performance.* Wheelock reminds us that traditional assumptions about intelligence and learning have often been severely skewed:

> For decades we have assumed that if we could only get the rewards and consequences "right," we could motivate students to work harder and improve achievement. The "right" incentives must be worthy of students' aspirations and dignity if they are to motivate students to work harder academically. . . . Programs that combine future financial scholarships for postsecondary education with structured tutoring, mentoring, and peer support motivate many middle grades students to persist in school.[6]

- *School norms about effort and risk taking drive students' success.* Wheelock contends that educators who want to make sure that school is a place where it is "safe to be smart" counter students' beliefs that learning depends on innate ability. For some teachers this attitude represents a substantial cultural shift professionally. Schools need to encourage all teachers to study the literature on motivation and achievement and to think through their private perceptions about actual or implied limitations that their instructional practices may place on student learning. Teachers should understand that praising students for taking on challenging assignments rather than praising them for less-challenging work leads to higher performance levels. "Motivating young adolescents depends in part on helping them understand learning in terms of expandable intelligence. . . ."

- *Detracking and heterogeneous (inclusive) grouping support the success of standards-based education.* Large numbers of middle-level schools have made progress over the past decade in overcoming the practice of tracking "like ability" students in classrooms in favor of heterogeneous classrooms. However, many teachers, principals, and parents remain uncertain about the practice. Wheelock responds by holding that tracking is incompatible with standards-based education and that such practices must change if it is to succeed. But the formation of flexible groups directed to accomplish a specific task or purpose is allowed, given that such grouping should be considered temporary.

(See also the following appendixes at the end of this chapter: Appendix 6-C, "Engaging Students: What I Learned Along the Way"; Appendix 6-D, "What to Expect Your First Year of Teaching"; and Appendix 6-E, "Creating a Learning Organization.")

# Creating a School Culture

- **Study the diagram in Appendix 6-A with a group of colleagues.** Consider each of the major characteristics of a school culture essential for implementing and sustaining a standards-based middle school. Collectively, they emphasize the need for dramatic behavior changes on the part of both students and teachers to support the principle that all students can and must meet rigorous academic standards. Discuss each of the major elements in the graphic and their presence in your school. Be generous in affirming positive evidence of each major element whenever appropriate. Be equally frank in identifying elements that need improvement or are missing. Develop proposals for doing something about the deficits. Organize your findings and share them with your principal.

- **To be effective, standards-based education must include a schoolwide commitment to differentiate instruction in accordance with the varied styles of learners as well as the differing strengths or deficits.** Yet there is overwhelming evidence that the majority of teachers do not differentiate instruction adequately, often because they have not been trained to do so. Assess your own ability to differentiate your students' learning experiences. Provide examples of ways in which you attempt to achieve this goal. How do you grade your effectiveness? Is there help you need? For example: What would be the most effective format for obtaining this assistance? District-level in-service classes? Mentoring? Peer coaching? Independent study? School-site seminars with colleagues? Other? Have you made known your needs to those in a position to act?

- **In your school what are the most pervasive and consistent behaviors on the part of teachers and administrators that project a caring attitude toward students?** Do you have suggestions for enhancing these behaviors? If so, suggest examples. Have you shared your thoughts with others, including the principal? If not, will you? When?

- **Sociologists emphasize how important the physical environment is to one's perception about the significance of what transpires within a school building.** Assess your own school in terms of its aesthetics, of the academic ambience it physically projects. On a scale of one to ten (with ten being high), is there evidence of pride in the exterior appearance of the school building and grounds? Is the interior—including entry, halls, and individual classrooms—bright, pleasant, and inviting? If you have given high marks, identify those factors that express that education is valued. If you have given low marks, how can the situation be improved? Who is accountable? What accountability do you have?

- **Effort and quality are among the most valued aspects of student work in determining academic proficiency in standards-based classrooms.** Discuss the role of effort and ways to keep it from becoming confused with true academic achievement in response to standards.

# Appendix 6-A

## Major Characteristics of a Middle School Culture Capable of Implementing and Sustaining Standards-Based Education

**Standards Based Education**

**Content**
**Performance Standards**
**Assessment**
**Accountability**

Successful standards-based middle schools are characterized by high-quality student work enhanced and enabled by excellent teaching and a supportive school culture.

**Learning occurs** in a context that values fairness, equity, justice, honor, civility, service to others, and democratic principles.

**Learning occurs** in a classroom setting that emphasizes the ability of all students to do quality work and to meet the standards for their grade and subject.

**Active learning** develops student proficiency through creative work involving problem solving and other tasks requiring complex reasoning.

**Learning emphasizes** direct and frequent interaction with real-life experiences:
- Field trips
- World of work
- School-to-Career
- Mentorships

**Learning occurs** in an attractive setting—no matter how old the school—that says to students and faculty: Education is valued here.

**Learning occurs** in classrooms that honor the richness of human diversity. The contributions of all ethnic, linguistic, and cultural traditions are celebrated.

**Learning occurs** in inclusive groups that emphasize caring teachers and differentiated instruction.

**Learning focuses** on the most important knowledge and skills. The significance of standards is made clear to all students.

**Learning emphasizes** the value of redoing, polishing, and perfecting work until it represents the highest quality of which students are capable.

**Learning takes place** in classrooms where students participate in selecting ways in which they will demonstrate their academic proficiency and have input in developing scoring criteria.

**Learning involves** locating information from print and digital sources and validating the quality and integrity of the content.

**Learning occurs** in a setting that values participation, cooperation, and collaboration among teachers, administrators, students, and parents.

# Appendix 6-B

# Learning to Manage Information
# in Twenty-First Century Middle Schools

*"The next best thing to knowing something is knowing where to find it."*
—Samuel Johnson

The significance of information management skills in twenty-first century middle schools is impossible to exaggerate. The continued exponential explosion of knowledge and the ever-increasing ease of instantaneous access through digitized library collections and other electronic media—particularly the Internet—make it an urgent priority to ensure that students have the ability to gain access to this massive database and to move into the exciting world of learning that *digital literacy* makes possible.

As middle school educators respond to this agenda, Alan November has noted that while technology plans are written that emphasize hardware, software, networks, fiber optics, and other issues, the most critical task relates to how such plans help teachers and students learn to manage effectively the information flowing into the classroom at the speed of light.

This means learning not only how to access the Internet and other digitized information bases but also how to discriminate among the many versions of truth that electronic media present on computer and television screens. In effect the Internet has democratized access to knowledge and has dethroned traditional gatekeepers of information sources. Such information access can be viewed as both a threat and an incredible intellectual breakthrough.

The ability to access, evaluate, and integrate efficiently the information available via the Internet, CD-ROMs, and other existing and emerging digital technologies lies at the heart of the meaning of *digital literacy.* Paul Gilster, internationally known author on cyberspace issues, emphasizes that the ability to evaluate and interpret information is critical. It is impossible to understand information found on the Internet, for example, without determining its origin and evaluating the legitimacy of the source.

The challenge is made even more demanding because data on the Internet not only are available in print format but also are transferable to video, audio, and photo formats that can be downloaded in seconds. Added to this are the multiple links to other Internet sites that start the process all over again.

Middle grade students are poised on the cusp of respectable proficiency in terms of digital information management. The kinds of instantaneous key word or key concept searches available on the Internet make it possible to gather digitized information from many sources around the world. Students soon learn that different searches of the Internet often turn up different information. The result can enrich and enlarge the data-gathering process—or hopelessly confuse it!

Digitally literate students can use the hardware and software required to access, import, process, merge, and save data from electronic sources. November believes that such skills can be learned effectively and relatively quickly, even though they involve a higher order of complexity for students who are doing serious research work.

Taken from an address by Alan November titled "Technology and the Future," presented at the School's In! Symposium sponsored by the California Department of Education, Sacramento, August, 1998.

November urges teachers who attend teacher-only technology workshops to seek permission to bring selected students with them each time and emphasizes that all should learn together. This strategy has the ability to expand rapidly the base of teachers and students available to teach, tutor, and mentor others with respect to the technical side of digital literacy.

November insists that technical skills are only the beginning of true digital literacy. Unless they are followed by the development of skills that enable users to evaluate and validate data sources, genuine threats exist to the integrity of learning based on digital technology.

Digital literacy also includes developing the ability to print data, transmitting it to others via e-mail, using it with news groups, talking about it in a chat group, or using it in other ways. What makes all of this so formidable in terms of its instructional potential is that data access, management, and retransmission can all happen instantaneously. An urgent aspect of digital literacy involves knowledge of federal legislation and international agreements that affect the use of digitized information, including the safeguarding of intellectual property rights.

While access to computer-mediated digitized information will never take the place of direct instruction by teachers, middle school students who lack digital literacy will be compromised in terms of their ability to gain access to the most valued learning opportunities.

# Appendix 6-C

# Engaging Students: What I Learned Along the Way

by Anne Wescott Dodd

When I was a first year teacher, I was concerned with survival. My attempts to control students led to many power struggles from which both the students and I emerged discouraged or defeated. . . . I wish someone had told me then that knowing my students was as important as knowing my subject. I didn't realize until much later that to motivate and engage students, teachers must create a classroom environment in which every student comes to believe, "I count, I care, and I can."

The best advice I could give to beginning teachers now is the secret of the fox in Antoine de Saint-Exupéry's *The Little Prince*: "What is essential is invisible to the eye." What teachers need most to know about students is hidden; unless they develop a trusting relationship with their students, teachers will not have access to the knowledge they need either to solve a classroom problem or to motivate students.

## I Wish I Had Known

As a novice teacher I didn't realize that a seemingly logical response to tardiness—detention—did not take into account students' reasons for being late, some of which were valid. If I had allowed students to explain why they were late before telling them to stay after school, I might have prevented hurt feelings and hostility. A sixth grader who hides from an eighth-grade bully in the bathroom until the coast is clear shouldn't be treated the same as someone who chats too long with a friend in the hall.

I wish I had found out sooner that simply asking students to tell me their side of the story could make such a positive difference in their attitudes. When I tried to understand situations from their points of view, students were willing to consider them from my vantage point. These conversations opened the way for us to jointly resolve problems.

But, most of all, I wish someone had told me that understanding students' perspectives was the best way to foster engagement and learning. Like other novice teachers, I wasted a great deal of time searching for recipes to make learning more fun. Only much later did I find out that the most effective veteran teachers reflect on their classroom experiences. Instead of thinking in terms of making learning *fun* (extrinsic motivation), they look for ways to make assignments and activities *engaging* (intrinsic motivation). Although they may express these ideas differently, effective teachers know that to become engaged, students must have some feelings of *ownership*—of the class or the task—and *personal power*—a belief that what they do will make a difference.

## From the Student's Perspective

Because beginning teachers often focus on what they will do or require students to do, they often overlook some important principles about learning.

First, learning is personal and idiosyncratic. It helps to view students as individuals (Marina, Hector, and Scott) rather than as groups (Period 1 Class, English). . . . Thus, teachers need to find out how students individually make sense of any lesson or explanation.

Second, every student behavior—from the most outrageous classroom outburst to the more common failure to do homework—is a way of trying to communicate something the student cannot express any other way or doesn't consciously understand. Punishing the behavior without learning its cause does nothing to solve a problem and, in fact, may intensify it.

From *Educational Leadership,* Vol. 53 (September 1995). Reprinted with permission from the Association for Supervision and Curriculum Development.

Third, teachers should never "assume" because too often they can be wrong. Low grades on tests do not necessarily mean that students haven't studied. Some students may have been confused when the material was covered in class. Incomplete homework isn't always a sign that students don't care. A student may be too busy helping care for younger siblings to finish assignments. The student who sleeps in class or responds angrily to a teacher's question may be exhausted, ill, or unable to cope with personal difficulties.

By inviting students to share their feelings and perceptions, teachers can establish positive relationships with them and . . . discover how to modify their teaching methods and personalize assignments in ways that engage students in learning.

### Getting Students to Open Up

- On the first day of class, give students a questionnaire to complete. Or invite them to write you a letter about themselves. The sooner you learn something about your students, the better equipped you will be to build personal relationships and address their concerns.
- Ask students who have not done their homework or who have come late to class to write a note explaining why. Establish this requirement on the first day of class, but don't present it as a punishment. Students should see these notes as an opportunity to communicate privately with their teacher.
- Ask students to write learning logs. Logs are especially useful at the end of a class in which new material has been introduced. For example, "Briefly summarize what you learned today, and note any questions you have." Don't grade the logs; just read them quickly for common problems to address in the next class. List names of students who

may need extra help. A note or smiley face shows students that you care about them as people. . . .

- Invite students to help you solve classroom problems. . . . Even if you wish to discuss an issue with students, having them write their ideas down will make the discussion more productive. Writing works because every student gets to share what he or she thinks, misunderstands, or needs to know. Teachers who depend on students to say aloud what they don't understand may be fooled into thinking that everything is okay when there are no questions.

### How to Personalize Assignments

- Give students some choice of topics for research, books for reading, and planning methods for projects or papers.
- Let students prepare a lesson and teach their classmates. For example, if teachers want students to be exposed to several aspects of a topic, . . . small groups of students can focus on the different parts of the larger assignment.
- Encourage students who understand a concept to help those who don't understand.
- Allow students to choose how to demonstrate their understanding. For example, draw the solution to a math problem or the plot in a novel. Write about it. Or videotape a real-life connection for it.

### Reflection Is the Key

Trying out a practice offers fertile ground for reflection even if the trial fails. As teachers look for new ways to engage students in learning, they are likely to find that the search itself will reenergize their teaching. . . . As teachers learn more about how students think and feel, they will be able to create classes where students enjoy learning because they are engaged in diverse, purposeful, and meaningful ways.

# Appendix 6-D

# What to Expect Your First Year of Teaching

## by Amy DePaul

*Without fail teachers give their colleges and universities high marks. But they suggest a number of initiatives they believe universities should consider. They concede, however, that there are issues for which no college or university could have prepared them. Here are excerpts from a book that captures fascinating and inspiring vignettes from the lives of a number of first-year teachers:*

When the bell rang at 8:15 a.m. on August 28, a new reality entered my mind, . . . *in loco parentis,* a legal term meaning in place of parents. I was taking on the responsibility of a parent! Following the first day, I expressed my concern to a fellow teacher, and he replied, *"Encargada!"* This is a Spanish term often used by Mexican parents when they are putting their child's life in a teacher's hands. It means we are handing our child over to you and now you are in charge. Wow! What responsibility! A couple of weeks passed, and I was still in shock. . . . I tried to create a nurturing, educational and safe environment for these students; then I would be fulfilling my job as an educator. Right? Surprisingly, I still felt the responsibility 24 hours a day! Teaching wasn't only my job; it was fast becoming my lifestyle.

—*Scott Niemann*

Before I became a new teacher, I never realized the social dimension involved with instructing eighth graders. . . . My students are dealing with issues I never imagined when I was a thirteen-year-old. AIDS, abuse, neglect, drugs, and sex are buzzwords I overhear in the hallways, classrooms, lunchroom, and library. As an individual I personally do not deal with most of these problems because they are not direct issues in my life. Yet as a teacher, mentor, and friend, I have to deal with these issues every day. I have students who have been physically and mentally abused, whose parents have been removed from their homes because of drugs, and who have had family members and close friends die of AIDS.

—*Melissa Luroe*

College did not prepare me for the student whose mother was murdered by a jealous boyfriend; for the student who witnessed a drive-by shooting; for the student who was removed from her home because of an abusive father. These realities do not exist in textbooks, yet they are, sadly, all too often the realities that people, with real lives and real problems, bring into my classroom. Perhaps universities could in the future focus on teaching teachers to teach students with a lot of problems. I find that I fill a million roles in a day (e.g., parent, teacher, friend, hero, disciplinarian, counselor). . . . Perhaps universities could focus on how to fill the many demanding roles of teaching. Doing this would better prepare teachers to meet the pressing needs of their students.

—*Lisa Shipley*

Teachers are the last bastion against darkness and ignorance. The intensity of this need was my surprise, and I know of no way my state college, in all its excellence, could prepare me for this life lesson. Only being a caring teacher can.

—*James Morrison*

Universities in general could help prepare future teachers by offering classroom management courses, by putting education majors in the schools earlier, by placing student teachers in settings that more closely resemble the assignments of typical first-year teachers, and by providing a postgraduation mentor program.

—*Stephanie Bell*

From *What to Expect Your First Year of Teaching.* Washington, D.C.: U.S. Department of Education, 1998.

It would have been ideal for my college to have instituted a mentoring program or to have aided students in establishing cohort groups. The experience of first-year teaching can indeed be one of isolation and self-questioning. The opportunity to have had a support group of other graduate students would have provided me with avenues for in-depth discussion and for brainstorming of ideas. I would have also benefited from learning about the varied experiences that my fellow students were encountering in their clinical and student teaching assignments.

*—Jeannette L. Whaland*

Along with being the "mender of hurts," where does the mender go to get mended? Teaching is an exhausting job. This was not a surprise. I did not, however, expect to be emotionally exhausted. I suppose the easiest way out of this dilemma would be to make myself emotionally unavailable to my students and become a true teaching machine void of any feelings. The maker of excellent lesson plans and doer of fantastic scholastic deeds, I could teach these students like they have never been taught before. I have no feelings. You can't hurt me! Don't tell me your problems, I am a teacher! Teachers don't do feelings and emotions. We teach. . . . Not this teacher. This teacher can't help but share some of these emotional moments. Maybe that's why they come to me so often. I can't turn off a portion of myself when I walk into the classroom. It's either the whole Mrs. Baer or nothing. And the whole Mrs. Baer needs to learn where she can go to remain whole. Could I have learned this at my university? I sincerely doubt it!

*—Allison Baer*

My first year of teaching has been full of many wonderful surprises. . . . But I was not prepared for the moment I first heard myself ask, "Does anyone in class not think that spitting on the floor is inappropriate behavior?" But most of all, I never thought that teaching would be such an exhilarating and rewarding career, continually pushing me in my quest to be a master teacher. . . . But there is one bit of wisdom that I would like to pass on to colleges regarding the first year of teaching. Don't focus in on the negative side of the profession. I must have spent hours listening to first-year teachers who appeared gaunt, malnourished, and exhausted drone on about how they were "coping." . . . Reinforce the intrinsic rewards that teaching offers. Stress that as a teacher you will experience the satisfaction of knowing that you make a difference, the ability to have a marked effect on the life of an emerging adult, and the excitement of advancing young minds."

*—Jeffrey Breedlove*

All of my life my career goal was to become a professional football player. After tryouts for the NFL, my dream began to fade. . . . I knew that with the help of God, I would choose another career that would give my life meaning, enable me to give back to my people; and emerge a stronger person with a sense of purpose. What better way could there be than that of a physical education teacher, just like my father, who dedicated 35 years of his life to the boys and girls of the D.C. school system. . . . From the first moment that I was alone with a class, there was no doubt in my mind that these students needed me, my experience, energy and dedication. . . . I would create a meaningful instructional program and environment filled with unlimited love and respect.

*—Neal Downing*

# Appendix 6-E

# Creating a Learning Organization

by Larry Lashway

According to some theorists, schools that dedicate themselves to systematic, collaborative problem solving can "continually" develop and implement new ideas, thereby not just improving but transforming themselves. Does research support this optimistic view? Or will the learning organization, five years from now, be just another entry on the jargon list?

Kenneth Leithwood and colleagues . . . define a learning organization as a group of people pursuing common purposes (individual purposes as well) with a collective commitment to regularly weighing the value of those purposes, modifying them when that makes sense, and continuously developing more effective efficient ways of accomplishing those purposes.

Although this is an inspiring vision, schools may be far from achieving it. Teacher isolation, lack of time, and the complexity of teaching present significant barriers to sustained organizational learning. . . .

Not surprisingly, researchers have often found that substantive changes in teaching practices are elusive. Richard Elmore and colleagues . . . discovered that even when teachers were willing to learn new methods, they often applied them in a superficial or inconsistent way, offering the appearance but not the substance of real change.

Despite this vein of pessimism, researchers have begun to identify schools in which entire faculties have become proficient in new forms of instruction, resulting in immediate impact on student learning and behavior. Several key findings from this work are highlighted below.

Beverly Showers, Carlene Murphy, and Bruce Joyce . . . studied three schools that undertook a systematic, sustained reform that focused on several models of teaching with a strong research base, including cooperative learning, concept attainment, and synectics. These models were designed to supplement teachers' existing strategies, not replace them.

The models were taught in three steps to all teachers. The first phase was designed to give teachers a theoretical understanding of the new concepts. This was followed by multiple demonstrations (mainly videotapes of classroom instruction) and opportunities to practice the new skills in the workshop setting.

Showers and colleagues note that this intensive workshop model is sufficient for teachers to introduce new strategies in their classrooms, but without additional support fewer than 10 percent will persist long enough to integrate the new skills into their repertoire. They . . . encouraged teachers to use the new methods immediately and frequently and to organize themselves into study teams for sharing, observation, and peer coaching.

The results were notable. At the end of the first year, 88 percent of the teachers were using the new strategies regularly and effectively. In one middle school promotion rates soared, while the average achievement test score jumped from the twenty-fifth to the forty-second percentile. In addition, disciplinary referrals dropped to about one-fifth the previous level.

Bruce Joyce and Emily Calhoun . . . note that schools are "both information rich and information impoverished." School personnel collect a prodigious amount of information, from test scores to attendance figures, yet rarely link this wealth of data to school improvement efforts.

From the *ERIC Digest*, No. 121, 1998.

Focusing on data confronts staff with hard evidence that may challenge existing perceptions of success; discrepancies raise sharp questions about what is happening and why. In addition, monitoring data provides a good way of tracking the effects of change efforts. Joyce and Calhoun point out that this is especially important in convincing faculty that students can achieve more than they thought possible. Finally, study of data often leads to a desire for more information. As reform efforts proceed, the school generates increasingly sophisticated data and uses it in a meaningful way.

Some studies point to changes in the workplace as a key to successful organizational learning. Schedules and assignments should allow time for collective inquiry. Joyce and Calhoun argue that significant reform is "nearly impossible" in a typical school workplace; at best, people will move forward as individual "points of light," but they will be unable to form a learning community.

Thus, schools must provide time for teachers to work and reflect together. Some schools, using early dismissal one afternoon a week, have been able to clear out significant blocks of time. In addition, Sharon Kruse and Karen Louis point out the importance of well-developed communication structures, such as e-mail and regular faculty meetings, as well as a common space for working.

Collective inquiry may be strengthened by more democratic forms of governance. Joyce and Calhoun advocate the formation of "responsible parties" to lead the school community in improvement efforts. These groups, composed of administrators, teachers, parents, and community members, would not be traditional parliamentary decision-making groups but would act as champions for extended inquiry.

Creating a learning organization requires a deep rethinking of the leader's role. Principals and superintendents must see themselves as "learning leaders" responsible for helping schools develop the capacity to carry out their mission.

A crucial part of this role is cultivating and maintaining a shared vision. . . . The vision provides focus, generating questions that apply to everyone in the organization. Learning becomes a collaborative, goal-oriented task rather than a generalized desire to stay current.

At a more mundane level, leaders must tend to the organizational structures that support continuous learning, squeezing time out of a busy schedule, collecting and disseminating information that accurately tracks the school's performance, and creating forms of governance that support collective inquiry.

Perhaps most important, leaders must view their organizations as learning communities, for faculty as well as students. . . . When the spirit of inquiry permeates the daily routine, schools are on their way to becoming true learning organizations.

> *"We must not, in trying to think about how we can make a big difference,*
> *ignore the small daily differences we can make which, over time, add up*
> *to big differences that we often cannot foresee."*
>
> —Marion Wright Edelman

# Team Teaching: Made to Order
# for Standards-Based Middle Schools

Certain instructional practices have received widespread acceptance in middle schools, including interdisciplinary team teaching. The reasons for this acceptance, according to principals and teachers, are the following:

- Greater flexibility in planning and implementing counseling programs and increased opportunities for tutoring and mentoring are provided because the teachers can work with the same students over longer periods of time.
- Teachers and students get to know one another better. As a result the students embrace the academic goals of the school.
- Teachers can work effectively with students who possess a wide range of learning abilities, thereby reducing the amount of tracking.
- Students experience a greater sense of personal identity, an enhanced ability to connect concepts across subject-matter

Recommendations 2, 3, 7, 13

areas, and an increased opportunity to engage in cooperative learning activities.
- At-risk students are identified more easily. As a result earlier intervention with alternative instructional opportunities is allowed in response to individual needs.[1]

## Major Types of Team Teaching

Often, however, the goals for team teaching have failed to materialize or have been significantly compromised. This chapter looks closely at some of the challenges. Specific attention is paid to the potential of interdisciplinary team teaching for realizing multiple instructional goals associated with middle-level education. When designed and implemented correctly, team teaching can effectively organize a broad range of instructional practices and support services directly related to the fundamental purposes of middle schools. Three major types of team teaching arrangements are discussed as follows:

### Chronological Team

The most basic team teaching model is the *chronological team.* Two or more teachers with

---

Marion Wright Edelman, Founder and President, Children's Defense Fund.

separate subject-matter specialization share the same students but teach in different classrooms. Most students in this situation may be unaware that they are part of a team. The thread that holds together the notion of team is time; that is, the same students rotate from one teacher to another at given intervals. Further, although the use of blocks of time may be flexible, the teachers rarely if ever meet consistently to plan instruction or address individual student needs. The teachers are responsible for their own subject matter and operate at the same level of independence found in self-contained classrooms.

### Cooperative Team

The *cooperative team* also typically involves assigning the same students to two or more teachers with separate subject-matter specialization. The teaching may or may not involve all students learning together through large- or small-group instructional activities. Although the teachers may plan together, they usually focus on allocating time and organizing instruction within a block schedule rather than on developing interdisciplinary connections. The cooperative team differs from the chronological team primarily in the amount of collaborative teaching time spent on addressing individual student needs. In this team arrangement the teachers are frequently more concerned with the social and emotional well-being of their students than with the design and teaching of interdisciplinary thematic units.

### Interdisciplinary Team

The *interdisciplinary team* ordinarily involves two or more teachers with separate subject-matter specialization who are assigned the same students in a common block of time.

But the team members are committed to working together to develop and teach interdisciplinary units. The primary instructional objective is to draw content from two or more subjects and focus the content on a specific topic or theme. Units are based on the topics or themes. The success of interdisciplinary units depends on the teachers' deep understanding of the separate disciplines and the use of the knowledge and skills associated with separate disciplines that allows the study of a topic or theme from several viewpoints. Students then develop a broader perspective on the issues. This type of team teaching is linked to the development of higher-order thought processes, including complex reasoning.

(See also Appendix 7, "Models of Team Teaching Showing Unique and Overlapping Features," at the end of this chapter.)

## Difficulties in Implementing Team Teaching

Genuine interdisciplinary team teaching remains out of reach for most middle schools. Even cooperative team teaching has been hard pressed to retain its original vitality. The reasons for team teaching encountering so many difficulties are many, although it still ranks as one of the most prized organizational arrangements among middle grades educators. Primary reasons for the difficulties and related recommendations for revitalizing team teaching are allocation of time and staff turnover:

### Unwise Allocation of Time

Time is one of the most fundamental factors that frustrate the intentions of even the most ardent supporters of team teaching. Time to plan! Time to teach! Time to learn! Block schedules are intended to provide more flexible use of time and more opportunity to allocate classroom time in relation to the nature of the immediate learning task. For example, expository teaching usually requires less time than does project or lab-oriented work. But time still remains rigidly apportioned in many middle schools. Block scheduling is often little more than a weak redefinition of conventional six- or seven-period school days.

The National Education Commission on Time and Learning notes that:

> Time is learning's warden. . . . If experience, research, and common sense teach nothing else, they confirm the truism that people learn at different rates and in different ways with different subjects. But we have put the cart before the horse. . . . The boundaries of student growth are defined by schedules for bells, buses, and vacations instead of standards for students and learning.[2]

Teaching teams need common planning time if new staff members are to be effectively inducted into the middle school culture. In addition, time is needed for team members to collaborate in planning instruction to meet a wide variety of academic, intellectual, social, and emotional goals. Common planning time should be provided during the school day through released time and extended-year contracts. Otherwise, frustration or regression to the least common denominator of teaming, the *chronological team,* may occur.

## Staff Turnover

Teacher transiency also lies at the heart of failed promises associated with team teaching. Team building among teachers is similar to team building in a professional sports franchise or in any other organization in which team play is essential. Each member needs time to get to know the strengths of one's teammates and time to practice the plays. However, teaching teams usually have only a few members; athletic teams have active players and reserves. When a change in the roster for an athletic team occurs, adjustments can be made. But when a member of a teaching team moves on, the consequences can be shattering. Entire middle school teaching teams can disappear because of retirement, transfer, leaves of absence, or other reasons.

The turnover of principals also causes team teaching to fail. To be very effective, middle school principals need sufficient time (at least five to ten years) in their assignments to provide consistency and continuity in communicating the philosophy of middle grades education to the staff. If interdisciplinary teams are to achieve the many accomplishments expected of them, the principal remains the single most important factor in reaching that goal. Effective teaching teams require long-range continuity and careful matching of new members with current members when changes do occur. As keepers of the vision and communicators of the middle grades philosophy, principals must be thoroughly involved in guaranteeing the integrity of the composition of teaching teams and must maintain close supervision during the transition period, when changes do occur.

The knowledge and skills associated with effective interdisciplinary teaming have been largely neglected in the preparation of new middle-level teachers. Consequently, many are thrust into team teaching with little knowledge of their new roles, even though they are expected to carry their weight from the first day. This is a recipe for failure for the new teacher and other team members as well. Principals who interview prospective teachers must usually give priority to the academic credentials and personalities of the candidates rather than to skills suitable for team teaching. To overcome this problem, schools must assume responsibility for inducting new teachers into the middle grades culture and providing mentoring and other help for them to function effectively in a team-teaching assignment.

## The Challenge of the Small School

Small schools, composed primarily of self-contained classrooms, may consider interdisciplinary teaming inappropriate. The full benefits of such teaching, made possible when two or more teachers blend their unique subject-matter competencies, may be hard to achieve in self-contained single-teacher classrooms. However, high-quality programs responsive to widely accepted middle grades educational principles and practices can be implemented successfully in such settings. Effective and appropriate instructional strategies must not be ignored or rationalized away because administrators and teachers feel unprepared or unable to use them. Principals have a responsibility to assist teachers in creating the best and most appropriate learning environments. If teachers, even in self-contained classrooms, are convinced that they can address more content standards by integrating selected core subject matter through an interdisciplinary focus, they should seek help if

they lack essential skills or enough flexibility to carry out their plans.

## Interdisciplinary Team Teaching and Standards-Based Education

At this point standards-based education and interdisciplinary team teaching intersect. No other change in either educational philosophy or practice in the past half-century holds as much promise for revitalizing interdisciplinary team teaching than the introduction of standards. When team teachers plan together to teach the most important knowledge and skills in an interdisciplinary approach, they will ensure not only that the standards will be taught but that their students will learn the connections between the various disciplines.

Many teachers are confused as to how to select the most important content for their students when faced with finite amounts of time at school. Standards-based education improves this situation. Content standards explicitly reflect the most essential concepts of what students should know and be able to do at each grade level, and performance standards measure and describe how well students are achieving those goals. Other industrialized nations with standards-based educational systems have learned that less is more: standards well taught provide a better foundation for future learning than does the traditional cover-the-book approach.

In conclusion, middle schools must focus on educational responses appropriate for young adolescents. Organizational structures and instructional practices must follow commitment to the essential elements of the middle grades philosophy: a caring, nurturing, student-centered learning environment that develops the intellect, contributes to emotional and social maturity, and results in high levels of academic achievement by all students in response to grade-level content and performance standards.

Interdisciplinary team teaching continues to offer promise to teachers and principals as one of the soundest methods for achieving a broad range of curricular and instructional goals. With standards-based education team teaching should become more focused and should help alleviate the pressure of time that has prevented the development of genuine interdisciplinary connections.

Middle grades teachers and principals cannot be passionate about developing appropriate programs and practices unless they believe in the underlying principles of middle grades education and understand the reasons for choosing particular organizational structures. Student-centered learning that enhances academic achievement is the hallmark of an exemplary standards-based middle school.

# Team Teaching

- **Team teaching, which makes good sense to large numbers of middle school teachers and principals, is widely considered one of the most important organizational characteristics of middle schools.** Yet it sometimes falls short of the mark, with few of its benefits realized. What has been your experience? Study the team-teaching diagram in the appendix at the end of this chapter. How do you characterize your team? Is it meeting your expectations? What are its strengths? Its weaknesses? What might help you and your team colleagues do a better job? If team teaching has worked well in your situation, describe the most important factors in the success. Find ways to share the information with other teams in your school that may be struggling.

- **How has standards-based education changed the way your teaching team operates?** Is your teaching more focused? Are standards prominently displayed in your classrooms? Are you and your team partners collaborating in designing student assessments based on standards and performance levels? Have you engaged in planning thematic units? What accomplishments are giving you the most professional satisfaction as you have sought to incorporate the elements of standards-based education into your team teaching? How might you do more? What kinds of assistance do you need? Who can provide it? Will you try to obtain the necessary resources?

- **How well has your school dealt with turnover among teachers and principals?** What threat has turnover posed to efforts to implement a successful middle school program? Are you facing personal challenges to your own team-teaching assignment and the ability to do your best work? If so, seek out a colleague with whom you can share your concerns. Become a catalyst in helping to resolve existing challenges so that your school's teaching teams will become stronger.

- **Are you teaching in a middle school where size or other factors are keeping you and your colleagues from having strong teaching teams?** What changes would you make? Does anybody else know your wish list? If not, are you prepared to share it?

- **Are genuine interdisciplinary teams a reality in your school?** If so, is a serious effort being made to organize content standards from several different subject areas according to important themes? Are students' assignments and benchmark assessments reflective of this integrative approach? Can you assess student work by using rubrics aligned with your instructional strategies? If you have experienced success, find ways to share your work with other teaching teams. If any of your answers are qualified, what kinds of assistance would benefit you and your team colleagues? Share this need with your principal.

# Appendix 7

# Models of Team Teaching Showing Unique and Overlapping Features

## Chronological Team Teaching

Same teachers, same students but assigned to alternate time blocks. Teachers typically working independently without seeking to integrate instruction.

*Unique features:*

- Traditional instruction—team in name only
- Little if any effort to coordinate instruction or to develop complementary units involving two or more subjects
- Little if any group guidance planned as team effort
- Each teacher typically responsible for own discipline
- Common planning time shared or not shared by teachers
- Students rotated between teachers and often unaware that their teachers belong to a team

*Features overlapping with cooperative team teaching:*

- Students typically not involved in interdisciplinary learning
- Collaborative instructional planning optional
- Teachers typically responsible for separate subjects taught in separate rooms

## Cooperative Team Teaching

Same students assigned to same teachers and same time block. Emphasis on effective use of time but little consistent effort to integrate instruction.

## Interdisciplinary Team Teaching

Same students, same time block, same teachers who collaborate on all phases of interdisciplinary instruction

*Unique features:*

- Interdisciplinary projects requiring complex reasoning and cooperative learning regularly planned by teams
- Shared comprehensive instructional strategy developed by teams
- Regular study and learning together by teachers

*Features overlapping with cooperative team teaching:*

- Common planning time for team members
- Provision of in-class remediation typical
- Group guidance provided regularly by teams
- Significant emphasis on differentiated instruction
- Instructional units frequently constructed around topics or themes
- Student disciplinary problems shared by team members

*Overlapping features of chronological, cooperative, and interdisciplinary team teaching:*

Special concern for developmental characteristics and social-emotional needs of young adolescents

Emphasis on caring teacher-student relationships

8

*"To him whose elastic and vigorous thought keeps pace with the sun, the day is a perpetual morning."*

—Henry David Thoreau

# Instructional Significance of Research on How Students Learn

Researchers increasingly agree that the human brain is constantly searching for meaning as it seeks new patterns and connections, including retention of new information. An interdisciplinary curriculum reinforces brain-based learning because the brain appears better able to retain information when presented as integrated rather than isolated. Implemented in the context of interdisciplinary instruction, standards-based education represents a powerful and practical application of brain-based learning theory.

## Effects of Multiple Intelligences on Instruction

Gardner's work on multiple intelligences during the past two decades is significant. He defines intelligence as "the ability to solve problems or fashion products that are valued in at least one culture." Conventional intelligence tests, he emphasizes, are unable to estimate a

Recommendations 2, 3, 10, 15

product's value or an individual's ability to produce a product. His theory appears to be particularly true outside one's own cultural experience and may help to explain why multicultural classrooms often challenge teachers and students as they seek to assign values to one another's unique contributions.

Gardner has identified seven intelligences: verbal/linguistic, logical/mathematical, musical/rhythmic, visual/spatial, body/kinesthetic, interpersonal, and intrapersonal. Everyone, he contends, has these intelligences in varying degrees. He and his colleagues continue to engage in significant research designed to confirm the theoretical basis of their work and, more important, develop practical ways to use their findings to improve teaching and learning. Teachers who use multiple-intelligence theories seek to present subject matter in ways that respond to the multiple intelligences of their students. Language, numbers, environment, sound, physical movement, and social skills, for example, are used to carry out various instructional approaches.[1]

(See also Appendix 8-A, "Multiple Intelligences Contribute to the Learning Potential of all Students," at the end of this chapter.)

# Effects of Learning Styles on Instruction

Attempts to define learning styles are intended to reveal how students differ in the ways they learn. Although all students can learn, they process and absorb new information differently. Twenty-one learning-style elements affect students' motivation and achievement. Students may perform poorly in a given subject not because they cannot learn but because the strategy used to teach them was inconsistent with their learning styles. And teachers and students alike often confuse mismatches in styles of teaching and learning with lack of ability. If underachievers are taught in ways that complement their strengths, research has found, they can increase their scores on standardized tests significantly. For example, students who are hearing oriented learn and recall information when they hear it. And students with more developed kinesthetic abilities may need to experience physically what they are to learn through such strategies as role playing and the use of manipulatives.[2]

Some ways to adapt the environment to accommodate the learning styles of students are listed as follows:

- *Noise.* Students who prefer a quiet, relaxed work environment for independent study are provided with individual desks or carrels and are allowed to listen to soft music. Those students who wish total quiet are provided headphones without cords.
- *Light.* Many students prefer to work with less light, particularly to avoid the glare of fluorescent lighting. Separate switches control several banks of lights in the classroom. Some banks have had all but one fluorescent tube removed. For those concerned about the effects of reduced lighting on students' eyes, current research reveals that even when the light is reduced markedly, the eyes will not be injured.
- *Temperature.* Mental work is done most effectively in a cool environment. Thermostats are set to 65 degrees. Students who prefer a warmer classroom are urged to wear sweaters, and those who prefer a cooler classroom are urged to wear layered clothing.
- *Design.* The aesthetics of the learning environment can affect students' perceptions about learning negatively or positively. A neat, clean, graffiti-free classroom is essential. The walls are painted in pleasing pastel colors, and wall decorations show the work of serious students. Evidence of work related to the content and performance standards is displayed prominently.
- *Sociological stimuli.* Students are engaged in learning activities emphasizing independent work. They work in pairs and in small groups. Those who need special supervision by the teacher (e.g., vision-impaired, hearing-impaired, and emotionally troubled students) are seated near the front of the room or near the teacher's desk.
- *Perception centers.* Instruction within the classroom or the instructional media center provides for auditory and tactile-kinesthetic learning modes, including access to listening centers and computers.
- *Intake (high metabolic rates).* Provision is made for a limited number of snack times during scheduled classes. Only healthful foods are provided in school vending machines.

Other learning styles are also worth considering. Sensitivity to the various learning styles of students on the part of teachers and principals is consistent with the attention paid by employers to the work environment of their employees.

Students need to be aware of their schools' efforts to respond to at least some aspects of their learning styles. The flexibility provided in a classroom adapted to differences in learning styles carries significant personal responsibilities for students. They should discuss the concept of learning styles with their teachers and should be urged to suggest improvements in their classrooms to enhance their learning. Those who identify the kind of learning environment in which they are the most productive should be asked to share that information with their parents, who then should be urged to create appropriate settings for study at home.

There are no good or bad learning styles— just differences in learning that frequently continue into adult life. Teachers and principals are aware of the kinds of work environments in which they experience the greatest sense of their own productivity. Helping students identify their learning styles and providing them with opportunities to capitalize on them are worthy goals. That process should be repeated with every new class at the beginning of the school year and with individual students who transfer in during the year.

It may take three to five years to develop learning environments responsive to the factors that influence effective learning. To do so is a sound educational investment. Providing for differences in individual learning styles benefits a whole range of students, including those identified as being learning disabled or experiencing attention deficit disorders.

## Characteristics of Differentiated Instruction

Differentiated instruction provides many more ways for students to take in new information, assimilate it, and demonstrate what they have learned in contrast with instruction aimed at the average student and delivered through uniform lectures, activities, homework assignments, and assessments. Unfortunately, few teachers modify instruction for struggling or advanced learners.

Three principles of cognitive research (the need for emotional safety, for appropriate challenges, and for self-constructed meaning) suggest that a one-size-fits-all approach to classroom teaching is ineffective for most students and even harmful for some. Some students need more repetition, fewer ideas presented at one time, clearer homework assignments, or more time to read instructions. Others require more individualized instruction, more time for independent hands-on problem solving, or tutorial help. The principles that point clearly to the need for differentiated instruction are listed as follows:

1. *Need for emotional safety.* Learning environments must feel emotionally safe to students for the most effective learning to take place. A student who needs an accepting and relatively open learning environment will be intimidated by a teacher who stifles wholesome spontaneity. Classrooms in which one right answer is always required will blunt creative minds that might otherwise invent valid alternative solutions to problems. A student whose first language is other than English and who struggles to make sense

out of what is going on will experience one emotional block after another when he or she cannot grasp key concepts. When students experience high levels of emotional insecurity, they may spend more time in figuring out how to cope than in how to learn. Although teachers cannot control all of the variables that contribute to emotionally unsafe classrooms, they can influence many of them.

2. *Need for appropriate challenges.* Students require appropriate levels of challenge. When students are confronted with content and performance standards well beyond their level of readiness, intense stress frequently results. The brain overproduces neurotransmitters (substances transmitting nerve impulses across a synapse) that impede learning. But if the curriculum is repetitive and lacks stimulus, the brain is not inclined to respond and therefore does not release the neurochemicals needed for optimal learning, causing apathy.

   A one-size-fits-all approach to teaching produces lessons pitched at a single-challenge level, virtually ensuring that many students will be overchallenged or underchallenged. Neither group will learn effectively. Research supports the conviction that all students should strive to meet the same content and performance standards, although many will do so at different levels of acceptable proficiency.

3. *Need for self-constructed meaning.* Students need opportunities to develop their own meaning as new knowledge and skills are encountered. They have different learning styles, process ideas and concepts differently, have varied backgrounds and experiences, and express themselves differently. All must be helped to assimilate new knowledge and skills within the framework of prior personal experiences.

## Effects of Cognitive Diversity on Instruction

The extent of students' cognitive diversity in a classroom means that effective teaching should focus more on concepts and the principles from which they are derived than on fact-based curriculum and instruction. Wise teachers help students develop intellectual processes, allowing them to draw conclusions logically and ascribe meaning to major concepts and principles in the core curriculum. But students are also taught that some knowledge has intrinsic meaning, represents an intimate part of their cultural heritage, and should be learned for its own sake. Our concepts of self, society, nation, and world are shaped by this knowledge. Major historic events and their significance, breakthrough discoveries and their impact on humankind, the great themes of classical literature, and the rich symbolism of the visual and performing arts represent this kind of learning.

Extensive cognitive diversity among students also means that content and performance standards should be taught in a context that allows students to see part-whole relationships and relate the content of what is being studied to real-life situations. The brain learns best when it does rather than when it absorbs. Students helped to process new knowledge and skills in ways relevant for them are more apt to acquire deep learning of the material embedded in the content standards. Youth-oriented context as well as content and programs such as school-to-career help students see future possibilities and give relevance to their learning. Middle school teachers and principals are encouraged to draw on the three major principles from cognitive research to develop differentiated instruction.

## Differentiated Instruction in Middle Schools

Differentiated instruction in middle schools includes the following characteristics:

- Teachers spend quality time learning all they can about their students' emotional security, readiness to address specific content and performance standards, and success in making sense of the curriculum.
- Classrooms are student centered. Students are not embarrassed by individual differences or learning difficulties. They are helped by their teachers to identify and value the similarities and differences each one brings to the classroom, show mutual respect for one another, and work together to create an emotionally safe environment.
- Teachers refine professional skills and practices, enabling them to function democratically in their interpersonal relationships with each student and the class as a whole. Professional qualities of openness and spontaneity are combined with a sense on the part of students that their teachers want to reduce root causes of emotional stress.
- Teachers vary their instructional practices in response to their students' learning styles and readiness levels to provide appropriate degrees of academic challenge for all individuals. Their doing so is not,

however, a license to lower standards for students with learning deficits. Rather, the goal is to work with students where they are and to make provisions for those who need more time, need to learn in smaller increments of content, need help in overcoming language barriers, or have other special needs.
- Teachers develop skills to present curricular content in multiple ways (e.g., deductively, inductively, aurally, orally, visually, hands-on) to respond to individual learning differences.
- Teachers frequently give choices to students concerning topics of study, ways of learning, ways of presenting evidence of learning, and learning environments. Care is taken to ensure that choices are consonant with grade-level content standards.
- All students are expected to demonstrate acceptable levels of performance in response to grade-level content standards. Varied but equally valid ways of demonstrating individual performance are provided.
- Teachers ensure that content and performance standards and the manner in which performance levels are determined are clearly and regularly communicated to students and parents.
- Teachers may assign students to work by themselves, in random groups, or according to similar or mixed readiness, similar interests or mixed interests, or similar learning profiles or mixed learning profiles. Students with acute physical, emotional, or intellectual deficits are mainstreamed as fully as possible. Effective schools use ongoing, formative assessments to regularly group and regroup their students to ensure

that they receive the most pertinent and highest quality instructional program possible.

- Teachers design homework to extend individual knowledge and skills. Parents are enlisted as fully as possible to monitor homework and are helped to understand which content standards are being addressed at any given time. They encourage their children to use rubrics in assessing the quality of their homework.

- Standardized tests are augmented by varied assessment options, including oral presentations, portfolios, real-life problems to be solved, research projects, and tests designed by students and teachers. Assessments seek to reduce emotional stress by providing varied and valid tasks that reflect the students' ability to apply knowledge and skills free of the pressures of time.

- Reporting of student progress reflects performance levels thoroughly understood in advance. Teachers and students frequently discuss these matters, and indi-

vidual students can tell with substantial accuracy where they fall in a continuum of acceptable performance. The reporting of progress employs formats designed to reflect standards-based education. Students who fail to reach acceptable performance levels receive appropriate support.

- Teachers are academic coaches who attend to the needs of individual students, groups of students, and the entire class. Their primary goal is to encounter all students where they are (those with learning deficits, those who are gifted, and all who are in between) and to move them forward as far and as fast as possible.[3]

The true account found in Appendix 8-B, "Lessons Learned from My Students in the Barrio," provides a particularly compelling description of a classroom in which the need for creating emotional safety is a dominant factor in establishing the conditions for effective learning.

# How Students Learn

- **In the preceding discussions of findings in cognitive research, did you reconfirm elements of your own instructional style?** Did you learn anything new that might influence your future teaching? In what ways? Can you implement the changes at once? Or would you need special training? Are you interested enough to let the appropriate persons know of your interest and possible need for staff development services?

- **Have you assessed your students' most productive learning styles?** Do you involve students in assessing themselves as to what kind of study environment works best for them? Are you consciously aware of your own learning style? In what kind of study environment do you feel most productive? Have you talked with other colleagues about this matter to develop greater sensitivity to the varied needs of students? How might you go about doing so?

- **Research indicates that teaching underachievers in ways that complement their learning styles can significantly increase their achievement.** How might you go about testing that finding in your classroom? How might you involve other teachers?

- **How do you assess your school's sensitivity to the various learning styles supported by research?** Are teachers and other staff members (especially library-media specialists) allowed to alter the learning environment, such as creating quiet zones, varied light intensities, and cooler temperatures? How do you rate the overall aesthetic quality of your classroom? Of your school? Is there a pleasant work environment that projects a message that what we do here is important? How is this purpose achieved? Do you have suggestions for improvements?

- **Emotionally safe classrooms are very important in fostering effective learning and preventing misbehavior.** Given the diversity present in every classroom, the data clearly suggest the urgency of differentiating instruction to develop an emotionally safe learning environment. Unfortunately, such instruction occurs consistently in only a small percentage of classrooms. How do you assess your classroom? What might you do differently—and better—to differentiate instruction? What would be needed to do so?

- **The account in Appendix 8-B shares the experiences of an inner-city teacher who struggles to develop *emotional and cognitive safety* in her classroom.** Do you see any of your own experiences in her personal account? If you were telling your own story, what would you most want to share with others? Would you be willing to do so either formally or informally?

# Appendix 8-A

## Multiple Intelligences Contribute to the Learning Potential of All Students

Harvard professor Howard Gardner has identified, through his extensive research, "seven intelligences" present to some extent in every individual. These intelligences, in combination, influence thinking and learning. The categories identified for each type of intelligence suggest useful instructional emphases for developing the learning potential of all students.

**Verbal/Linguistic**
- Reading
- Vocabulary
- Formal speech
- Journal/diary keeping
- Creative writing
- Poetry
- Verbal debate
- Impromptu speaking
- Humor/jokes
- Storytelling

**Logical/Mathematical**
- Abstract symbols and formulas
- Outlining
- Graphic organizers
- Number sequences
- Calculation
- Deciphering of codes
- Forcing of relationships
- Syllogisms
- Problem solving

**Body/Kinesthetic**
- Folk/creative dancing
- Role playing
- Physical gestures
- Drama
- Martial arts
- Body language
- Physical exercise
- Mime
- Invention
- Sports games

**Visual/Spatial**
- Guided imagery
- Active imagination
- Color schemes
- Patterns/designs
- Painting/drawing
- Mind mapping
- Pretending
- Sculpture
- Pictures

**How We Learn**

**Intrapersonal**
- Silent reflection methods
- Metacognition techniques
- Thinking strategies
- Emotional processing
- "Know-thyself" procedures
- Practice of mindfulness
- Focusing/concentration skills
- Higher-order reasoning
- Complex guided imagery
- Centering practices

**Interpersonal**
- Giving feedback
- Intuiting others' feelings
- Using cooperative learning strategies
- Communicating person to person
- Practicing empathy
- Dividing work
- Developing collaboration skills
- Receiving feedback
- Sensing others' motives
- Participating in group projects

**Musical/Rhythmic**
- Rhythmic patterns
- Vocal sounds/tones
- Musical composition/creation
- Percussion vibrations
- Humming
- Environmental sounds
- Singing
- Tonal patterns
- Musical performance

See, for example, Howard Gardner, *Multiple Intelligences: The Theory in Practice* (New York: Basic Books, 1993), for more complete information.

# Appendix 8-B

# Lessons Learned from My Students in the Barrio

By Myrna W. Gantner

**This was my first day at an inner-city middle school. . . . The boys and girls who walked into my room that day reflected the changing demographics in the United States, where the Hispanic population is growing at a rate five times faster than that of the general population.**

For the uninitiated, inner-city schools can be difficult places in which to teach. Bashing stereotypes and respecting differences set the stage for successful learning. They walked into my classroom giggling and jesting with one another in Spanish. When they saw me, they immediately became somber and sat down, watching every move I made. I looked into a sea of apprehensive, questioning faces. This was my first day at an inner-city middle school. I had taught school in a private setting for seven years, and I was ready for something new. I wanted to expand my experience base to the public schools, particularly schools where students were different from those with whom I had worked previously. Now I had my chance!

The boys and girls who walked into my room that day reflected the changing demographics in the United States, where the Hispanic population is growing at a rate five times faster than that of the general population. Many of my students were first-generation Americans and were just learning to speak English. Others, although born in the United States, spoke Spanish at home. Almost all of the youngsters were from low-income households. These students came from a culture that was very different from mine.

## Learning from One Another

During my teacher certification process, I took a class in multicultural education. I learned about different ethnic groups and how our varied perspectives of life cause us to view our worlds in very different ways. I learned much more in my classroom. I knew that because I was working with students who spoke English as a second language, I needed to speak slowly and clearly and to use simple vocabulary. I thought I was doing just that until a student asked me to repeat the instructions I had just given. I repeated the instructions but asked the student to listen more closely that time. The look on his face immediately told me that I had made a mistake. Later, as we spoke privately, he blurted out, "Miss, you talk too fast! I just don't understand you!" I was dismayed. I really believed I had slowed my speech sufficiently. I knew I was making a conscious effort to use vocabulary my students understood and to define the words they needed to learn. The problem was that I hadn't carried my adaptations far enough. I apologized to the student and worked hard to speak more slowly and clearly.

My students and I corrected each other and learned from each other daily. My red hair and blue eyes were fascinating to these

From *Educational Leadership,* Vol. 54 (April 1997). Reprinted with permission from the Association for Supervision and Curriculum Development.

children. "Miss, do you paint you hair?" was a question I was asked every year. I appreciated the fact that they felt comfortable enough with me to ask such a personal question. "No, this is natural, but the word you want to use is dye your hair. In English we use paint for painting signs, buildings, and artwork." They would giggle and correct their terminology.

It was my time to learn when I mispronounced the last name *Guereca.* One of my students taught me how to say it correctly. "Don't say the *g* like the word *go.* Say it like this." She demonstrated it again, several times. To me the *g* sounded like an English *w* and the *r* resembled a very soft *d.* I now pronounced the name something like "wedeca" but hardly enunciated the *d.*

Suddenly I was improving, and my students grinned. "Miss, that's better!" The three years I spent at this school were filled with both joy and sadness. The joy came as we made progress and learned about one another. I also experienced overwhelming sadness at times, particularly when I realized there were some students I could not help. I remember one boy, a fourteen-year-old gang member, who told me life didn't matter to him because he knew he'd be dead before he was twenty-one.

**A Difficult Challenge**

One of the most difficult challenges I faced was convincing my students to become more assertive when they felt they were mistreated or misunderstood by other teachers. Hispanic parents often teach their youngsters that the teacher is always right. I encouraged my students to speak up for themselves but to do so in a gracious way. Assertion is different from disrespect, I would tell them. There are right ways and wrong ways to handle these situations. Yes, you must respect your teachers, but it is not disrespectful to talk to them privately and confide that a particular statement made you uncomfortable or hurt you. While some of my students began to act on this instruction, others just listened. I still believe the ones who only listened were tucking the information away for a later time when they felt a little more confident.

**Shared Frustration**

During the school year my students shared some of their frustration with me. The following statements are representative of what I heard time and time again from my eighth graders: "We want to be treated with respect." Unfortunately, some teachers believe that inner-city students do not merit the same amount of time and attention they would give to more affluent students. It is impossible to hide such an attitude. The students know when teachers think less of them, and they retaliate by misbehaving and being disrespectful in the classroom. It's important to remember that all of us respond better when treated with dignity and respect. "Don't prejudge us. Not all of us are bad, use drugs, or belong to gangs."

Inner-city students grapple with problems far beyond those faced by the average middle-class student. Many of my students were struggling to stay away from drugs and avoid violence. It's as though they were hanging on by threads. They needed support and encouragement, not disapproval. "Don't laugh at our English. When teachers laugh, it makes us not want to try anymore." The more our students speak English, the more successful they will be in the classroom. We must do everything possible to make the learning environment comfortable and safe for students. "We know you hear bad things about the barrio on TV. It's not really like that. There are just some people who do those things."

> Unfortunately, some teachers who would thrive in the inner-city classroom never consider applying because they hear only the negative news. The rewards of teaching these children are immense.

Unfortunately, some teachers who would thrive in the inner-city classroom never consider applying because they hear only the negative news. The rewards of teaching these children are immense. They appreciate teachers who care for them, and they verbalize it frequently. They are very grateful for teachers who hold high expectations and show them how to achieve their goals. The parents, too, are appreciative of teachers who work to make a difference in their children's lives. "Don't judge us by the way we dress." That's one complaint I heard often.

## Easing the Transition

Too few teachers are willing to work in inner-city schools, helping the students who face so many difficult challenges. And too few of those who do have had enough preparation. Although preservice university classes are helpful, such classes are not sufficient to adequately prepare the teacher who has never worked with inner-city youngsters. We must do more.

The barrio was a different culture and a new experience for me. I would like to have spent some time in the neighborhood before my first day of school. An in-service program before the school year started, designed to address my students' special needs, also would have helped immensely. But despite the difficulties I would not trade the three years I spent in that classroom. The youngsters I taught were among the most appreciative students I have ever had the pleasure to work with. Together, we learned to recognize and value the differences we saw in one another. And we built a wonderful relationship that was grounded in trust and caring.

*"Remember, people support that which they help create. . . . Always get the commitment of others in any undertaking. Have them take a piece of the action so it's their action as well as yours. Involvement begets commitment. Commitment begets power."*

—Herb Cohen

# Providing Time for Standards-Based Education

Time is one of the most critical variables in standards-based education. How it is spent speaks volumes about the things that count most in a school. Spent well, time enhances students' learning opportunities; spent poorly, it robs students and teachers of the most precious commodity in the school environment. In relation to standards-based education, time must be viewed on a continuum, including the regular school day, the critical hours after school, weekends, intersessions, summer vacations, and extended school years. Standards-based education depends on highly focused instruction that addresses the most important knowledge and skills in each area of the curriculum. Time must be closely managed and tightly focused to ensure that all students have maximum opportunities to learn and demonstrate their ability to meet or exceed performance standards.

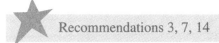 Recommendations 3, 7, 14

## Wise Use of Time: The Challenge

The master schedule is the most basic expression of a school's philosophy. It must facilitate the access of all students in a middle school to the full array of instructional resources and opportunities to learn. Allocation of time for each student's instruction must be made wisely. To recognize the truth of this statement, one has only to consider the limited amount of classroom time available to students versus the amount of time spent in watching television or participating in activities that have little or no connection to school.

Administrators, teachers, and counselors—anyone who helps build master schedules or make student course assignments—need to accommodate the most demanding mix of courses, programs, and services and make them universally available. The many instructional demands of standards-based education make the acquisition of expertise in sophisticated scheduling an urgent priority for principals and teachers.

---

Herb Cohen, motivational speaker

If the essential elements of standards-based middle schools are to be realized, the allocation of time must be fundamentally reexamined. Provisions must be made for flexible block scheduling, team teaching, differentiated instruction, remedial support programs, accelerated learning opportunities, active and cooperative learning experiences, advisory or similar types of guidance programs, tutorials, extended-year learning opportunities, intersessions, and summer school programs. Every desirable program element must be accommodated.

Schedules must also ensure that teachers can do their jobs effectively. Standards-based professional work requires additional time beyond the contact time scheduled with students. It is essential to schedule time for collaborative planning, benchmark assessment development, and scoring and evaluation of student work. Beyond professional work, regular opportunities for professional development, collegial mentoring, and coaching are also important contenders of available time.

Some schools have negotiated blocks of time for noncontact professional work by extending the contact time each day by a few minutes and banking the additional minutes in exchange for regular minimum days.

## Block Scheduling

Block scheduling combined with interdisciplinary team teaching provides a basic means of encouraging the effective use of time. The combination allows the flexibility needed to overcome many of the teaching constraints imposed by conventional six- or seven-period days. Although many variations of block scheduling exist, the simplest involves breaking the school day into fewer but longer time segments, each segment equivalent to three or four conventional periods. Teams of teachers responsible for two or more subjects then collaboratively apportion time within the block according to the nature of the specific instructional goals.

Differentiated instruction, one of the hallmarks of blocked interdisciplinary team teaching, includes learning activities requiring varied lengths of time for active and passive teaching strategies. Expository teaching, an essentially passive instructional mode, predictably requires less time than active learning, which emphasizes tasks that require doing. The latter include creative writing, problem solving, experimenting, constructing, perfecting visual and performing arts skills, and other activities that link knowing and doing abilities. In addition, one of the major corollary benefits of block scheduling is the flexibility provided for professional collaboration during the school day.

Block-scheduled schools tend to emphasize staff development at the school level, increased attention to instructional programs, and more differentiated instruction as well as significant improvement in students' attendance and grade point averages.[1]

## Guidelines for the Use of Time

The guidelines presented here are intended for schools that use block scheduling or conventional scheduling. Emphasis is placed on the finiteness of time, the urgency of using time well, and the intrinsic relationship between standards-based education and school schedules:

- A commitment is made to the proposition that any program element associated with a standards-based middle school is administratively possible to implement. If it is educationally sound, it can be scheduled. Time is viewed as a factor supporting learning, not a boundary that marks its limits.
- Time is no longer viewed within the context of six- or seven-period days five times per week. Rather, the total number of available instructional hours becomes the primary criterion in creating the school schedule.
- The hours available are divided into a larger number of increments of shorter duration than regular periods. The increments provide needed flexibility in determining the amount of time required for different instructional tasks. Flexibility of this kind is essential for block scheduling, advisory programs, assemblies, service-learning experiences, and other needs.
- Blocks composed of any number of time increments are made as long as needed to accomplish instructional goals. For example, the extended amount of time blocked for interdisciplinary teaching teams provides for differentiated instruction, including active and cooperative learning experiences within the context of an integrated curriculum.
- Time is allocated differentially to allow for courses that require setup and takedown time for instructional purposes. Science laboratories, exploratory programs, school-

to-career, shops, instrumental and vocal music classes, visual arts programs, physical education activities, and computer laboratories fall into this category. The same logic is applied to other than regular instructional programs, such as tutoring programs, mentoring programs, and advisory programs.
- When a village or house organization exists, the school's master schedule provides substantial flexibility in sharing staff time and instructional facilities.
- All teachers are assigned a planning period each day consistent with contract provisions. Members of the teaching teams are assigned common planning time each day—again, consistent with contract provisions. For those who are not members of a teaching team, efforts are made to provide common planning time when the teachers share assignments or when other program considerations suggest that doing so would encourage professional collaboration.
- Advisory programs or guidance activities are accommodated within the students' schedules in ways that emphasize their significance.
- Opportunities for school-based and community-based service-learning experiences are accommodated within the students' schedules to ensure that instructional time remains uncompromised. The same holds true for the students' access to health care providers, human services agencies, and other health support services. Conflicts with regular classroom learning activities should be avoided unless emergencies exist.

- When block scheduling is used, passing time is reduced. Only part of the student body moves on any given passing bell. Consequently, the amount of in-class instructional time is increased.
- Passing bells are replaced by chimes or soft music to avoid interrupting classes that remain in place and to improve the school environment.
- Early research on adolescent sleep habits has prompted some schools to consider later start times to give students an extra hour or so of sleep (see Chapter 13).
- Roll taking, announcements, and similarly disruptive activities are reduced to their absolute minimum. The time saved is reallocated to instructional priorities.
- Computerized scheduling is used to ensure that predefined time specifications for each course, program, service, or activity are incorporated into the master schedule. The best minds and available technology should be used to ensure that the schedule is of the highest quality and is creative.
- Students' schedules that reflect regular classes and other learning experiences (e.g., tutorials, exploratory classes, service-learning projects, and performing groups) should be generated by computer. The likelihood that students will be placed correctly within the master schedule is thereby ensured.
- Every decision about instructional or other program priorities related to the master schedule should be subordinated to achieving full implementation of standards-based education. Time must be visualized as a resource to be used in a number of ways (altered, refined, lengthened, shortened, banked, rotated, molded, or otherwise configured) in the pursuit of that goal.

(See also Appendix 9, "Designing the Master Schedule as a Mosaic," at the end of this chapter.)

# Providing Time

- **An examination of middle school master schedules frequently reveals a failure to consider major priorities that should serve as the basis for allocating time.** Consider your own middle school master schedule. What do you believe are the most basic criteria used in justifying its structure? Does it facilitate instructional activities known to work well with young adolescents? Does it clearly honor the professional role of teachers in a standards-based system by maximizing flexibility in making decisions, planning time, and evaluating student work? Does it minimize classroom interruptions? Are the rigorous academic goals of standards-based education facilitated? Develop a simple analysis of your responses to these and similar questions. Then suggest ways to improve your present master schedule. Invite several colleagues to join you in the activities and share your thinking as appropriate.

- **Is there a single program element you would like to see incorporated into your school's schedule?** Is it explained away as being "a good idea but we can't schedule it"? Does that program element occupy a significant priority in the minds of other staff members? Using a modified version of the mosaic strategy described in the appendix at the end of this chapter, explore ways of solving the scheduling problem and suggest the best options to your principal.

- **The United States Department of Education's Commission on Time and Learning estimates that in many schools students actually spend less than half their time in the classroom on academics.** Among reasons given for this situation are excessive interruptions from outside the class and too much time spent on activities, such as drill and practice routines, that contribute little to the mastery of academic content standards. Schedules should provide more time for rigorous assignments that engage students in tasks allowing them to demonstrate their academic proficiency. Evaluate your own teaching. Can you make better use of the instructional time allotted to you? You might be tempted to ask, "Who couldn't?" However, consider to what extent your instruction focuses systematically on the content standards. Be generous to yourself in terms of what you are doing right and doing well. But be equally candid in identifying (1) ways in which you might improve; and (2) things others might do to eliminate unwanted interruptions and intrusions into your teaching time. Share your thoughts with colleagues. Suggest to your principal a faculty seminar on the subject.

- **Analysts of school master schedules estimate that as much as one hour each day could be redefined for instructional purposes through the more creative use of time and the elimination of disruptive traditional routines.** Consider how you can create an extra instructional hour each day for each student by the most ingenious and workable ways you can devise. If you are the principal, challenge all teachers to do the same and reward the best ideas. Then plan ways to implement them.

- **This chapter identifies the master schedule as the single most important factor in communicating a school's philosophy.** Think through this assertion with a group of colleagues. Compare your educational commitments with schoolwide priorities reflected in the use of time. Are they congruent? Can there be a better match? How might it be achieved?

# Appendix 9

## Designing the Master Schedule as a Mosaic

Very few resources provide scheduling strategies and examples of finished products. One reason for this lack is that each school is based on a unique configuration of time, talent, and teaching. Someone has suggested that the most likely source of help in designing a school schedule is a good book on creating mosaics. That suggestion is not far off the mark because a good school schedule is much like a mosaic.

Select the most important pieces of your master schedule "mosaic."

Like a finished mosaic, a school schedule should reflect a logical process and an end product that is aesthetically pleasing rather than a random juxtaposition of pieces with no apparent definition. Unfortunately, many school schedules appear to be made randomly rather than being produced by an artful process.

The metaphor of the mosaic has proved to be helpful for principals and teachers in designing school schedules. The artist who designs a mosaic begins by identifying the pieces of material that are to be incorporated into the work and assigns them their relative prominence in the finished design. Likewise, those responsible for the school master schedule begin by identifying the program features they want to include and assigning them relative priorities. Time is defined in terms of equal intervals of instruction or in blocks of multiple intervals. Time for professional planning and

collaboration is identified as another piece. It is specified for advisory programs, service-learning, tutoring and mentoring, independent study, lunch, any unique instructional features, and every desired program.

All identified program features are seen as pieces of the completed schedule mosaic. Like the artist who refuses to leave any piece out of the mosaic for fear of compromising the completed work, the designers of the school schedule strive to include every significant program variable.

This is the moment for specifying and defending every proposed feature of the school program. All features are then represented by individual squares of cardboard with different colors to represent each one. The pieces are moved about on a tabletop or attached to a vertical surface with Velcro.™ Principal and staff collaborate in arranging program elements in various designs as consensus builds as to the most attractive and inclusive schedule. An instant camera is available for keeping track of potential designs while others are being examined.

The scheduling process takes time. It involves commitment and collaboration. The task cannot be rushed any more than an artist rushes a finished work of art and is not complete until the majority of those affected are able to step back and say, "Aha!"

The task is not complete until the majority of those affected are able to say "Aha!"

*"Unless you try to do something beyond what you have already mastered, you will never grow."*

—Ronald E. Osborn

# Academic Literacy: Key to Equal Access and High Standards of Achievement

California's diverse student population comes from many different ethnic groups, speaks a variety of languages and dialects, varies in English proficiency, and comes to school with a variety of experiences, academic and nonacademic. The state Language Census for 1999-2000 revealed that 2.27 million students enrolled in California public schools use a primary language other than English and 1.48 million are identified as English learners (limited-English proficient). English learners represent 24.9 percent of the total California school enrollment and speak more than 56 languages, as reported by their school districts in 1999-2000. The languages most commonly spoken by English learners are Spanish (82.6%), Vietnamese (2.7%), Hmong (1.9%), Cantonese (1.7%), and Pilipino (1.2%).

By no means do these students enter California schools only at the primary grades. Significant numbers of English learners are enrolled in the middle grades, and schools need to accommodate their needs. Large numbers of

Recommendations 1, 2, 5, 12

middle grades students, including native speakers of English, lack what is termed *cognitive academic language proficiency.* Although they may be proficient in the basic language skills used in everyday social interaction, they frequently lack the specialized subject-matter vocabulary unique to each area of the curriculum and the generalized academic language functions, structures, and vocabulary needed to master standards at the middle grades.

Academic language is defined in the *Reading/Language Arts Framework* as "the language of literacy and books, tests, and formal writing." It differs from conversational speech in terms of "language function, vocabulary, background knowledge, text structure, syntactic complexity, and abstract thinking."[1] Another way to think of the academic language is to recognize that it represents a much higher level of literacy, a level basic to the full development of complex thinking skills. This chapter addresses some of English learners' needs; elements of the chapter may be useful in considering ways for native speakers of English to develop academic-language proficiency as well.

## Instructional Programs for English Learners

Two groups of English learners at the middle school level must be considered in program planning: students who have limited prior academic experience or literacy in their primary language and those who are literate in their primary language. "Students who enter school . . . with little prior schooling and limited English must be quickly identified and assessed to determine their level of reading and writing skills in their primary language and in English." Students needing *English-language development* "require intensive, systematic instruction in oral and written language, . . . individualized instruction, and additional assistance. . . . From the earliest stages of their academic careers and in concert with instruction in reading and writing, English learners participate in an instructional program that supports their acquisition of informal English and teaches them the patterns of formal academic English. The instruction is designed to provide for students' experiences with English that are understandable and meaningful and enable the students to communicate with peers and adults and thereby participate fully in the academic program."[2]

English learners entering middle school with strong literacy skills in their primary language have the advantage of being able to concentrate on acquiring and learning English rather than having to receive initial instruction in reading and writing. English-language development instruction is necessary for all English learners, from the beginning level of English proficiency to the advanced. Particularly in the middle grades, where many English learners languish at the intermediate level of English-language proficiency without making notable progress from one year to the next, it is critical to move students to more advanced levels of language proficiency so that they can fully participate in the core curriculum and master content standards. *Specially designed academic instruction in English* (SDAIE) originated to help second-language learners who have basic literacy in their primary language and rudimentary proficiency in English learn grade-level content in the core curriculum while being instructed in English-language development. Other strategies designed to enhance academic literacy are described further in this chapter and are helpful to both native and nonnative speakers of English.

## Providing English-Language Development Instruction

English-language development (ELD) requires purposeful, daily instruction during specific times in accord with students' proficiency levels. Although there are many opportunities in a language-rich classroom environment for language learning, merely being exposed to, even engaged in, activity in English is not sufficient to ensure the development of full academic language proficiency. Approaches to teaching ELD have undergone rethinking in recent years. The state English-language development standards emphasize the connection of ELD and literacy and encourage reading and writing instruction early in learning English. Various authors have argued for renewed emphasis on direct teaching of new language concepts, greater attention to the features of English language, increased practice of complex language skills, and appropriate corrective feedback within the context of meaningful and rich language learning and interaction.[3] The California Reading and Literature Project, in its Professional Development Institute for Teachers of English Learners, proposes that English-language development include:

- Forms—grammatical structures and word usage
- Fluency—ease of comprehension (listening and reading) and production (speaking and writing)
- Functions—purposes and uses of language (e.g., make statements, joke, inquire, compare) in formal and informal settings
- Vocabulary development

Of special importance to middle schools is the idea that English-language development instruction should continue for students at the intermediate levels of language proficiency and beyond. Whether in specialized ELD courses or through the English–language arts program at the school, students' academic language must be continuously developed and explicitly taught as its own area of study and within all subject areas. Higher-level ELD students need explicit instruction and practice using advanced phonology, morphology, syntax, semantics, and pragmatics.[4] Gersten and Baker observe that SDAIE or sheltered content instruction often emphasizes content acquisition over the building of English–language abilities, leading to sacrifices in learning English.[5]

In particular, English-language development instruction should target the student's level of proficiency (beginning, early intermediate, intermediate, early advanced, or advanced) and include many opportunities for student-to-student practice at that proficiency level as well as systematic teaching of language skills at the next level of proficiency. When students "use, but confuse" language elements, the teacher should model the academic language and provide practice. The targeted skills should be taught at the level of what students can already do (understand, say, read, write) "plus one." In other words students will need many opportunities for scaffolded use of a word, phrase, verb tense, or sentence structure before they are able to produce or understand it independently, orally or in writing. To develop high levels of language proficiency, the teacher must provide comprehensible instruction, clear modeling, many opportunities for practice, accurate and timely feedback, and reasons to apply new language skills in new ways. Particularly in settings with few native English-speaking models, teachers need to create many opportunities for English learners to hear and use academic language for the purpose of building the linguistic competencies required to achieve grade-level content standards.

## Providing Specially Designed Academic Instruction in English

The broad repertoire of instructional skills offered through SDAIE has become increasingly popular in classes for students at all levels of English-language ability, including native speakers of English. For this phenomenon to be understood, it must be viewed as more than an attempt to meet the needs of English learners who no longer receive extended periods of instruction in English-language development or sheltered English. Extensive classroom observation reveals that not only second-language learners but also large numbers of native speakers of English lack proficiency in academic language. In a time of standards-based education, therefore, many students will struggle to achieve even the most minimally acceptable levels of proficiency.

The challenges posed by a lack of proficiency in academic language (academic literacy) are especially acute in the middle grades. The level of academic success achieved in grades six, seven, and eight is pivotal in determining the extent to which students will be prepared to pursue progressively more demanding curricula in high school. Development of proficiency in academic language is closely linked to a commitment to provide equal access to the most valued curriculum for all students. Aptly characterized as an effective educational practice, SDAIE allows teachers to present rigorous academic content to all students by scaffolding for linguistic complexity based on the teachers' knowledge of the students' levels of proficiency.

A significant component of English-language development and SDAIE is *scaffolding*, which the *Reading/Language Arts Framework* defines as the "temporary support, guidance, or assistance provided to a student on a new or complex task."[6] Scaffolding involves the teacher in modeling and demonstrating skills and providing supports at strategic points in the lesson to help students assimilate new ideas and strategies. "Scaffolding . . . does not involve simplifying the task; it holds the task difficulty constant, while simplifying the child's role by means of graduated assistance from the adult expert."[7] In pursuit of that goal, students often work collaboratively in small groups, a strategy especially powerful in heterogeneous classes.

Collaborative learning in small groups allows students to practice and apply content taught by the teacher and encourages students with conflicting viewpoints to attempt to clarify, analyze, synthesize, speculate on, and evaluate their views as they work their way toward solutions to problems or carry out other tasks. This process (1) promotes refinement of meaning based on the diversity of the group; and (2) encourages the members to reflect on their own understanding of the curriculum content. Teachers assist students in making connections between ideas presented in class and their prior knowledge—in effect, to move gradually from street-level literacy to academic literacy.

An emotionally safe learning environment is essential for most students to learn successfully. An anxiety-free classroom is necessary for the kind of risk taking required to expand language development and promote other kinds of cognitive growth. An appropriate learning environment is fostered by having students collaborate in small groups and encouraging them to use expressive oral language in presenting their thoughts, feelings, and opinions about the material being studied. By deepening their understanding and mastery of ideas and concepts, they increase their academic literacy.

Similarly, complex reading and expressive writing provide opportunities for students to use their new academic-language skills. This process is as effective for native speakers of English as it is for those still acquiring English. Students are encouraged to connect new ideas, concepts, and vocabulary through, for example, reflective logs, quick writes, and essays. In mathematics and science students are encouraged to provide written explanations of solutions and processes used in problem solving, investigations, or research projects.

Health, physical education, and history–social science also provide many opportunities for writing assignments that involve interpretation of important activities, issues, or events in the context of real-life experiences. Literature and the visual and performing arts equally provide opportunities for students to use expressive writing as they (1) explore their individual responses to historically or culturally significant works; (2) explain the intent of the authors or artists; or (3) analyze and clarify their ideas and connect them to other works. (See also Appendix 10-A, "Developing Academic Literacy for *All* Students: SDAIE and Other Strategies," at the end of this chapter.)

All teachers of English learners are reading and language development teachers, regardless of their content area. In planning effective instruction, content-area teachers should consider:

- Content-specific vocabulary required for conceptual understanding
- Language complexities, including language forms
- Demands of the text structure of textbooks and other readings, including chapter and section headings, charts, graphs, and maps
- Reading strategies required for comprehension of that type of text
- Ways of both accessing and building student background knowledge of the content
- Cognitive processes students must employ to meet content demands
- Ways in which to engage students' interactions to further both linguistic and conceptual goals of the lesson

Effective SDAIE includes consideration of these areas. Simply accessing prior knowledge and ensuring student motivation and interaction—while critical—are not enough to ensure student learning. As teachers plan instruction, they must thoughtfully consider language, content, and the cognitive process involved in the learning task.[8]

## Developing Academic Literacy Through Scaffolding

The use of scaffolding may range from learning basic knowledge and skills to understanding complex principles and higher-order thought processes. Scaffolding requires that teachers observe their students and gradually hand over responsibility to them. Among the most important elements of scaffolding are the tools listed below.[9] They represent functional approaches to instruction, emphasizing the movement of students from dependence to automaticity and independence and the development of academic-language proficiency through expressive oral and written communications.

- *Modeling and demonstrating.* The teacher directly models and demonstrates, showing students *how,* by walking them through the steps of an activity, process, or skill until they understand how to proceed and can demonstrate their ability to do so. The number of times a teacher needs to model and demonstrate desired learning will vary according to the needs of individual students.
- *Bridging.* The teacher uses the personal experiences of students, including prior knowledge or skills, to provide a bridge

from the known to the unknown concepts. Teachers help students make a personal connection with the content, leading to the internalization of new learning.

- *Contextualizing.* The teacher helps clarify and bring to life abstract concepts by using pictures, manipulatives, or other objects and by creating analogies or metaphors based on the students' own experiences.

- *Schema building.* The teacher helps students establish the connections that exist between and across concepts that may otherwise appear unrelated. This strategy helps students gain perspective about where ideas fit in the larger scheme of things. For example, diagrammatic outlines and other graphic organizers are used to compare concepts and show interrelationships.

- *Metacognitive development.* The teacher involves students in using strategies to monitor their own learning. In metacognition, the process of thinking about thinking, students are helped to understand how they learn and how they know. The teacher consciously focuses students' attention on strategies for accomplishing academic tasks and helps students internalize them for later use.

- *Text re-presentation or alternate presentations.* The teacher helps students extend their understanding and apply them in novel formats. Students use different modes to present material being learned, including oral, written, or graphic formats, to ensure that they understand the material.

For most middle grades and high school students, the lack of academic literacy may be the result of prior schooling. And for students who entered the United States recently, the lack may be attributed to insufficient time to learn new vocabulary and use it in assignments that call for using higher-order thinking skills and learning complex concepts.

## Developing Academic Literacy in the Middle Grades

Every middle grades teacher should become proficient in teaching reading and writing so that the students can develop basic skills in literacy. Learning strategies designed to develop academic literacy should include ensuring that students understand the significance of grade-level content and performance standards in each subject area. They should also be provided with the scoring criteria by which their performance levels will be determined. Emphasis is placed as follows:

- Standards are reviewed with students and explained prior to the start of each unit or other curricular increment. Content standards and performance standards are written at a basic adult reading level. Most middle grades students who are reading at grade level should not have difficulty reading the California content standards. For English learners and other students with reading difficulties, teachers may want to simplify the language without losing the significance of complex concepts.

- Students are helped to understand the difference between fluency in social language and proficiency in academic language. Teachers explicitly teach academic-language functions and structures and design opportunities for students to practice and apply them. In academic language the meaning must be derived from written material standing on its own. Prior association with ideas, events, or surroundings in the lives of students that help them derive meaning is limited. The ability to derive meaning from written or spoken communication lacking familiar interpretive cues lies at the heart of academic literacy.

- Vocabulary building emphasizes new terminology associated with the study of core subjects. The selection of words, phrases, or concepts is determined on the basis of language essential to deep learning of content standards. Those choices are based on language ordinarily used by professionals for a given subject. Vocabulary lists are developed collaboratively by teachers and supplemented by students.
- Students frequently participate in small study groups in which assignments are tailored to the subject and content standards being addressed in the curriculum. Small-group assignments include problem-solving or issue-oriented tasks requiring students to use new academic vocabulary and concepts.

## Developing Academic Literacy Through Complex Reading

The next set of examples suggests strategies designed to practice and apply academic-language proficiency through complex reading experiences:

- *Oral reading* with advanced vocabulary is practiced frequently in small, heterogeneous study groups. Essays, stories, articles, or other reading materials are selected collaboratively for their relevance

to the subject and content standards. Students take turns reading aloud to improve listening skills, build academic-language proficiency, and ensure comprehension of complex ideas. Although reading aloud is typically used to promote the study of literature, it can also contribute to an understanding of complex concepts in all curriculum areas.

- *Reading aloud* with advanced vocabulary is a variation of oral reading in which students follow the text while their teacher or a guest reads portions aloud, emphasizing fluency, expression, and clarification of complex ideas. The underlying emphasis is placed on comprehension and the use of academic language. (See Appendix 10-B, "Reading Aloud to Students of All Ages," at the end of this chapter.)
- *Team reading* involves pairing a more able reader with a less able reader. The subject matter is linked to the curriculum. Through this approach the weaker reading skills of the less able reader are not exposed to the class, and the other team member knows that he or she is serving in a helping role. Sometimes, more able readers are recruited from the higher grades. In this approach the less able reader, feeling emotionally secure, is able to concentrate on improving his or her academic literacy. The more able reader, given extra credit, is trained to be an effective helper.
- *Tutorial reading* involves a teacher, a trained aide, or a tutor leading a small group of students (or sometimes an individual student). Under the leader's direction they read, talk, think, and question their way through a book or other material

related to the curriculum. Each participant should have a copy of the material being read. The leader helps the students ask questions about the reading selection and questions they might pose to the author. Advanced vocabulary is emphasized. The students are helped to find meaning in their reading as they explore concepts and use complex thinking skills.

- *Classroom community reading,* a variation of the previous strategy, involves having the entire class read and discuss the same book or other reading material, preferably one related to the curriculum. The teacher guides the discussion, emphasizing new vocabulary, themes, and complex ideas and generally focusing on academic-language proficiency. When done in moderation, whole-class reading, as opposed to reading in small groups, is an excellent way for teachers to know students better, observe their attitudes toward reading, examine how they read, and build a classroom-based reading community.

- *Independent reading of advanced material* engages students, with their teacher's approval, in reading materials selected by the students. Self-paced, independent reading involves periodic individual conferences with the teacher, a trained aide, or a tutor. The students may meet in small groups to discuss their independent reading selections. The primary focus is placed on building confidence in reading and developing complex reasoning skills. The students continue to build academic-language proficiency, using advanced vocabulary and growing in their ability to manage complex ideas.

## Developing Academic Literacy Through Complex Writing

The next set of examples suggests strategies designed to practice and apply academic-language proficiency through complex writing experiences:

- *Writing of topical drafts* preferably takes place in small groups. Topics are selected from the curriculum and linked to content standards. Emphasis is placed on writing short, focused drafts that involve new vocabulary and concepts. The process often begins with a brainstorming session about the topic to involve the students in the subject. The students share their writing and help one another clarify ideas. The teacher helps the students understand that writing good drafts is an essential part of academic literacy.

- *Special-interest writing* occurs when students write about a particular interest related to their present learning. Or they may choose through independent study to become the class "expert." Students who feel at ease about the subject matter often write more naturally and creatively than they would otherwise. They are asked to read the completed work of other students or read aloud to one another. They enjoy learning about the "expertness" of their peers.

- *Writing with a scribe* involves a student working with a teacher, a trained aide, or a tutor to compose a written assignment. This approach is suitable for students experiencing unusual difficulties in writing or being unable to write or use a computer keyboard because of a physical disability. The teacher, aide, or tutor acts as the scribe. The content results from a process in which meanings, choice of words, and topics are decided jointly. Students see that their ideas can be translated into meaningful written content and that clear thought leads to clear writing with good structure and logical expression.

- *Quick writing* encourages fluency of thought and self-confidence. It provides short, timed writing assignments requiring students to write about a subject related to their studies as quickly as possible and without editing. They are also told to use new vocabulary and are reminded that the task is intended to show proficiency in academic language.

  Quick writing can be used to free up students' knowledge and understanding of a particular subject or issue because it avoids constricting the students' thoughts to the limits of their ability to write correctly. Quick writing is especially useful in working with second-language students or native speakers of English whose writing skills are limited because of learning deficits.

- *Essay writing* illustrates a student's ability to take a point of view and, through a series of logical arguments based on factual information, lead the reader to a reasoned conclusion. Essays are to be measured not by their length but by the depth of their content. They are especially attractive to teachers because they can provide substantial insight into the levels of academic literacy achieved by the students. Although essay writing is appropriate for any content area, it should relate to the content standards for the class.

- *Process writing* describes problem-solving strategies, experimental procedures, and summaries from which a narrative outline of activities is produced. Because process writing is usually subject specific, it provides strong evidence of students' ability to use specialized vocabulary correctly and effectively, thereby demonstrating their levels of proficiency in written academic language.

- *Academic journaling* provides an ongoing record of learning by individual students, differing greatly from an ordinary diary. Rather than providing a free flow of ideas and emotions related to personal issues, academic journaling involves focused writing in which students reflect on their assignments. Examples of appropriate subjects for academic journaling are observations, new knowledge, and skills.

  Unlike the situation with diaries, students understand that their journals will be subject to teacher review because their content provides a valid means of assessing important aspects of individual progress. Included is the ability to demonstrate academic-language proficiency through use of subject-specific vocabulary, conceptualize complex ideas, and engage in effective written communication of information. When teachers are sensitive to and respectful of their students' efforts to do journaling, they often observe dramatic success. The process then becomes an integral part of the curriculum. (See also Appendix 10-C, "When Students Write Home," at the end of this chapter.)

# Academic Literacy

- **This chapter calls for the development of a more advanced level of literacy, *academic literacy,* so that students may achieve deep learning of the more complex knowledge and skills embedded in and defined by grade-level content standards.** Consider specific examples of the standards that you teach. To what extent do they already reflect an emphasis on academic literacy? Can they be improved? Do they need to be simplified or more clearly explained to English-language learners? Are they clear to struggling readers?

- **English-language development (ELD) is presented as an essential program component for all English learners, even those at higher levels of English proficiency.** Do all the English learners in your classes have access to a full program of English-language development? Is ELD included in English–language arts courses for students at the intermediate level of proficiency or higher? What strategies for ELD instruction are employed? What is the specific content of ELD instruction?

- **SDAIE strategies are presented as appropriate for all students, not just second-language learners, as they strive to develop both basic and advanced literacy levels.** Do you find that a significant number of your native speakers of English have difficulty with subject-specific vocabulary and the concepts that the vocabulary is intended to convey? If so, to what extent are you using the suggested SDAIE strategies? Prepare a checklist, using the discussion provided. Are there suggestions not yet part of your repertoire of instructional strategies that you would like to attempt? If so, try them out and keep a journal of the results. Share the process with potentially interested colleagues. Invite them to take part with you.

- **For teachers of subjects other than English–language arts: Do you regularly incorporate grade-level reading and writing skills development with your daily instruction?** If your answer is yes, what kinds of experiences have worked best for you in your efforts to help your students achieve a higher level of literacy? Are your expectations based on the grade-level English–language arts content standards? Consider the recommendations related to reading and writing activities described in the text. Which have the most relevance for your own teaching situation? Find ways to mix and match your choices and, if you are not already doing so, integrate them into your teaching on a regular basis. Let your principal know what you are doing and provide her or him with a periodic progress report.

- **Proficiency in academic language is linked to equal access to the most valued curriculum.** Yet even basic literacy skills, much less academic-language proficiency, still present a difficult challenge in many schools. How can your school more aggressively ensure that basic reading and writing skills are consistently taught by every

## Academic Literacy (Continued)

teacher? What would it take to move beyond this level to the development of academic literacy skills? Included are the ability of students to (1) use effectively the formal language of each discipline; and (2) engage in assignments calling for complex reasoning based on their ability to read and interpret challenging material from grade-level texts and other sources. Ask your principal to convene interested members of your staff to pursue these issues.

- **Does your school have a literacy council (a committee of staff members dedicated to the goal of achieving a significant level of academic literacy for all students)?** If not, encourage its creation. Focus on the development of schoolwide efforts to develop a comprehensive literacy program that incorporates multiple strategies and involves every staff member at the most critical point—daily classroom instruction.

# Appendix 10-A

# Developing Academic Literacy for *All* Students: SDAIE and Other Strategies

SDAIE, specially designed academic instruction in English, originated from earlier efforts to help second-language learners develop their English-language skills while they address grade-level content in the core curriculum. But extensive classroom observation has revealed that not only second-language learners often lack academic-language proficiency. Large numbers of native speakers of English frequently experience the same problem.

In implementing strategies to build academic literacy, teachers should:

- Begin by rewriting content standards in simple yet precise terms and posting them prominently in your classroom.
- Provide examples of excellent student work. Let the students see clearly the level of academic proficiency they should be striving to achieve.
- Speak slowly but naturally. Avoid condescending behavior.
- Enunciate clearly. Let the students hear correct English spoken well. Demonstrate respect for primary languages other than English.
- Use controlled vocabulary. Be deliberate about introducing new words and concepts specific to the subject being learned.
- Avoid the extensive use of idioms. Check for meaning and explain the origin of the idioms.
- Use nonverbal language, including gestures, facial expressions, and dramatization, to make a point.
- Use manipulatives and props as you introduce new material. Employ as many of the students' senses as possible.

- Use illustrations, comparisons, and examples from daily experiences to clarify key points until the students progress to the point where they can derive meaning from abstract ideas on the printed page.
- Check frequently for understanding. Ask the students to rephrase key definitions and ideas.
- Provide an emotionally secure learning environment where it is safe to make mistakes as long as they are used as a basis for learning how to correct errors.
- Record material on tape for later review by the students.
- Rewrite key concepts from texts and other materials in simpler language to communicate difficult ideas without losing the integrity of the meaning.
- Engage the students in cooperative learning experiences. Ensure that every student in a cooperative learning group is responsible for learning new concepts and skills.
- Use peer, cross-age, and adult tutoring whenever possible. Recruit support actively.
- Use active learning strategies designed to reinforce students' conceptual learning (e.g., experiments and projects).
- Ask the students regularly to refine and polish all important assignments until they represent the students' best effort.
- Grade the students on their level of proficiency in response to performance standards rather than on a class curve.
- Reinforce key concepts frequently. Watch for opportunities to do so naturally.

- Wait a sufficient amount of time for the students to think and to respond to questions. Keep from succumbing to the temptation to answer your own questions.
- Engage the students in complex reasoning experiences. Teach the students the scientific method. Involve them regularly in using it.

- Ask the students to verbalize in speech or in writing when they are ready. Help them find alternative ways to express difficult ideas, such as using visual representations.
- Summarize and review frequently. Involve the students in the process.

# Appendix 10-B

# Reading Aloud to Students of All Ages

*"Books are like ships, and libraries and classrooms are the ports from which readers may sail on voyages of high adventure."*

—Anonymous

Experience shows that people of all ages enjoy having someone read aloud to them. From early childhood and on through life until one is too old to hold the book or see the print (and even then), being read to is a pleasurable experience and should happen much more frequently for students regardless of age or grade level. Use of school time for that purpose, no matter what the regular subject matter may be at the moment, is time well spent in building fundamental and advanced literacy skills.

A few of the reasons we read aloud to students are helpful to consider. We read aloud to help them experience the joys of reading and to develop the art of listening. We read aloud to model clear diction and the art of inflection in making content come alive. Perhaps most of all we read aloud to expose students to a rich array of adventures of the mind and to awaken them to a more active reading life of their own.

These and other similar justifications fit directly with the efforts of educators to help all students achieve basic and advanced levels of literacy, including the *academic literacy* emphasized in this chapter.

*Students benefit from being read to because they:*

✔ Extend their knowledge of human relation-ships and important events across the centuries to the present even as they antici-pate the future.

✔ Deepen their understanding of the essential differences between written and spoken language.

✔ Develop new vocabulary and conceptual understanding of the world in general and of specialized areas of human experience in particular.

✔ Experience the interaction of their own minds with the minds of authors past and present. The popularity of dead poet societies illustrates the attractiveness of this kind of intellectual experience for many students.

✔ Learn about new writers and new ideas consistent with their age and interests— intellectually stimulating experiences for all students.

✔ Become familiar with different genres and forms of writing. They learn that there is more to the life than textbooks and comic books.

✔ Enjoy content understood aurally even when they cannot comfortably read by themselves. Students are challenged to pursue their own reading and comprehen-sion levels, the essence of literacy.

✔ Have the door opened to a world of previously unknown source material to complement formal academic study or provide pleasure.

*Students have positive read-aloud experiences when:*

✔ Books or other reading materials are carefully selected for their interest, appro-priateness, style, and capacity to hold the attention of listeners. Suspense is always a winner and can be found in works that represent either fact or fiction.

✔ Reading is fluent, paced, and inflected appropriately. Teachers do not have to have golden throats to be effective oral readers. Reviewing the material in advance, practicing challenging passages, and checking on vocabulary that may be unfamiliar are just a few of the things that can be done to be more effective.

✔ Passages of appropriate length are selected that are long enough to capture the imaginations and short enough to fit the students' attention spans and the class time available. It is better to stop reading at a suspenseful point than to risk listener fatigue.

✔ Reading done in a series of episodes should always be prefaced by a short review of the previous material. Engage students in this process. Ask leading questions (e.g., "What was the most important point so far?" "What is the author or specific character trying to say?").

✔ Interruptions at key points are allowed to enable students to imagine outcomes, interpret or clarify events, check word meaning, or otherwise interact with the reader and the author.

✔ Reading occurs in a relaxed environment, which will differ for varying age groups. Having the students sit quietly with their eyes closed works for children of nearly all ages. However, there is no magic formula. The teacher's judgment should always prevail.

✔ Reading aloud is viewed as something to be anticipated, even a reward, yet always in the context of a substantive learning experience. When reading aloud can be tied directly to the subject matter being studied, so much the better.

✔ Reasons for reading aloud are clearly communicated to the students. The students themselves, depending upon their age and maturity, should be encouraged to develop their own reasons. The depth of their insight may be surprising, ranging from simple enjoyment to the more subtle yet powerful contributions the process makes to developing basic and advanced literacy skills.

✔ Time is provided to reflect on what has been read, identify key insights and new knowledge, or otherwise draw major lessons from each experience, depending on the nature of the subject matter.

Being read to and reading aloud to others represent lifelong sources of enjoyment, shared experiences, new knowledge, and the ever-present thrill of setting sail on voyages of the mind. Never apologize for reading aloud to your students, no matter their age or sophistication, out of fear that others will not understand.

# Appendix 10-C

# When Students Write Home

## by Madeline Brick

*Consider adopting this strategy to improve standards-based reports to parents about each student's academic proficiency.*

To help bridge the gap between home and school, I decided to try a new approach with my seventh-grade heterogeneously grouped English classes. Instead of the regular midterm progress reports (a cursory checklist of test grades, behavior, and homework completion), I wanted to encourage my students to assume more responsibility for their learning.

I asked my seventh graders to write letters to their parents about their progress in English class. Many of my students had never written to their parents. The prospect was exciting to them but somewhat formidable. I assured them that I would help.

### Writing the Letters

To begin, I asked them to think about the work they were doing. Together, we reviewed the daily and weekly progress reports that I asked them to keep: grades, books read, homework completed, my comments on papers

handed back, peer feedback, and so on. We discussed possible ideas to include in their letters: journal entry responses, writing read aloud in class by the teacher, projects displayed on the Writing of the Week and Writing in Progress board, short stories, poems, their thoughts on process writing, whether their grades accurately reflected their work, and specific ways to improve with help from home.

We also created sample letters to illustrate how to write about negatives in a positive way and how to accentuate their strengths. Students drafted, edited, and revised letters before showing me the second (sometimes third or fourth) draft for my review. . . . I was very impressed with the letters, and we addressed the envelopes. My students had suggested that mailing the letters from school would ensure the authenticity of the effort. Here are two excerpts from my students' letters:

Dear Mom,
I am not doing so well because I have missed a lot of assignments. I am trying hard to catch up on all my work. . . .
I have read "The Stepsister," and now I am reading "Problem with Love."
Mrs. Brick wrote on my journal that I am thinking more about my writing. . . .

Love, Grethel

Dear Mom,
I haven't been very honest with you. Whenever you asked if I had homework, I would say no, even though I did. I would end up never doing it. That is why I am missing nine out of 21 assignments. I haven't really given it all my effort, and my attitude has been very poor in English class. I am very sorry for that, and I will try a lot harder. Of course you already know all of this, but I wanted to tell you myself! . . .
Love, Justin

From *Educational Leadership,* Vol. 50 (April 1993). Reprinted with permission from the Association for Supervision and Curriculum Development.

## Responses from Parents

The students were excited when the letters started arriving. And parents did write back—94 percent! Mothers and fathers wrote lovely, caring, proud, moving, and sometimes apologetic letters. Some wrote of their childhoods. Others wrote of their dreams. One wrote of her secret ambition to be a mystery writer. A few parents wrote in their native language. One mother spoke her response in Spanish into a tape recorder that I had provided. Although my primary concern was that students communicate their progress with parents, almost all of them wanted to share the letters from home with me. Here are some excerpts:

> Dear Kelly,
> In the future, I would be happy to spend more time helping you with assignments. All you need to do is ask. I have plenty of confidence in you. . . .
> Love, Mom

> Dear Justin,
> Your mother and I are proud to see how well you can write. Your letter was really well done. We're also pleased to see that you're determined to work more diligently on the requirements of your studies, especially in English. . . . Please count on us to support your worthy efforts. . . .
> Love, Dad

> Dear Joanna,
> Dad and I continue to be very pleased with your work habits. Sometimes we know you would rather watch television, but you seldom give in to temptation. We know that working to the best of your ability is important, and we are proud for your efforts. . . .
> Love, Mom and Dad

What did the students think of their parents' responses? Here are some of their comments:

> "I finally could be honest with my mom in a letter. I wasn't telling her the truth before."

> "It's weird writing to my parents and having them write back."

> "I never knew this about my mom."

> "I never expected my dad to write."

> "My mom said she wrote four drafts back to me. She needed to make it sound right."

## Partners in Learning

Much more than the routine progress reports, the letters prompted my students to think about themselves as learners and to involve their parents in that thinking. Parents reciprocated by offering to help with their children's studies. For many of my students, an important bridge was crossed as they learned to assume responsibility for their learning. As one student wrote in a letter to her mother and father:

> I am sorry that I am not doing as well this term as I hoped to. . . . I will try to bring up all my grades to A's. I might need some help from you, but I will do it.

11

*"When you starts measuring somebody, measure him right, child, measure him right. Make sure you done taken into account what hills and valleys he come through before he got to wherever he is."*

—Mama, in *A Raisin in the Sun,* a play by Lorraine Hansberry

# Social Promotion and Grade Retention: Issues and Challenges

Nowhere else among the 50 states does there exist a greater challenge than in California to analyze the root causes of student failure and identify those with a reasonable chance of being successfully addressed by educators, working with legislators, parents, and others. California's educational and political leaders have joined a national chorus of reformers calling for demanding subject-matter content and performance standards accompanied by increased levels of student performance and professional accountability. The seriousness of the agenda continues to be accentuated by changes in policy at the federal, state, and local levels. This chapter focuses on the related issues of social promotion and grade retention. Further, it examines ways to increase significantly the number of students able to demonstrate acceptable proficiency according to grade-level standards.

 Recommendations 7, 8, 11, 12

Responding to the demands for action, the California Legislature enacted Assembly Bill 1626, which was approved by the Governor in 1998. The bill is described in the official legislation summary as follows:

> [AB 1626] requires all school districts to adopt promotion and retention policies that require students to demonstrate basic proficiency in certain subjects and certain grades before they progress to the next grade. Stipulates that pupils shall be retained unless retention is "not the appropriate intervention" or if the pupil participates in summer school or interim session remediation programs. Requires parental notification and consultation with the teacher and principal before any final determination regarding retention can be made.

## Grade Retention and Social Promotion

*Grade retention,* the practice of having low-performing students repeat a grade, is not a new phenomenon. Data from the 1988 *National Educational Longitudinal Survey* show that 20 percent of all eighth graders had repeated at least one grade. The proportion climbed to 33 percent for eighth graders from low-income and minority families. More recent data from the *National Longitudinal Study of Adolescent Health* show that 22 percent of all adolescents had been retained in grade.

*Social promotion* is the practice of advancing students from one grade to the next without sufficient evidence that they have adequately learned the course content. Although social promotion is often spoken of disparagingly by parents, politicians, and the general public, educators often defend the practice as an unfortunate but necessary way of responding to almost insurmountable obstacles to teaching every child successfully.

This research on grade retention reveals that higher achievement and renewed commitment to educational values are not among the outcomes of the practice. Students who repeat a grade typically do worse academically than those in carefully matched control groups who are promoted. In districts with a high percentage of students retained in the elementary grades, many students reach middle school already overage for their grade. If they experience retention again during the middle grades, they begin to disengage from schooling altogether.

Far from stimulating students to perform at standard, being over-age for one's grade level during early adolescence erodes students' belief in their ability to be successful. The effects on African-American students are especially severe. Over-age students in the middle grades also often end up in the lowest-

ability groupings—the antithesis of the reason for their retention. Often, the most vulnerable students experience the most diluted curriculum and the most diminished opportunities to learn.

Wheelock summarizes the dilemma of grade retention for middle grades students as follows:

> In districts and schools that couple grade retention with high-stakes standardized testing in the name of standards, many students, especially the most vulnerable, lose more than they gain from so-called standards-based reforms. For retained [students]—bored with their schooling and overage for their grade, sometimes by two years by the time they leave the eighth grade—the threat of withholding a diploma rarely stimulates them to engage in school. Many of these students ultimately develop the belief that "school is not for me" and drop out; and many under pressure of high-stakes testing drop out earlier in their school careers. Indeed, being overage for grade is a better predictor of dropping out than below-average test scores.
>
> Current grade retention policies may seem to be the logical outgrowth of the demand for higher standards. However, the fallout from such policies does not bode well for schools or students. In particular, with grade promotion determined by test scores, such policies deflect attention from the greater need to build schools' capacity to reform teaching and learning so that students receive the support they need to produce work that meets genuinely high standards of quality.[1]

## AB 1626—Ensuring That All Students Get the Supports They Need

When the California Legislature enacted Assembly Bill 1626, its intention was to ensure that all students get the support and the interventions they need for success in the state's new results-driven educational system. The legislators used their ban on "social promotion" as a means of communicating to students, teachers, administrators, school boards, and the general public the depth of their concern for students whose needs had been ignored for too long.

The legislation is aimed at school districts, requiring them to identify as early as possible students who may be at risk and to provide effective interventions so that no student will be left behind. In that way the negative effects of grade retention that the research literature has identified for students will be avoided altogether. An effective early intervention system that enables all students to meet standards on time stops both the deleterious consequences of promoting students who do not have the skills they will need for future success and the stigmatization that occurs when a student must be retained.

## Instruction for Students with Learning Deficits

Implementing rigorous standards helps all students, including those with learning deficits, advance successfully toward expected achievement goals because those expectations are clearly defined. (For the purpose of this discussion, the term *learning deficits* refers to students who are performing below a basic level and who may be several grade levels behind in relation to the standards.) Some basic suggestions for teachers are offered as follows:

- Lower standards should not be set for students with learning deficits. Every student is entitled to aspire to the highest curriculum a school offers. Establishing high expectations creates a self-fulfilling prophecy for students and their teachers.
- Students must be engaged where they are, not where their teachers wish them to be, but the target is always "forward focused." Learning deficits accumulated over many years will take time to overcome. However, under optimum conditions remarkable progress can be made in overcoming the learning deficits of many or even of most students in a fraction of the time already spent in school. A middle grades student receiving appropriate specialized instruction can, in one school year, be helped significantly to overcome several prior years of dysfunctional learning.
- Teachers should not be held responsible for everything that has happened in their students' lives. But they must be held responsible for the standards-based learning experiences they provide during the time the students are under their supervision. Although teachers may be able to influence only a few of the many events and experiences that affect their students, those few can be potentially powerful. Firm, fair, consistent, and caring classroom interaction, together with a sense of humor, can help set the stage for successful learning experiences.

- One of the most basic tasks for teachers of all students, including those with learning deficits, is to find reliable ways to pre-assess what the students can and cannot do in relationship to grade-level standards. This assessment provides critical data for planning instruction. Standardized tests can be used to assess literacy and computational skills, and performance assessments are invaluable in determining how well students can use higher-order cognitive skills, particularly those related to logical and analytical thinking used in the classroom. Teachers often discover that many students with learning deficits do very well in thinking things through logically and solving complex problems in their daily lives. The challenge to be faced is to find ways to focus that ability on academic tasks.
- Students falling below basic performance levels may need supplemental assistance opportunities in addition to classroom instruction. The results of standards-based pre-assessments helps target remedial and accelerated instruction.
- The familiar curriculum spiral (the ability to learn each new skill being based on the mastery of essential prior skills) must be honored in principle. But a teacher is not required to ensure that every possible prior learning associated with a lower grade level has to be mastered before the content standards for the present grade can be introduced.
- Teachers focus on their grade-level standards but provide scaffolding lessons that refresh all students on requisite areas that have been identified through assessment as "weak" before introducing the grade-level standard(s). Teachers remain "forward focused."
- Students with identified prerequisite weaknesses requiring more than the initial scaffolding lessons may be appropriately grouped for additional instruction and support in and out of the classroom.
- The teacher makes every effort to improve the literacy skills of all students, particularly those with significant deficits. Achievement of literacy, especially academic literacy, may well represent the most important academic goal in any subject.
- Students needing intense help in achieving the standards and academic literacy should receive the support of other professional staff, including reading specialists, aides, and peer and adult tutors. But an absolute minimum of time for this purpose, if any, should be taken from the instructional time assigned to core subjects. Instead, the teacher should attempt to bring available help into the classroom. Aides and tutors should work closely with the teacher and selected students so that assistance in reading and writing is tied directly to classroom instruction. Too often, pullout programs isolate students from classroom activities, putting them further and further behind. The teacher should not be afraid to ask for extra help, making every attempt to collaborate and wisely use all available school-based resources, both staff and volunteers. Peer tutors may be available from another class and may succeed where adults are unable to break through the shell of a reluctant learner.
- Students should be involved in written and oral communication focused on explaining

how they solved a problem or completed a task. Consistent, long-term efforts by students to write and speak about their thought processes can accomplish significant incremental gains in academic literacy and academic achievement.

- The law requires that some type of written individual learning plan be developed for students needing assistance to demonstrate proficiency in response to content and performance standards. Students with learning deficits may need an individualized plan the same as or comparable to the individualized education program (IEP) used in special education for a student with a disability. With the passage of the 1997 amendments to the Individuals with Disabilities Education Act, all states must now include students with disabilities in state-wide and districtwide educational assessments (Section 612[a][17][A]). Fundamental questions must be asked about students with disabilities, including the most appropriate ways for them to provide evidence of their standards-based levels of proficiency. Many will be enrolled in inclusive classrooms; others may be enrolled in a more specialized learning environment. Teachers of inclusive classes must receive specialized guidance as they plan alternative assessments for students with documented disabilities. To assist those teachers, principals must create the conditions enabling the teachers to plan how to engage students with disabilities in the standards-based curriculum successfully and to ensure that alternative assessments are established. (See also Appendix 11-A, "We Need Not Exclude Anyone," and Appendix 11-B, "Sample Scoring Rubric for Alternative Assessments," at the end of this chapter.)

- Interventions at the school or in the classroom are most effective in helping students catch up on essential academic knowledge and skills. Teachers can monitor their students' progress as remedial help is being delivered. Although teachers should not be held accountable for all remedial efforts, they need to be involved as fully as possible in ensuring that their students know of and participate in opportunities for learning assistance.

- Professional staff development in strategies for delivering specially designed academic instruction in English (SDAIE) should be provided in schools enrolling significant numbers of students with limited reading and writing skills. Used successfully by thousands of teachers with all types of students, SDAIE provides a repertoire of easily learned and applied instructional techniques to enhance communication during instruction. It can be used effectively in introducing grade-level content standards for students with many types of learning deficits.

- Parents must be helped to understand that their child's teachers are working hard to overcome the child's past learning deficits. At the same time the teachers are helping the child achieve basic mastery of a significant number of grade-level content standards. According to reports from teachers, parents who have given up on school gain new confidence and increase their level of home support when they find a teacher with high expectations for their child.

## Teachers and Principals Working Together

The challenges of grade retention carry added intensity because standardized testing is to be used as a primary criterion for determining whether students qualify for promotion. The anxieties of teachers and principals, further exacerbated by the need to teach English learners in English, are well founded. They affect not only teachers and principals but also central office administrators, school board members, and, most especially, parents.

Specific comments and recommendations are, therefore, addressed to principals and their staffs as follows:

- Absolute answers to the multitude of challenges students bring to their classrooms do not exist.
- The reality must be accepted that, at least for now, some students will fail to meet the desired levels of performance despite the best efforts of teachers and administrators. They may be living in situations so complex and disabling that for them the school represents little more than a holding place. In that event everything possible should be done to connect such students and their families with appropriate social services agencies.
- Accepting that reality must not, however, be permitted to excuse the majority of students who fail to meet the standards required for promotion. Most students with learning deficits can perform at a much higher level of academic proficiency than that for which they are being held accountable. That assumption must be the corner-stone of all school initiatives to improve student achievement.
- Preventive education is the best way to ensure that grade retention gives way to student success. Clearly focused standards-based education is designed to achieve that goal. How? Standards provide teachers and students with clear guidance on the most important things students should know and be able to do in each subject for each grade. Instructional time and energy must be focused not on extraneous learning tasks but on the content standards. Those standards are measured by a performance standard system, which provides the primary basis for determining acceptable levels of student proficiency. Guesswork about readiness for promotion to the next grade gives way to a new level of objectivity and precise data.
- Principals and teachers must give high priority to brokering participation in district remediation efforts for students in danger of being retained. The principal ensures that the status of all students is closely monitored and that all who need special help receive it.
- Dependency on district-level remedial efforts must not be seen as the sole recourse for principals. School-level programs must also be planned and implemented.
- Available resources are tightly controlled. More often than not, cash infusions from other sources may be required. Principals redefine and reallocate local resources when necessary; lobby for staff, materials, or extended hours; or seek other resources that make possible extraordinary instructional initiatives.

- Resources available to principals include professional talent, time, and energy. Severely troubled schools reallocate their resources according to their highest standards-based priorities. "Revolutions" brought about by the advent of standards-based education are already occurring in many schools. If required, principals must be willing to become "revolutionary" figures in their schools and communities to raise the levels of academic proficiency for all students.

- Principals and teachers work hard to prevent their struggling students from being exposed to remedial efforts that are nothing more than failed, glossed-over versions of previous school experiences. Remediation involves effective and experienced teachers possessing a range of teaching skills, offering differentiated instruction, and using supplemental strategies that are of high interest to the middle grades student.

- Principals must mobilize the faculty to develop schoolwide efforts to make every student academically literate. Achievement of academic literacy based on grade-level standards is the most pervasive shared responsibility of every faculty seeking to ensure the academic success of the greatest number of students.

- Principals and teachers involve parents, many of whom will support efforts to help their children. However, many parents must be taught to understand the gravity of failure so that they can intervene in time. Too often, parents are the last to know that their child is failing. Principals and teachers collaborate to devise ways to overcome that obstacle.

- Principals recognize that although many others share in providing remedial and preventive responses to student failure, the individual school remains the most effective place for promoting change. Principals and teachers may become so caught up in the complexity of the issues involved that they lose their perspective about their power to intervene and achieve major results. Principals are especially encouraged to maximize networking opportunities enabling them to talk, share, and plan ways to make their schools the center of leadership in standards-based reform.[2]

- If a student must be retained, he or she must not be subjected to a mere repetition of what failed previously but must be provided with a different instructional experience focused on the student's specific identified needs.

(See also Appendix 11-C, "Students Deserve More Than Talk: They Need Extra Help and a Second Chance!" at the end of this chapter.)

# Social Promotion and Grade Retention

- **Issues related to the passage of Assembly Bill 1626 (1998) continue to be vigorously discussed throughout California.** How has this legislation affected your school? Your own professional practice? What kinds of preventive measures are proving to be the most successful in enabling all students to receive the help they need to succeed?

- **Standards-based education is considered one of the most important developments in educational reform.** It can equip teachers and principals with a strategic focus capable of reducing the number of students who might otherwise fail to achieve the level of academic proficiency required for promotion and, ultimately, graduation from high school. To what degree has standards-based education been implemented in your school? What are the most important next steps? Who is accountable? What is your role?

- **Are all the students in your school included in standards-based instruction and assessment (see Appendix 11-A at the end of this chapter)?** How are you attempting to help students with special needs (1) work to achieve academic proficiency; and (2) demonstrate their learning? Do you need help in those areas? What kinds of assistance would be most valuable? Do other colleagues share these needs? Share your findings with your principal.

- **Critics often use unkind words to describe the schools' seeming inability to overcome obstacles to higher student achievement.** In your opinion, what are the most unfair criticisms? The most fair? Do you have specific suggestions for addressing criticisms that you judge to be fair? If so, share two or three examples. Have you ever shared your suggestions? Have you acted on your convictions? If not, what would be required for you to do so?

- **Enlisting parent support is seen as one of the most effective and desirable approaches to the problem of underachievement.** Yet parents of middle school and high school students are often among the last to know that their child is failing. What is the situation in your school? Is there a need to improve teacher-parent communications? How might that task be accomplished?

- **Are there any immediate actions that your school might take that would result in significant improvement in overall student achievement and reduced failure rates?** If so, what would it take to effect the changes? Who is accountable? Do you have any personal ownership? What can you do now? Will you act?

# Appendix 11-A

# We Need Not Exclude Anyone

by Jacqueline Farmer Kearns, Harold L. Kleinert, and Sarah Kennedy

One key to ensuring high expectations for every student is requiring that everyone is included in measures of educational assessment. With the passage of the 1997 Amendments to the Individuals with Disabilities Education Act (IDEA 1997), all states must now include students with disabilities in statewide and districtwide educational assessments (Section 612[a][17][A]). No longer can a disability exclude students from assessments or exclude their scores from state and district reports.

States will have to ensure that students with disabilities receive appropriate accommodations to participate in assessments. For students who cannot participate in assessments even with modifications, states and districts must develop alternative assessments by July 1, 2000. An alternative portfolio assessment can be designed specifically for those students for whom the regular assessment program does not provide a meaningful measure of learning, even with accommodations.

*The alternative portfolio designed for use in Kentucky follows this appendix (see Appendix 11-B).* It reflects the same set of learner expectations identified for all students. Although the alternative portfolios assess the same academic expectations, students with significant disabilities may demonstrate those outcomes in other ways. For example, [students] can demonstrate the expectation [for] assessing information by appropriately requesting assistance across multiple school and community settings. Students can [also] demonstrate the expectation [by] using technology effectively through appropriate assistive technology applications, such as using an augmentative communication device or operating a computer program through single-switch access.

The following are essential components of every alternative portfolio:

- *Evidence of how the student communicates,* including any special assistive devices or procedures
- *The student's daily or weekly schedules,* including those associated with academic expectations
- *A student's letter to the portfolio reviewer,* including a discussion of the portfolio entries
- *A résumé of work experiences for twelfth graders,* including highlights of real-life vocational experiences
- *A letter from the student's parents or guardian,* including comments about their level of satisfaction with the portfolio
- *Five academic entries,* selected from language arts, mathematics, science, social studies, arts and humanities, physical education, and vocational studies (Student products as well as systematic instructional data may serve as evidence of academic expectations.)

*Here is a true account:*

> Bobby, a middle school student with a moderate disability, completed a folklore project for his eighth grade U.S. history class. Students completed six projects that ranged from constructing a family tree to recording oral history. Bobby chose three of the six activities for his portfolio. He constructed a family tree, took pictures of family members, and with a partner took pictures of local historical sites. Together, he and his partner gave a presentation to the class.

From *Educational Leadership,* Vol. 56 (March 1999). Reprinted with permission from the Association for Supervision and Curriculum Development.

[Appendix 11-B] provides the five dimensions of the scoring rubric used to evaluate alternative portfolios: (1) performance of targeted skills within the context of academic expectations; (2) appropriate supports that lead to independence; (3) performance in multiple settings to enhance the generalization of skills; (4) social relationships that support the development of appropriate social interaction skills and the development of social networks; and (5) age-appropriate performance with opportunities for making choices and decisions.

*Recommendations:*

- Ideally, rather than create alternatives for distinct populations, assess all learners together. Many students, with and without disabilities, may not perform well on any given large-scale assessment, but that should not exclude them from the assessment.
- Carefully consider how students with disabilities can participate with appropriate accommodations. The remainder of students—the small percentage who, even with accommodations, cannot meaningfully participate in the large-scale regular assessment—may be the target population for the alternate assessment.
- Determine how state or district standards apply to students who will take the alternative assessment. Alternative assessments must align as closely as possible with state standards determined for all students.
- Convene a stakeholder group, with general and special education teachers, administrators, and parents, to assist with decisions about the standards as well as assessments.
- Determine the assessment format that is consistent with other forms of student assessment. Use a portfolio, for example, if other students are also developing portfolios. Teachers may want to think about how to assist students with moderate and severe disabilities to highlight their individual achievements.
- Decide how to report the student scores to the public in a manner that is useful and yet protects individual student identities.
- Implement the assessment. As teachers, students, and parents engage in conversations about student work, they will refine the assessment, which will lead to improved results for students.

# Appendix 11-B

# Sample Scoring Rubric for Alternative Assessments

Used for students with disabilities and for whom the regular assessment program does not provide a meaningful measure of learning, even with accommodations.

| | Advanced | Proficient | Basic | Below Basic |
|---|---|---|---|---|
| **Performance** | Student work indicates progress on specifically targeted skills that are meaningful in future environments. Evidence exists of planning, monitoring, and evaluating progress. Evaluation is used to extend performance. Evidence of academic expectations appears in all entries. | Student work indicates progress on specifically targeted skills that are meaningful in current and future environments. Student consistently plans, monitors, and evaluates own performance. Most entries show academic expectations. | Student performs specifically targeted skills that are meaningful in current and future environments. Planning, monitoring, and evaluating are limited or inconsistent. Some evidence exists of academic expectations. | Student participates passively in portfolio products. No clear evidence exists of targeted skills. Little or no linkage to academic expectations is evident. |
| **Support** | Support is natural. Evidence exists of adaptations, modifications, or assistive technology. | Support is natural, with students learning together. Use of adaptations, modifications, or assistive technology is appropriate. | Support is limited to peer tutoring. Use of adaptations, modifications, or assistive technology is limited. | No clear evidence exists of peer supports or needed adaptations, modifications, or assistive technology. |
| **Settings** | Student performance occurs in an extensive variety of integrated settings within and across all entries. | Student performs targeted skills in a wide variety of integrated settings within and across most entries. | Student performs targeted skills in a variety of integrated settings. | Student participates in a limited number of settings. |
| **Social Relationships** | Student has clearly established mutual friendships with nondisabled peers. | Student sustains social relationships with peers over time. | Student has frequent social interactions with nondisabled peers. | Student's social interactions are limited. |
| **Contexts** | Evidence exists of student choice and control in age-appropriate portfolio products within and across all entries. | Student consistently makes choices in a wide variety of portfolio products. All portfolio products are age-appropriate. | Student makes choices in a variety of portfolio products. All products are age-appropriate. | Student makes limited choices in portfolio products. Products are not age-appropriate. |

Adapted from Kentucky's "Alternative Assessment Scoring Rubric," developed in response to the Kentucky Education Reform Act of 1990.

# Appendix 11-C

## Students Deserve More Than Talk: They Need Extra Help and a Second Chance!

### by Anne Wheelock

Schools that are developing a culture of high standards communicate "caring rigor" by making sure that every student receives the support needed to meet standards for grade promotion. Educators in such schools know that grade retention undermines achievement and is a poor substitute for good teaching and learning. To avoid grade retention and ensure that students are prepared for the next grade, these schools offer . . . effective help early and often during the school year, before rather than after students fail. . . .

Schools that assert that every student can learn take concrete steps to saturate school life with opportunities to access the extra help they need to succeed in their age-appropriate grade. The steps they take vary from school to school, but effective approaches have several characteristics in common: they are offered early and often as a normal part of the school routine, and they are often multidimensional, with supports for academic achievement made available in a variety of ways.

Effective solutions are school-based solutions designed and owned by each individual school. Schools that practice "caring rigor" and "rigorous caring" (terms coined by Theodore Sizer) anticipate that students will need extra help to achieve. In these schools teachers take responsibility for the success of every student. Their commitment reflects Sizer's observation that "the new assumption, which has emerged in the past 15 years, is that if a kid does not get it in the usual way, the school should try to help him to get it another way. Everybody has to get it. No one can be sorted out."

Schools that operate on the assumption that "everybody has to get it" recognize that some students whose work lags behind acceptable standards need numerous opportunities for extra help in order to succeed. . . . With the growing number of students retained in grade in the name of standards, the need to develop extra-help responses with personalized support at the individual school level is urgent. Schools must offer extra-help strategies in their appropriate grade level, not as add-ons but within a school culture that reflects schoolwide commitment to equal access to knowledge, a "press for achievement," and research-based professional teaching practices.

Efforts to mandate grade retention and districtwide summer school or programs that shuffle failing eighth graders off to a separate transitional school may be well intentioned, but such programs are likely to fall short of expectations. . . . The knowledge that "there's always the district summer school" may tempt schools to tolerate failure within their own walls. . . . Likewise, separate transition programs represent less a second chance than a dead-end placement, the last step before dropping out. In contrast, . . . schools committed to ensuring that all students meet standards in the company of their peers illustrate that alternatives to either grade retention or social promotion are within the reach of all schools willing to use resources to design and implement them.

Students require more than talk. . . . Schools [must] back up the expectation that students will work harder by providing extra help and second chances for turning incomplete work into work that meets standards as regular features of school life.

From *Safe to Be Smart: Building a Culture for Standards-Based Reform in the Middle Grades.* Columbus, Ohio: National Middle School Association, 1998. Used with permission.

*"Innovation and creativity create opportunity. . . . Quality creates demand."*

—Anonymous

# Creating High-Quality After-Hours Academic Programs in Middle Schools

Using after-school hours to further the goals of standards-based education in middle schools has unlimited potential. Momentum for developing programs and services that meet the intellectual, physical, emotional, and social needs of young adolescents between the close of the school day and early evening continues to grow throughout California and the nation. High-quality after-hours programs should provide safe, engaging environments that stimulate students and combine academic, cultural, recreational, enrichment, and health-related activities both attractive and productive.

The role of after-hours programs in helping young adolescents is described by the Carnegie Council on Adolescent Development as follows:

> Fundamental changes in American families have strained the capacity of parents and kin to provide the care and guidance [that] young adolescents need to tackle everyday challenges. . . . The passage through early

adolescence should result in positive outcomes. For increasing numbers of young adolescents, that is not their experience. Instead of safety in their neighborhoods, they face chronic physical danger; instead of economic security, they face boredom and stagnation; in place of respect, they are neglected; lacking clear and consistent adult expectations for them, many youth feel deeply alienated from mainstream American society.

Each day 20 million young adolescents decide how they will spend at least 40 percent of their waking hours when not in school. For many these hours harbor both risk and opportunity. For some, particularly those supervised by adults, the out-of-school hours offer opportunities to be with friends, play sports, pursue interests, and engage in challenging activities. For many home alone the out-of-school hours present serious risks for substance abuse, crime, violence, and sexual activity leading to unwanted pregnancy and sexually transmitted diseases, including AIDS. Time spent [unsupervised] is not the crucial contributor to high risk. Rather, it is what young people do during that time, where they do it, and with whom that lead to positive or negative consequences.[1]

 Recommendations 2, 3, 5, 12, 14, 15

Fundamental concerns for the health and safety of students during the critical after-school hours provide much of the energy behind the momentum for after-hours programs. Educators, community leaders, and the public at large also view the critical hours as outstanding opportunities to address a variety of academic challenges that cannot be accommodated adequately during the normal school day. Consequently, this chapter focuses on creating, for the middle grades, after-hours academic programs and services provided in a safe, caring environment and designed to foster academic success and general intellectual enrichment for every student.

The development of community-based after-hours programs requires an exceptional commitment from all participants. For example, the roles, responsibilities, expectations, relationships, and schedules of institutions and organizations may require change. And changing any of those variables, much less all of them, will almost certainly guarantee frustration, even failure, unless all parties genuinely agree to work together. Those essential commitments can lead to a series of steps involving a definition of needs, goal setting, and strategic planning, followed by program implementation and evaluation.

## Consensus Building and Goal Setting

Students' needs are identified and priorities assigned when after-hours academic programs for middle schools are being implemented. The priorities should be stated as program goals and should focus on the activities and experiences most likely to provide the greatest benefit to the largest number of students. Facilitating the initial stages falls heavily on teachers and administrators, who must work closely with their partners in the community. Goals should reflect the students' learning needs assessed in the classroom.

Successful consensus building is tested when the goals and priorities of schools and their community partners appear to conflict. For example, some community partners may feel poorly prepared to deliver services identified as priorities by school personnel. Potential conflicts involving roles, relationships, expectations, and responsibilities must be reconciled. Where goodwill exists, difficult goals can be met. The ultimate challenge in the goal-setting process may lie in determining whether each goal of the after-hours program can help students achieve the expected levels of academic proficiency.

## Structure of After-Hours Academic Programs

Items to be considered in discussing the structure of after-hours academic programs include organization, coordination, communication, management, staffing, supervision, and professional development:

### Organization

After-hours academic programs depend on individual schools or networks of schools linked with institutions and other entities, public and private. The manner in which after-hours programs are organized varies according to (1) the particular constellation of partners;

(2) the programs developed—whether they are to serve individual schools or networks of schools; (3) funding sources; (4) staffing; and (5) the degree to which school district offices are involved. Those who devise after-hours academic programs should work in settings characterized by close collaboration, effective communication, substantial flexibility, and a carefully conceived accountability system.

## Coordination

Effective coordination involves assurances that all parts of after-hours programs fit together in ways easily understood and communicated to students, parents, and community members. "Turf wars" must be avoided. When participating institutions understand their functions, they can focus on the most creative, effective ways to do their jobs. Coordination is best achieved through a council or similar structure on which the local school or schools, together with each participating organization or other institution, are represented. The representatives become the primary links between the programs and their sponsoring bodies and provide critical policy guidance to those who supervise the programs.

## Communication

Faculty members served by after-hours academic programs should be aware of the services available and direct students and their parents to those programs that best fit individual needs. Materials describing program goals, services, and benefits should be attractively packaged in multilingual formats when appropriate and should be distributed to students, their families, and members of partner organizations. The materials and

communication strategies should be professionally designed to project quality, continuity, and importance. Communication must also be viewed as an ongoing process and should include regular information updates, newsletters, press releases, and public-service announcements. Each partner should assign a high priority to its role in promoting the services.

## Management

After-hours programs require effective management to survive. Those involving several organizations usually rely on a paid manager because volunteer managers usually do not function well when a program demands their services full-time. When funds are limited, some programs extend the contract of the school principal or one of the leaders of a partner organization. The urgency of sound management is reflected in the federal Twenty-first Century Community Learning Centers Initiative (Elementary and Secondary Education Act of 1994, Title X, Part 1).

Effective management of successful after-hours academic programs involves developing annual operating budgets, maintaining accurate bookkeeping systems, and determining affordable fee structures if required. Program managers must also be skilled in developing funding sources and in-kind support, continually developing proposals to be sent to potential contributors, including foundations, corporations, public agencies, and the companies of program participants.

The managers must also enforce policies protecting students and staff. Included are assurances that participating entities meet licensing requirements, provide adequate liability coverage, maintain appropriate records systematically, meet building code specifications, and conform to necessary health and safety practices. Participants must also comply with the Americans with Disabilities Act, ensuring that after-hours academic programs include all students. Program managers must also help ensure that high-quality services are provided. To be effective, managers should develop strong working relationships with the administrators of the schools where students attend the after-hours programs and with the community partners.

## Staffing

Staffing varies in after-hours academic programs. Staff members must be qualified and committed, have appropriate experiences and realistic expectations, and be caring persons. They must also be responsive to the challenges faced by many students and their families, cooperate with one another, and interact productively and collegially with the regular school staff, whether or not the after-hours program is school based. Included on the staff may be certificated teachers, licensed members of allied professions, paraprofessionals, and college or university student interns. Others involved in the effort may be parent and community volunteers and others from various walks of life (e.g., sports, law enforcement, houses of faith, corporations, the helping and healing professions). All are expected to serve in various roles, including mentoring and tutoring.

## Supervision

After-hours academic programs must meet consistently high standards. Reviews by administrators, community councils, school boards,

and public agencies are among the more common types of program monitoring. Day-to-day supervision of paid and volunteer staff members, the foundation of a program's quality and integrity, is required. Formal reviews of the paid staff are also required periodically. Because college and university student interns are usually awarded academic credit for their participation, they must be evaluated regularly. The activities of volunteer mentors and tutors should be coordinated, and frequent opportunities for professional consultation and support should be provided for them. Also requiring supervision and encouragement are all other volunteers. Faithful adherence to these practices will guarantee the success of after-hours academic programs.

## Professional Development

Although paid and volunteer staff members may initially be well prepared for their roles, they require continual professional development for the long-range success of an after-hours academic program. And for the program's quality to be developed and sustained, they should be given many opportunities to refine their professional knowledge and skills. The priorities for staff development should be the special challenges posed by the different ethnic, linguistic, and cultural backgrounds and learning deficits or disabilities of young adolescents. Therefore, staff development programs should be directed to the teaching and tutorial practices effective in differentiating instruction. Further, those who work in tutorial, homework, literacy, and academic enrichment centers must have expertise in subject matter, including being able to teach skills in reading and writing.

## A Sampling of After-Hours Academic Programs

After-hours programs can provide young adolescents with a range of safe, stimulating, enriching, and healthy alternatives to being home alone, watching television, or hanging out on the streets. These programs should be attractive and engaging to all of the school's young adolescents and their parents. In addition to providing academic assistance, programs can provide students with opportunities to extend their academic learning in new situations or to acquire additional skills in the arts, career exploration, computers, sciences, or community service.

Although attendance at an after-hours academic program may be mandated by the school board for students needing remedial academic assistance, it should not be perceived as a place to which only those students needing remedial academic assistance are "sentenced" because they do not meet performance-level targets. The after-school, particularly a school-based, program can be a powerful vehicle for ensuring that students needing remedial assistance get the targeted help they need, but positive student perceptions and attitude about the after-school program are essential to what they get out of it.

Parents of students needing remediation must also be convinced of the value of the after-school program. The program is a potent response to helping their child obtain necessary skills and a preventive strategy to possible grade retention.

Content and supervision must project professional competence, caring attitudes, and curricular substance so compelling that young adolescents will attend regularly and voluntarily. A parallel level of parental support, including payment for some services if needed and close supervision of the children's involvement, is also required. Information on grant programs that are available to develop after-hours programs may be accessed through the California Department of Education's Web site <*http://www.cde.ca.gov*>.

Some of the after-hours academic programs being offered are as follows (see also Figure 12-1, which displays a sampling of after-hours programs that a middle school could implement in support of its students):

### Homework Centers

Students receive help in completing take-home assignments in supervised settings called homework centers, which are staffed by persons capable of assisting. Popular sites for the centers include YWCAs, YMCAs, and houses of faith. Many homework centers recruit college or university student interns, who volunteer as unpaid staff and earn academic credit. In addition, whenever other qualified volunteers with special qualifications are available, their assistance is also provided. Well-designed homework centers provide facilities responsive to varied styles of student learning (see Chapter 14), especially quiet places for independent work and settings for small-group tasks.

Homework centers should provide computers with word-processing software and Internet and e-mail connections, lists of textbooks currently adopted in each curriculum area, supplemental texts, specialized references, dictionaries, and encyclopedias. If school districts and county offices of education have

After-hours academic programs must be responsive to individual needs. Identified here are programs that focus on remedial assistance, service-learning, literacy, the arts, mentoring, and GATE-related academic enrichment experiences. Any and all of these options can be mixed and matched to create other opportunities.

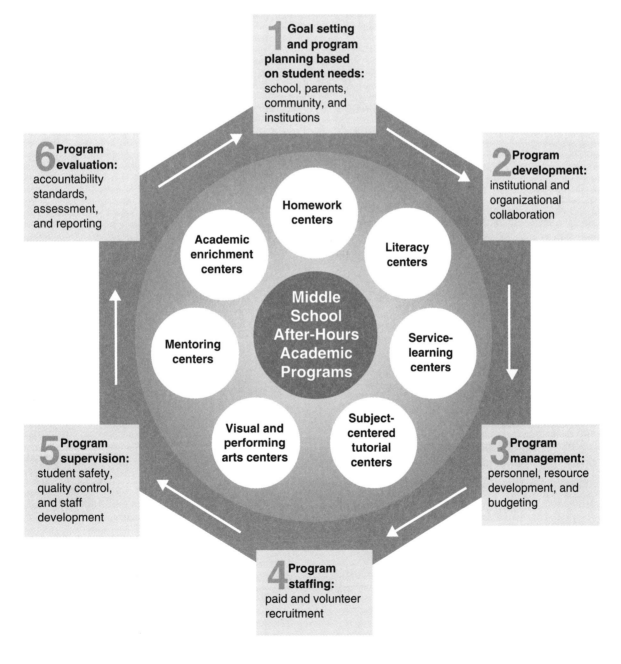

**1 Goal setting and program planning based on student needs:** school, parents, community, and institutions

**2 Program development:** institutional and organizational collaboration

**3 Program management:** personnel, resource development, and budgeting

**4 Program staffing:** paid and volunteer recruitment

**5 Program supervision:** student safety, quality control, and staff development

**6 Program evaluation:** accountability standards, assessment, and reporting

Homework centers

Academic enrichment centers

Literacy centers

Mentoring centers

Middle School After-Hours Academic Programs

Service-learning centers

Visual and performing arts centers

Subject-centered tutorial centers

homework hot lines, the centers should be given access to those services. Periodicals for teenagers, a small collection of good paperback books, and music CDs and tapes for listening on headphones should be made available for use after the students have completed their assignments and before they are scheduled to leave the center.

## Service-Learning Centers

According to the California Service-Learning Task Force report titled *Service-Learning: Linking Classrooms and Communities,* service-learning centers can be administered by current staff members: "These staff members would become the contact for community partners and help [other] teachers and community partners who are implementing service projects. The staff may be credentialed educators who know the community or professionals from the community who understand how schools operate. Support staff must also be available to coordinate service-learning as part of their existing job."[2]

The centers are designed to provide a planned, supervised setting and broker a wide range of experiences for students. In its report the Service-Learning Task Force calls for school districts and communities to use service-learning to connect youths to their communities, thereby reinforcing academic standards, assessments, and accountability. Service-learning is more than community service. Service-learning links community work directly to classroom learning. Ideally, service-learning should be integrated into the academic curriculum and provide opportunities to demonstrate civic responsibility.

Nonprofit groups and local entities are very receptive to having students assist organizations and agencies responsible for maintaining art museums, natural history museums, care centers for the aged, hospitals, zoos, parks and recreational facilities, social services, and environmental protection. Once the purposes of service-learning are explained to private-sector businesses, many of them will also participate in the program.[3]

(See also Appendix 12-A, "Service-Learning Makes the Grade," and Appendix 12-B, "The Nurturing Potential of Service-Learning," at the end of this chapter.)

## Literacy Centers

Students are helped to develop their reading and writing skills in literacy centers, which should provide not only instruction in fundamental reading and writing skills but also activities designed to develop academic literacy. The operation of the centers should be supervised by professionally trained staff, who, in addition to being proficient in teaching reading and writing related to grade-level standards, should be skilled in recruiting and training volunteer tutors.

The volunteers might include student peers, parents, retirees, and college and university interns. Especially valuable in centers serving students whose primary language is other than English are bilingual volunteers. The supervisory staff must work closely with the teachers in the regular school program who make available appropriate assessment data, daily assignments, or information on specific learning difficulties to facilitate the efforts of staff and volunteers. The work of literacy center volunteers will be most successful if it is aligned to classroom expectations and targeted to individual student needs.

Because literacy centers depend on professional staff and specialized instructional materials and facilities, they are often located in the school and are operated as extensions of the regular school program.

### Subject-Centered Tutorial Centers

In subject-centered tutorial centers, students with learning deficits receive specialized help for each curriculum area. These centers differ significantly from homework centers, which are designed to enable students to have a secure learning environment to do their homework. In addition to providing a secure environment, the tutorial centers offer specific academic assistance provided by tutors with specialized knowledge of the subject matter. Although the tutors may be recruited from many different sources, college and university interns are perhaps the most commonly selected. However, because the interns predictably have little if any formal knowledge about an effective tutorial role, they must be trained. The formal institutional connection does produce a stable, disciplined source of qualified personnel.

Not all college and university students participating in tutorial programs volunteer their time, even though they receive academic credit. Some may be paid for their services. A number of the most effective tutors for middle grades students are recruited from nearby high schools. Some may participate in their own school's service-learning program; others may be seeking after-hours employment.

A very important responsibility of the tutorial center staff is to develop close working relationships with teachers in the regular school

program. The connection helps ensure that students are focusing on appropriate content and performance standards. The centers should be viewed as planned extensions of the regular school program for students with learning difficulties. Ordinarily, attendance should be mandated by the school board. The number of eligible students participating may, however, exceed the capacity of the facilities used by the sponsors of other after-hours programs. In that event the school itself should become the primary site of the tutorial center.

### Visual and Performing Arts Centers

Attractive after-hours learning experiences can be provided by visual and performing arts centers for large numbers of students. But such programs should never lead to neglecting those arts in the regular school program. Rather, the learning that each can provide should be integrated into the curriculum. Visual and performing arts organizations, park and recreation services, and other similar entities are natural community partners in planning visual and performing arts programs. Successful centers provide opportunities for students to participate in activities in many areas, including music, the visual arts, dance, and dramatics.

Program personnel often schedule special presentations, miniconcerts, demonstrations, and other types of arts enrichment experiences provided voluntarily by talented professionals. And in urban areas especially, field trips to art museums and natural history museums or concerts are popular activities, as are walking tours or bus tours of public works of art, including monuments and buildings. Field trips made to sketch or paint are also popular. The possibilities are limited only by the creativity of those who plan the center's programs.

Student interns, local artists, museum personnel, and recreational specialists are among the many possible sources of volunteers and paid personnel.

After-hours visual and performing arts centers require an extra measure of flexibility, given the nature of the instructional services they seek to provide. Because supervising staff face special challenges in coordinating the diverse services, establishing quality controls at the outset is essential.

## Mentoring Centers

The word *mentor* comes from Greek mythology. Mentor, a friend of Odysseus, was entrusted with the education of Odysseus' son, Telemachus. Thus the term has come to mean a trusted counselor or guide.

One of the most valuable after-hours education programs is provided in mentoring centers. Older students and adults frequently mention that, apart from parents and teachers, they have been influenced the most by mentors in making critical decisions.

The sources of mentors are almost unlimited. The supervisors of the mentoring centers must give careful attention to selecting mentors and must be skilled in identifying adults who can communicate effectively with young adolescents. Successful mentors must be able to respond to the adolescents in ways that evidence an understanding of the fundamental goals of mentoring.

Supervisors of mentoring centers, with the assistance of parents, professional colleagues, and others already experienced as mentors, should be held accountable for developing criteria describing the mentoring function and the goals for the local program. Each center will have its own statement, even though common factors exist for all centers.

Mentors and the students they assist are expected to make important commitments to each other. Accordingly, they must be matched carefully. Qualified professional personnel should interview potential mentors and student participants separately. Because of the inherent closeness and duration of the relationship, mentors should be persons whom students, parents, and school personnel trust completely.

Mentors may be adults of any age who are mature in thought and experience. Often, those whose backgrounds are comparable with those of the students they assist and who have achieved successful careers are the most effective. And mentors and students who share common vocational or recreational interests often have an advantage in developing a successful relationship. Mentors must be helped to understand that their role is to show by their lives a strong commitment to educational values and personal effort.

Planning, implementing, and supervising an after-hours mentoring center for middle grade students involve complex operations. The center's primary objective in linking mentors and students is to remove as many variables as possible. Carefully defined policies and procedures for recruiting, screening, and selecting mentors and matching them with students, together with efficient operations, are essential for long-term success. With coordinated planning more students can be expected to receive assistance from tutors. Therefore, staff who supervise and coordinate mentorship programs must work diligently to locate the best possible candidates.

A basic link exists between mentoring programs and school-to-career programs. Although mentors and students do meet regularly, they do not meet daily unless involved in another after-hours program. When time is available, therefore, the students should be given wide exposure to career options and be made aware of the levels of academic achievement needed to reach certain professional and vocational goals. Presentations by guest speakers, field trips, and other similar experiences help to achieve those purposes. The mentoring program's supervisor must maintain a close working relationship with the counseling and guidance personnel in the regular school program. Doing so will prevent duplication in school-to-career planning and ensure that the progress the students are making in the mentoring program will become known to their teachers.

(See also Appendix 12-C, "The Hewlett-Packard E-Mail Mentoring Program," at the end of this chapter.)

### Academic Enrichment Centers

The term *academic enrichment* applies to a broad spectrum of student interests, aptitudes, and abilities. Therefore, academic enrichment centers should be viewed as much more than catchalls for middle grades students whose needs may not be addressed in other after-hours programs. Instead, the centers should be viewed as extensions of the regular school program.

Qualified professional personnel and adequate learning facilities should be made available to students participating in academic enrichment centers. Formal classes with low pupil-teacher ratios and independent study

projects should be encouraged. Examples of academic enrichment activities include learning new computer software applications, carrying out research projects, studying a foreign language, and writing creatively, including publishing original work. In fact, academic enrichment encompasses any worthy intellectual pursuit whose primary goals are reasoning and deep learning. One of the most important challenges of after-hours enrichment centers is to help students work to achieve the highest levels of academic proficiency. Although other types of academic centers also share that goal, only in academic enrichment centers are students deliberately pressed to exceed performance standards.

Although academic enrichment centers may be especially attractive to gifted and talented students, they are intended for all students seeking to excel in schoolwork. Supervisors should work closely with the regular teachers and guidance and counseling personnel to encourage all high achievers to take advantage of enrichment opportunities. Student work should be assessed in determining individual levels of academic proficiency.

(See also Appendix 12-D, "USC Neighborhood Pre-College Enrichment Academy," at the end of this chapter.)

## Summary of the Chapter

The range of after-hours academic and enrichment programs is more extensive than the sampling provided. Furthermore, those and other types of after-hours programs can be matched in various ways to serve more students by promoting health and physical well-being, personal and social competencies, school-to-career experiences, and leadership development. They can be expanded to encompass Saturday school, intersession, and summer school.

Although after-hours programs are often discussed in the context of urban inner-city communities, they are appropriate everywhere. They can provide safe, attractive places to learn, serve, and play as well as opportunities to develop secure, stable relationships with caring peers and adults in pursuing educational goals. Students are able to sharpen study habits, expand academic skills and knowledge, and increase the likelihood that they will achieve or exceed expected levels of academic proficiency.

# After-Hours Academic and Enrichment Programs

- **Has your school implemented after-hours academic and enrichment programs?** If so, how do you rate the level of cooperation between program staff and the staff of the regular school program? What factors have contributed to effective cooperation? What suggestions can you offer for improvement? Share the information with others.

- **After-hours academic and enrichment programs require the same kind of rigorous attention to planning, management, and supervision as that required for the regular day program.** Are after-hours academic programs at your school the product of a carefully developed consensus involving school staff, parents, and partner organizations? How can consensus building and shared decision making be strengthened? Can your ideas influence the process? What might you do next?

- **After-hours academic and enrichment programs fill a critical void in the day of an average young adolescent student and provide specific support.** If your school has after-hours academic programs, do the students, the regular teachers, the after-hours staff, and the parents understand the purpose of the programs? If so, how is that purpose apparent? If not, what specifically can be done to improve the chances that students will benefit from the programs? How are these programs advertised and promoted?

- **After-hours academic and enrichment programs can be very effective in extending the regular school day.** The programs are also viewed as a potent response to threats of failure and grade retention. If your school offers after-hours academic programs, are students actively recruited and enrolled? Are content and performance standards for the regular classroom linked with the instructional support available in the after-hours programs? If so, what has contributed most to your school's success in realizing those goals? If not, what can be done to improve those critical connections?

- **If your school does not offer after-hours academic programs or lacks careful planning, management, or supervision for the programs you do offer, can you provide leadership to improve the situation?** Do you know of colleagues who might help?

# Appendix 12-A

# Service-Learning Makes the Grade

## by Rich Cairn and Susan Cairn

*"... Many teachers insist that service-learning must allow for the unplanned learning outcome—not always related to a previously identified standard—that may be the most profound result of the experience."*

How can students learn and serve at the same time? Nathan Vetter, an eighth grader, participated in a service-learning project for his history class. The class project was to re-create historically accurate European immigrant and native American gardens. The project held added importance because students planted rare Native American seed stock to help replenish the local state university's genetic bank.

Nathan and his fellow students planted their gardens on the grounds of a center that commemorates an 1851 treaty between the U.S. government and the Dakota people. Students experienced two radically different sets of cultural practices. Neat, orderly European gardens follow straight lines, whereas Dakota corn, bean, and squash hills conform to complex symbolism.

Students constructed and used deer antler rakes and shoulder bone plows, and they also used European-style steel implements. Since service-learning is a particularly strong example of performance-based learning, students in this project created portfolios that included site maps, drawings, journals, and research reports which were used in teacher assessments.

What did Nathan learn? Nathan himself observed, "I got to know I did a good job by the effort I put into the garden and by how good the crop came out." Such a response is typical from someone involved in a service-learning project where students apply knowledge and skills learned in the classroom while providing a genuine community service.

Students also get real-world feedback from professionals. For example, in Nathan's case it came from the local historical society and the local state university.

Service-learning advocates are enthusiastic supporters of standards-based education. Yet concerns exist. As with any large scale, systemic change, the implementation of new standards requires extra time during start-up. Further, some teachers fear that too much assessment might sap the very power of service-learning by channeling student's attention away from the community and back toward their own gain.

Most significantly, many teachers insist that service-learning must allow for the unplanned learning outcome—not always related to a previously identified standard—that may be the most profound result of the experience.

In spite of these challenges, teachers who try service-learning projects tend to come away as supporters of the process because of the expanded opportunities for learning, the emphasis on student accountability, and the potential link to content standards in many different subject areas.

From *Educational Leadership,* Vol. 56, No. 6 (March 1999). Reprinted with permission from the Association for Supervision and Curriculum Development.

# Appendix 12-B

# The Nurturing Potential of Service-Learning

by Sandra Krystal

*"Service-learning should be at the core of every school's curriculum because it gives young people purpose and nurtures their spirits as few experiences can."*

Today's youth lack positive connections with their communities. Service-learning is a method by which young people learn and develop through active participation in thoughtfully organized experiences led by qualified adults. It brings young people into their communities to make positive changes. It also helps youngsters connect school learning to the world outside the school building.

Young people have to participate in activities that help them make meaningful connections between themselves and the vast world they inhabit. They need to be guided in real-life situations to develop a moral code and a sense of civic pride.

Service-learning is a transforming experience. Practitioners in the field witness these dramatic changes in students every day. Surly youngsters who are turned off by school and refuse to participate in school life suddenly look forward to their service-learning.

What transformed these young people from sometimes unruly adolescents into serious, caring, thoughtful young adults? They were needed, they were involved in a meaningful activity, and they were discovering talents that they never knew they possessed.

Service-learning should be at the core of every school's curriculum because it gives young people purpose and nurtures their spirits as few experiences can. How is the spirit nurtured? From the feeling of accomplishment; from knowing they have achieved goals; from the rewards of giving and realizing how much they have received; and from knowing they have made a difference in someone's life or in the community.

From *Educational Leadership,* Vol. 56 (December 1998/January 1999). Reprinted with permission from the Association for Supervision and Curriculum Development.

# Appendix 12-C

# The Hewlett-Packard E-Mail Mentoring Program

The Hewlett-Packard Company has developed and funded the HP E-Mail Mentoring Program to improve achievement in mathematics and science in grades five through twelve in several countries. The company has also given special attention to increasing the number of females and minorities studying and teaching mathematics and science.

## Formal Applications Required

Working in a one-to-one mentoring relationship by e-mail, students and HP mentors collaborate in classroom activities, such as science projects and mathematics lessons, under the direction of a classroom teacher. Admission to the program is requested by the teachers on behalf of their students. The teachers are required to submit lesson plans for individual projects that the students and mentors use as they work together and for which the students will receive a grade on completion of the assignment. The students' teachers serve as the primary supervisors for the program. The teachers and participating students must have appropriate Internet and e-mail addresses.

## Mentors Around the World

Students selected by their teachers to participate are directed to the HP Mentoring Program Web Site, where they complete an application and a survey. The mentors are HP employees located worldwide who have submitted an online application to the HP Mentor Program staff. They are responsible for communicating with their students at least two to three times weekly throughout the 36-week school year.

## Preconditions for Mentors

As a condition for participation, mentors agree to be positive role models, encourage their students to excel in mathematics and science, use appropriate grammar and communication skills, encourage their students to use the Internet as a learning resource, and correspond by e-mail with their students' teachers and members of the HP Mentor Program staff. The latter commitment is particularly important for ensuring program quality controls. Mentors are scattered worldwide at HP corporate operations. They may never personally meet members of the program staff or the students whom they mentor.

## Student Commitment to Serious Study Required

The HP Mentor Program staff matches students and mentors according to specific criteria, including the kinds of science or mathematics projects involved, common career interests, academic studies, and hobbies. The mentoring program includes a specific commitment by students and mentors that they will work together on rigorous projects integrated with the regular school curriculum. Since being founded in January 1995, the program has served several thousand students in schools throughout the United States, Canada, Australia, and France. At the time of this writing, 2,900 Hewlett-Packard mathematics and science mentors were serving worldwide.

# Appendix 12-D

# USC Neighborhood Pre-College Enrichment Academy

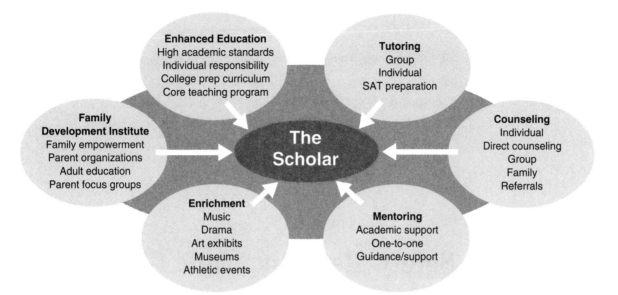

Efforts to support families with children who are troubled or gifted sometimes overlook families with children who are good learners with average school performance and no behavioral problems. The University of Southern California (USC) launched a program for the latter in 1991 as part of its Neighborhood Academic Initiative, designed to offer services mostly to children of working-class families living close to the Los Angeles campus. Each year the university selects 70 seventh graders with a C average from two nearby schools to attend its six-year Pre-College Enrichment Academy. The reward for graduating is a fully paid four-year tuition scholarship to the university.

*What parents do:*

Parents sign a contract, pledging to fulfill their responsibilities to the academy and the academic initiative; ensure that their children study at least three hours every evening; agree to notify academy staff of troubles their child has at home, at school, or in the community, including changes in behavior or attitude;

participate in 24 Saturday Family Development sessions each year to discuss such subjects as family conflict resolution, employment skills, and enhancement of cultural awareness; and attend all academy-sponsored special activities and help with at least one program each year.

*What academy scholars do:*

Students agree to maintain at least a C average and grade-level proficiency in reading, writing, and speaking English; attend at least 90 percent of their classes and arrive at school on time; have no drug, gang, or criminal involvement; and sign a contract, pledging to fulfill their Academy responsibilities and follow a scholar's Code of Ethics.

The program asks a lot from participants. The students, known as Academy Scholars, attend classes at their schools and go to USC each weekday and Saturday for more than 14 hours of additional college prep courses, tutoring, and enrichment activities. The first class of Academy Scholars is scheduled to graduate in 2001.

Adapted with permission from the University of Southern California Neighborhood Academic Initiative.

*"Many kids passing through classrooms these days are like chewed-on pencils. . . . They've been worn down, battered, chewed up by life. . . . But they're capable underneath it all, in the hands of teachers who can see past the bite marks to the strong lead inside, who don't mind getting spit on their hands, who'll keep working that sharpener again and again."*

—Sandy Banks

# Health, Safety, Resilience, and Civility: Correlates of High Academic Achievement

The physical and emotional health and general well-being of students are some of the most significant issues to be addressed in implementing standards-based education in California's middle schools. The situation facing young adolescents is described in a Carnegie Council on Adolescent Development publication as follows:

> The years of early adolescence, roughly from ages ten to fifteen, mark the end of childhood and open up new vistas of the future, of goals and options, inviting speculation about adulthood in a world that holds all of the possibilities of personal triumph and encourages dreams of glory. Early adolescence can be wondrous years, marked by significant physical, cognitive, and psychological growth that transforms social

relationships with peers, parents, other adults, and their communities.

Early adolescence can also be frightening years—a time of self-doubt, of loneliness, of fear of failure, of ambivalent relationships with peers and adults. These feelings can even raise the question of whether life is worth living.

All adolescents are at a crossroads: they face the opportunity to transform a period of high risk into one of high hopes. Fateful choices confront them. Many adolescents will choose paths toward productive and satisfying lives for themselves, their families, and communities. But others will flounder, and some will be lost altogether. If adolescents are to choose wisely, they need adult understanding and help.[1]

When students experience serious distractions in their lives resulting from poor physical health, self-doubt, fear, a sense of isolation, family disruptions, or other problems, they should not be expected to set their problems aside at the entrance to the classroom. Although

 Recommendations 8, 14, 15, 16

Sandy Banks, *Los Angeles Times* reporter

responsibility for all the personal and social ills suffered by students should not be assigned to the schools, those problems must be examined as fully as possible. And interventions within the purview of teachers, principals, and other school personnel and in close collaboration with parents must be attempted.

## Health Problems Among Adolescents

The overall health of adolescents has been declining over the past few decades. From the age of ten to the early twenties, youths frequently engage in high-risk behaviors that have serious and often life-threatening consequences. About three-quarters of the deaths among those in that age group were found to be caused by motor vehicle accidents (29 percent), murder (20 percent), suicide (12 percent), or unintentional acts, such as drowning or poisoning (11 percent), according to the Centers for Disease Control and Prevention.

Data also show that American youth have increased health risks related to the lack of healthy food choices and inactivity. Excess weight, high blood pressure, fat-rich diets, and other indicators, Stanford University researchers found, tend to be more common among African-American and Mexican-American youths than among whites and show up earlier in life. The researchers also found that the smoking rate (16 percent) for white teenage girls was four times greater than that for Mexican-American girls and eight times greater than that for African-American girls. Mexican-American youths were found more likely to be overweight and physically inactive, to be diabetic, and to have higher levels of

untreated or uncontrolled high blood pressure in comparison with their white cohorts.

The lack of sleep among America's adolescents is often a silent problem. In addition to having trouble concentrating, sleepy adolescents are more prone to increased use of stimulants, negative moods, behavior problems, and difficulty controlling emotions, all of which are critical to school success.[2]

Other data revealed that more than one-half of all Americans are overweight. If the trend continues, within a few generations virtually every adult in the United States will be overweight, experts predict. The percentage of overweight citizens has increased by about one-third in the past 20 years, and more than 25 percent of youths are overweight. Obesity increases the risk of diabetes, cancer, heart disease, and other chronic disorders. For significantly overweight persons, some studies show, the risk of premature death is increased by 60 percent.[3]

In contrast, studies have found a preoccupation with thinness among some young females. One of the first major studies on the eating habits of middle grades students found that 42 percent of females wanted to lose weight and 31 percent had dieted. Despite those data and the troubling incidence of eating disorders, however, health professionals are more concerned about the harm caused to youths from eating food high in fat, sugar, and sodium.[4]

## Medical Care, Nutrition, Exercise, and Sleep

For middle school students, who are being held accountable for significantly increased academic achievement, appropriate medical care, proper nutrition, regular exercise, and plenty of sleep are essential.

## Appropriate Medical Care

Adolescents rank among the most underserved for medical care. Although they constitute approximately 17 percent of the population, they make up only 11 percent of those seeking medical services. Further, less than 20 percent receive routine or preventive care annually, and about 15 percent lack health insurance.

A reason adolescents do not go to the doctor more often can be found in the gap that exists between pediatric medicine and adult-oriented internal medicine. Although pediatricians have the technical expertise needed to deal with the medical needs of adolescents, many are uncomfortable in coping with the psychological and social problems associated with that age group. Those problems often lie at the core of severe health problems. Adolescent medicine as a specialty is still coming of age, and more physicians need to focus on the developmental characteristics of young adolescents and develop practices that respond to their medical needs. Until that change occurs, many adolescents will not receive proper health care. The fact remains that 80 percent of adolescents still fail to receive annual preventive medical care. The current medical situation for adolescents is described as follows:

> Dr. Martin Fisher, president of the American Society for Adolescent Medicine, [states that] there are 1,000 doctors in the society, about 300 of whom have been board certified in adolescent medicine. Only 33 percent of visits to doctors [by adolescents] involved physician use of the counseling recommendations in the

> *Guidelines for Adolescent Preventive Services,* developed by the American Medical Association and backed by the American Academy of Pediatrics and the Society for Adolescent Medicine.

> Educators should encourage parents to ask their pediatrician or family doctor whether he or she is comfortable in dealing with the developmental concerns of a young adolescent. The student should also be asked whether he or she is comfortable in dealing with the pediatrician or family doctor. If the answer is negative in either case, the parents should find someone the youth can trust and should do so before a health crisis occurs.[5]

(See also Appendix 13-A, "State's Children Fare Poorly in U.S. Survey," at the end of this chapter.)

## Proper Nutrition

People tend to be affected in mind and body by the food they eat and the manner in which the body processes nutrients. Young adolescents experience greater freedom in their food choices. This growing independence is often reflected in less healthy food choices that may result in inconsistent behavior and may impact the readiness to learn. Too often meals are skipped and foods high in fat, salt, and added sugars are substituted for more nutritious foods. One nutritional consequence of such behavior is iron deficiency anemia, which can lead to shortened attention span, irritability, fatigue, and difficulty with concentration.

Many middle school students arrive at school after eating little or nothing for breakfast. And what they have eaten often does not provide enough nutrients to meet their daily needs. Explanations for this problem range from situations in which the parents of latchkey children leave for work before their children leave for school to those in which students struggle just to get up and go to school, neglecting to eat breakfast.

As noted previously, the legitimacy of the traditional school day has been called into question by researchers, given that 20 years of research into sleep patterns show that circadian rhythms change temporarily during adolescence. Consequently, young adolescents often cannot fall asleep until nearly midnight and have great difficulty in rising from sleep in the morning. Whatever the causes for not eating breakfast may be, the lack of nutrients at that time has been shown to hinder effective learning for many students.

Breakfast, the breaking of the period of fasting begun ten or 12 hours earlier, provides the first surge of fuel to the brain for the day. True, the brain does use stored-up glucose or blood sugar to operate on when we first awaken. But lacking breakfast to replenish that temporary nourishment, students and adults alike tend to become tired, irritable, and distracted. Further, 75 percent of students who skip breakfast fail to obtain their daily requirement for calcium, and one-third fall short of their requirement for protein.

(See also Appendix 13-B, "Food for Thought," at the end of this chapter.)

### Physical Activity

Physical activity should be a vital part of every student's total health program because it improves weight control, cardiovascular fitness, and strength and also produces a sense of emotional and physical well-being. Exercise and proper nutrition go hand in hand. The right balance of protein, fat, and carbohydrates is essential for supplying the fuel for a physically active lifestyle.

But young adolescents often do not realize the benefits of nutrition and exercise. Many not only fail to eat correctly but also do not participate enough in sports or other aerobic activities. Those who watch four or more hours of television a day are significantly fatter than those who watch two hours per day or less, researchers have found. Nationally, 26 percent of all youths watch television more than four hours a day. For black youths the figure is 43 percent; for Mexican-American youths, 31 percent.

Most boys engage in at least three 20-minute episodes of vigorous physical activity per week. Girls, however, do not do as well. Only 35 percent of teenage girls get the minimum recommended amount of vigorous exercise, and 20 percent get no exercise. Black and Mexican-American students exercise less than white students, perhaps because of concerns about neighborhood safety, according to some experts.[6]

The data on exercise are especially troubling because regular, moderate exercise is the key to health and longevity. Although health authorities say that students should have daily physical education classes throughout their high school years, reaching that goal is becoming increasingly hard to achieve. Where physical education classes are offered, data reveal, they often include only a restricted exercise routine for as little as ten minutes at a time. The situation is especially bad for students whose parents cannot afford the time or money needed to take the students to soccer, ballet, or other physical activities after school. For those students a strong school-based physical education program is essential.

(See also Appendix 13-C, "Experts Try to Lighten Kids' Packs," at the end of this chapter.)

## Plenty of Sleep

According to Richard L. Gelula, National Sleep Foundation's executive director, "We hear many remedies for improving the education of our teenagers, remedies that address low test scores, behavior problems, class size, and teacher quality. But we rarely hear about a vital key to every child's success in the school classroom—adequate sleep." He also notes that "sufficient sleep on a regular basis must be high on the list in discussions about criteria and standards for high quality education."[7]

The National Sleep Foundation has issued a "Wake Up Call" to address the problem of the nation's sleep-deprived adolescents. The following suggestions form part of that "Wake Up Call":

- *Establish sleep-smart schools.* School schedules and activities should be structured to accommodate adolescents' sleep needs and behaviors and circadian rhythms. Later school start times, which could result in teens being more alert and able to learn, is one approach that school systems should review.

  Principals, superintendents, and school boards should consider integrating sleep-related education in curricula so students can learn about the physiology of sleep, the consequences of sleep deprivation, and the importance of sleep to their overall health, along with nutrition and exercise.

  Teachers and other school personnel must be educated about adolescent sleep needs and patterns, taught to recognize signs of sleep-related difficulties among their students, and report such symptoms to parents and school health providers.

- *Create sleep-smart homes.* Parents/guardians must make sufficient sleep and a regular sleep schedule for their adolescents a top priority at home, which may require lifestyle changes for everyone. Adults should be on the alert for a teen's sleep problems and bring them to the attention of teachers and health professionals.

- *Encourage teens to be sleep-smart trendsetters.* Empower adolescents to be messengers and role models for a good night's sleep. They can keep a diary of their sleep experience, describe the advantages of a good night's sleep from a personal point of view, and encourage their peers to make adequate and regular sleep a priority daily activity.[8]

(See also Appendix 13-D, "Today's Kids: Overscheduled and Overtired," at the end of this chapter.)

## Recommended Practices

Although much research remains to be done on the relationship between developmental changes associated with early adolescence and their impact on learning, a great deal that is known can guide policies and practices in middle schools as follows:

- Students should be helped to understand that proper nutrition is profoundly important for young adolescents in ensuring that their body chemistry is balanced and that they will be able to engage effectively in complex learning tasks.

- Adolescents need 60 minutes of physical activity daily. Students should be helped to understand that this level of physical activity should become a lifelong goal unless restricted on the advice of a physician.
- All young adolescents should receive age-appropriate instruction in nutrition.
- All young adolescents should eat a healthy breakfast to ensure mental alertness and healthy emotional responses to normal stress. When appropriate, schools should provide guidance to students and parents as to which breakfasts contain adequate servings of grains, a dairy product, and some kind of fresh fruit. Parents have a fundamental obligation to ensure that their children eat a balanced, nutritious breakfast.
- In the cafeteria and throughout the campus, schools should offer such healthful food choices as fruits, vegetables, and whole grains.
- School personnel should regularly emphasize to students the importance of making healthful food choices for breakfast, lunch, dinner, and snacks.
- Both obesity and eating disorders such as anorexia and bulimia are serious medical issues that may become life threatening. Students affected by weight gain or loss outside the range of normal for their height should be referred for appropriate professional counseling in consultation with their parents.
- Young adolescents, their parents, and the education community need to be aware of the relationship of sleep to academic performance and social behavior. Studies have established that adolescents need from $8^1/_2$ to $9^1/_4$ hours of sleep every night.

## Safe, Violence-Free Middle Schools

Tragedies involving violence in middle schools and high schools that occur periodically create great anxiety among students, parents, educators, and the general public. Simplistic explanations for such violence do not provide guidance to administrators, teachers, counselors, and parents trying to prevent such behavior. However, although no single explanation for the violent acts is apparent, a good deal is known about the warning signs that must be attended to if troubled students are to receive timely help.

The authors of *Early Warning, Timely Response: A Guide to Safe Schools* hold that well-functioning schools foster learning, safety, and socially appropriate behaviors. They have a strong academic focus and support students in achieving high standards, foster productive relationships between school staff and students, and promote meaningful parental and community involvement. Most prevention programs in well-functioning schools address many factors and recognize that safety and order affect the healthy social, emotional, and intellectual development of all students. Those perceptions have special significance when the challenges posed by middle school students are being addressed.[9]

(See also Appendix 13-E, "Creating Healthy Environments for Youth," and Appendix 13-F, "Early Warning Signs of Violent Behavior by Students," at the end of this chapter.)

# Recommendations for Safe Schools

Prevention, intervention, and crisis-response strategies work best in schools and communities that adhere to the following recommendations:

## Emphasize Academic Achievement

Safe schools believe that all students can achieve academically and behave appropriately while they continue to value individual differences. Adequate resources and a variety of programs and experiences help to ensure that the high expectations are met. Responsibility and accountability for using resources and participating in preventive programs are based on agreements involving students, school personnel, and parents.

## Involve Families Meaningfully

When families are involved positively in their children's education, the children are less likely to become involved in antisocial behavior. Many parents report a distancing between themselves and their children during early adolescence. Safe schools seek ways to promote frequent communication between teachers and parents, preferably face-to-face and with the involvement of the student. Every classroom should have a telephone and a printout of the home telephone numbers of students. Increasingly, schools are encouraging home visits by teachers in accordance with the provisions of the teachers' contract with the school district.

(See also Appendix 13-G, "The Role of Parents in Helping to Create Safe, Violent-Free Middle Schools," at the end of this chapter.)

## Develop Links to the Community

Safe, academically successful schools uniformly report close ties with families, social services providers, law-enforcement agencies, the faith-based community, and other organizations and institutions that list students' well-being among their goals. Many valuable resources can help students feel that they are valued and will be supported whenever personal emergencies or family crises occur. When community links are weak, the risk of school violence increases, and opportunities to serve students at risk of violent behavior decrease.

## Emphasize Positive Relationships

A positive relationship between a student and an adult who can provide needed support is one of the most critical factors preventing student violence. Students often look to their teachers and parents or to other adults in the community for guidance. Because many middle school students experience a wide range of emotions linked to rapid physiological changes, including temporary hormonal imbalances, their rapid mood swings can create fear, panic, isolation, and depression or even feelings of invincibility, leading to high-risk behaviors. Safe middle schools ensure that all students have quality access to trusted adults. Special training is a valuable but not necessary condition for adults who listen well, know how to encourage, and obtain professional help promptly when indicated.

## Discuss Safety Issues Openly

Students bring many different ideas to school about matters of life and death. They are bombarded with images of violence seen in video games and on television news programs, where guns are commonly observed being used for legitimate and illegitimate purposes. Whether encountered in movies, on television, on the Internet, or in the print media, good and evil blend together. Adults' perceptions of students' abilities to separate good and evil may often be inaccurate. Because young adolescents are powerfully motivated by peer pressures, the culture of some peer groups may conflict with the values taught in the home and at school. The risk of adolescent violence can be reduced by the schools if a strong, sustained effort is made to teach students about the dangers involved in using firearms and about strategies for coping with their emotions.

## Stress Responsibility and Accountability

Emphasis should be placed on responsibility and accountability for one's actions. Explaining away violent behavior by an individual because of external events or the actions of others is inexcusable. Although other persons or events may create the conditions for a violent response, most individuals can choose right from wrong. Parents should be made aware of efforts by the school to equip students with the knowledge and skills needed to work through their emotions, acknowledge their ability to choose good over evil, and recognize the terrible consequences that can result from aggressive actions. Parents should be urged to reinforce the school's efforts in this matter.

## Treat All Students with Respect

A major source of conflict in many schools is perceived or actual bias and unfair treatment of students by peers or staff members because of, for example, the ethnicity, gender, race,

social class, religion, disability, nationality, primary language, sexual orientation, or physical appearance of the students. Students who have been treated unfairly may be subjected to further harassment and may become targets of violence. In other cases victims of unfair or violent acts have themselves become aggressors. The circle of violent, aggressive behavior can then rapidly expand to involve others, including gang members.

If schools are to curb violent and aggressive acts effectively, they must find ways to communicate to students, parents, and the larger community that all students are valued and that unfair treatment of any student will not be tolerated. That process involves more than words and printed pronouncements. Ways must be found to forge caring relationships. Further, teachers and principals must seek to identify students who seem alienated and provide support for them.

## Create Ways to Report Trouble

Peers and siblings are often the most likely to know about potential school violence in advance. Therefore, programs to prevent violence must create ways for students to report with safety any troubling behavior on the part of friends or siblings. Unfortunately, adolescents frequently observe a mistaken "code of honor" based in part on their childhood experiences with tattling. Because tattling is seen as infantile behavior, the opposite extreme is folded into the norms of the peer culture. Even the most responsible students participate in denial and cover-up, even in the face of potentially disastrous events. Coping with the code of honor represents one of the most difficult challenges to those seeking to prevent school violence. Even adults often waffle when faced with moral and ethical dilemmas related to illegal or potentially harmful information in their possession. No easy solutions are available to solve this problem. Talking with students in the class-room, with advisory groups, and with others in different forums can help expose the fallacy of defending honor at the expense of the lives of innocent victims. *(Note: Students who report information about potential violence must be protected. Anonymity in reporting critical information should be guaranteed, given its wide acceptance in adult society.)*

Schools must support strong risk-trust relationships among teachers and students before the students can be expected to provide information that will expose them to legitimate fears of retaliation. Students should be helped to reflect on the possibility of saving lives and having an adult life free of guilt because they responded to a higher code of honor when a matter of life and death was involved. Although the issues are among the hardest to deal with, they should not be ignored.

### Help Students Express Their Feelings Safely

Students need help in expressing their emotions, needs, fears, and other anxieties in nonthreatening ways. When they have access to caring adults with whom they can share their feelings, they are less likely to act out. Some of the most profound emotions, including those involving suicidal tendencies, are experienced by abused or neglected children. California schools, which are legally obliged to report such situations, should have an established system for prompt referrals. The needs of

abused and neglected students are complex. Although community agencies can sometimes provide safe havens, such students may still bring with them to school deep, disabling emotions. Caring teachers and counselors are vital in helping these students.

### Offer Extended-Day and Summer/Intersession Programs

School-based before- and after-school programs can help reduce violent behavior. Programs need to be well organized, adequately funded, properly supervised, and appropriately staffed. They should provide a range of options, including centers featuring organized games and other types of sports, homework support, literacy development, and service-learning experiences. Vacations and intersessions should provide similar opportunities.

Generally, elementary school students have many opportunities to participate in activities involving youth groups, and high school students can work part time. But in many communities such opportunities are few. Consequently, school-based before- and after-school programs are appropriate for students in kindergarten through grade twelve. Participation in such programs generally requires parental consent and some kind of payment. Schools must work closely with parents and the community to encourage student participation and should obtain the resources needed to guarantee that no student will be denied access to the program for economic reasons. (See Chapter 12.)

## Promote Good Citizenship and Character Development

Schools have been given significant responsibility for helping students become good citizens. They are at the forefront of communicating the civic values enshrined in the U.S. Constitution, including the Bill of Rights. Those values include freedom of religion, speech, and press; equal protection; nondiscrimination; and fairness and due process under the law. Schools also promote shared social values, such as responsibility, honesty, kindness, and respect for others.

A renewed commitment to those aspects of the school's mission is needed at a time when many influences work against the positive values that students are expected to internalize. Recognizing that parents are the primary moral educators of their children, the schools must work in partnership with them. In turn, parents must understand that schools are facing as never before the stark realities of a violent society. Although violent crimes have not occurred in most middle schools, crimes against persons have been reported as being substantially higher among young adolescents in middle schools than among students in elementary schools or high schools. The report, provided by the California Safe Schools Assessment, is accompanied by a firm reminder that:

> Such facts [must] be used to educate the public and the media and to implement programs for students about anger management and conflict resolution. The finding that crimes against persons occur most often at the middle/junior high school level confirms research that prevention efforts to curb such behavior must begin in the early elementary school grades.[10]

## Identify Problems; Assess Progress

Schools successful in preventing violent behavior are those that examine carefully situations that appear to be potentially dangerous, including those in which members of the larger school community feel threatened. Safe schools continually monitor situations within the school building and on school grounds that present actual or potential problems as well as situations faced by students as they come to school or leave for home. Direct observation and formal data gathering can provide an effective school and community profile of gang behavior, student harassment, drug trafficking, and other threats. The information is often gathered in cooperation with local law-enforcement agencies.

Information on activities that threaten harm to students should be shared with students, their parents, and the community. Safe schools continually work to eliminate circumstances likely to result in violent crimes. Actions may range from changing the school environment (e.g., improving lighting, using concealed cameras) to using hall and grounds monitors, obtaining assistance from law-enforcement agencies, and having offenders prosecuted. Parents and the community share responsibility with the school in guaranteeing the safety of all students at all times before, during, and after school.

## Risk, Resilience, and Academic Achievement

Despite their personal vulnerability during a time of rapid development, middle school students potentially have an amazing amount of *emotional resilience,* the ability to adjust to change and even misfortune. However, this predisposition to adjust to one's circumstances successfully will be realized for many students only when they receive significant support from caring adults.

Most students can transform their lives, no matter how strained their circumstances, if they receive needed help. For example, researchers have examined the lives of students growing up in extremely high-risk environments, such as in poverty-stricken or war-torn communities, and in families in which alcoholism, drug abuse, physical and sexual abuse, and mental illness have been present. Remarkably, close to 70 percent of the affected children grew up to be successful according to social indicators and were "confident, competent, and caring." The more that is learned about resilience, the higher is the probability that the percentage can be increased. Every student possesses the seeds of innate resilience.

Being resilient includes the ability to build positive relationships with others, engage in successful problem solving, develop a sense of personal identity and autonomy, and plan for the future. Those capacities emphasize developing personal assets rather than focusing on fixing what is broken. Although many students may suffer from severe physical and emotional disabilities requiring professional interventions, the vast majority will survive the middle years with higher levels of personal resilience and positive academic achievement. In achieving those goals, students once again depend on the critical help of caring adults.

Teachers and mentors can, often unconsciously, tip the scale from risk to resilience, providing and modeling factors that buffer risk and enable positive emotional development to occur. In doing so, they provide for the most basic psychological needs of youth: safety, love and belonging, respect, power, accomplishment and learning, and, ultimately, personal meaning.

The three areas of adult influence that help to determine whether students move toward or away from resilience are the following:

1. Teachers and parents can convey loving support by listening to young adolescents, validating their feelings, and demonstrating kindness, compassion, and respect.
2. When teachers and parents have high expectations for youths, they encourage students to excel beyond the limits they may have set for themselves.
3. Teachers and parents who tip the scales from risk to resilience let students express their opinions and creativity, choose, solve problems, work with others, and return their gifts to the community in a physically and psychologically safe, structured environment.

Shifting from risk to resilience occurs not in programs as such but at the deeper level of relationships, beliefs, and expectations. However, certain kinds of programmatic approaches can provide the context within which emotional resilience can be fostered, including the following:

- *Teacher support.* Just as teachers can create a nurturing classroom environment, administrators can create a school environment that supports *teacher resilience.* They can promote caring relationships among colleagues; demonstrate positive beliefs about the ability of effective teaching to make a significant difference in the lives of students; set high expectations for professional performance and student achievement; set the stage for enduring relationships of trust by being a person with whom teachers can build a strong risk-trust relationship; and provide continuing opportunities for collegial reflection, dialogue, and shared decision making.

- *Professional development.* Teachers can reflect on their personal convictions about resilience and, as a staff, describe experiences about overcoming the odds. They can read and discuss the research on resilience, including reports of successful schools in difficult settings. The accumulated research on resilience represents one of the most important factors behind the assumption that all students can succeed in a rigorous, standards-based curriculum.

- *Student strengths.* Frequent efforts should be made to communicate with students about their ability to overcome obstacles and reach goals thought to be beyond their capacity. Many young adolescents, even the most emotionally healthy and academically successful, have serious self-doubts about being intelligent enough to meet the high expectations. Many others walk a tightrope between success and failure because they have heard more about what they cannot do than about what they might be able to achieve.[11]

## Focusing on Youth Assets Rather Than Deficits

Although identifying youth deficits and the warnings they signal are important, an equally compelling need exists for schools to focus on youth assets and their contributions to being emotionally healthy and academically successful.

Over the past two decades, the Search Institute in Minneapolis has conducted research using national samples of more than 450,000 adolescents in grades six through twelve. This research has discovered that the presence or absence of *developmental assets* in a young person's life is highly predictive of whether the student engages or does not engage in high-risk behavior. These investigations have shown that the more developmental assets (see Figure 13-1) that are identified as present in a young person's living situation, the less likely it is that the young person will become involved with high-risk behaviors (such as using illicit drugs, becoming depressed or suicidal, committing violent acts, or becoming affiliated with a gang).

Researchers have organized *developmental assets* under two major headings, *external assets* and *internal assets. External assets* are divided into *support assets, boundaries assets,* and *structured use of time assets.* Using *support assets,* students draw on the strengths of parents, teachers, and other significant adults to experience caring relationships, mature guidance, open communication, and a safe environment in the home and at school. *Boundaries assets* help students learn and internalize standards for appropriate conduct, experience consequences when the standards are broken, recognize the rights of parents to know of their whereabouts and with whom they will be, and give and receive strength from friends who share positive values. *Structured use of time assets* are reflected in

*Asset type and name*

*Asset definition*

**External assets**

**Support**

1. Family support — **Family** life provides high levels of love and support.
2. Parents as social resources — **Student** views parents as accessible resources for advice and support.
3. Parental communication — **Student** has frequent in-depth conversations with parents.
4. Other adult resources — **Student** has access to nonparent adults for advice and support.
5. Other adult communications — **Student** has frequent in-depth conversations with nonparent adults.
6. Parental involvement in schooling — **Parents** are involved in helping student succeed in school.
7. Positive school climate — **School** provides a caring, encouraging environment.

**Boundaries**

8. Parental standards — **Parents** have standards for appropriate conduct.
9. Parental discipline — **Parents** discipline students when a rule is violated.
10. Parental monitoring — **Parents** monitor "where I am going and with whom I will be."
11. Time at home — **Student** goes out for recreation three or fewer nights per week.
12. Positive peer influence — **Student's** best friends model responsible behavior.

**Structured use of time**

13. Involved in music — **Student** spends three hours or more per week in music training or practice.
14. Involved in extracurricular activities at school — **Student** spends one hour or more per week participating in school sports, clubs, or organizations.
15. Involved in community organizations — **Student** spends one hour or more per week participating in organizations or activities or clubs outside school.
16. Involved in house of faith — **Student** spends one hour or more per week attending programs or services.

**Internal assets**

**Educational commitment**

17. Achievement motivation — **Student** is motivated to do well in school.
18. Educational aspiration — **Student** aspires to pursue post-high school education.
19. School performance — **Student** reports school performance is above average.
20. Homework — **Student** reports six hours or more of homework per week.

**Positive values**

21. Values helping people — **Student** places high personal value on helping other people.
22. Is concerned about world hunger — **Student** reports interest in helping reduce world hunger.
23. Cares about people's feelings — **Student** cares about other people's feelings.
24. Values sexual restraint — **Student** values postponing sexual activity.

**Social competence**

25. Assertiveness skills — **Student** can stand up for what he or she believes.
26. Decision-making skills — **Student** is good at making decisions.
27. Friendship-making skills — **Student** is good at making friends.
28. Planning skills — **Student** is good at planning ahead.
29. Self-esteem — **Student** has high self-esteem.
30. Positive view of personal future — **Student** is optimistic about her or his future.

**The Protective Consequences of Developmental Assets: Grades 6–12**

These assets are *negatively correlated* with high-risk behaviors, including use of alcohol, tobacco, and illegal drugs; promiscuity; depression and suicide; antisocial behavior, including violence; school failure; and vehicular recklessness. *The fewer the number of developmental assets in a student's life, the greater is the risk in every category of high-risk behavior.* For example, students with zero to ten assets had a 51 percent chance of committing violent behavior and a 42 percent chance of depression and/or attempted suicide. On the other hand, students with 26 to 30 assets had only a 6 percent chance of committing violent behavior and a 1 percent chance of failing in school. *Researchers propose a national goal of at least 21 or more of the 30 developmental assets for every youth.*

participation in hobbies, sports, community organizations and activities, and houses of faith.

*Internal assets* enable students to call on their inner strengths. Under that heading are *educational commitment assets,* involving motivation, aspiration, achievement, and a serious commitment to success in school. *Positive values assets* focus on helping others, reducing world hunger, showing concern for the feelings of others, and postponing sexual activity. *Social competence assets* emphasize the development of inner knowledge and strength needed to stand up for what one believes, make good decisions, develop positive friendships, plan, achieve a positive self-concept, and develop an optimistic perception about the future.[12]

## Civility, Ethical Behavior, and Social Consciousness

In less-advanced cultures of the non-Western world, community elders take their young adolescents aside for ceremonial rites of passage and initiate them into their roles as adults. In Western industrialized nations, that passage is much less straightforward and poses dramatic challenges. Concerns about the behavior of young adolescents in middle schools are frequently heard from parents and the community.

Williamson and Johnston, reporting on their study of four diverse communities, found, among other important responses, significant parental anxiety about the lack of kindness and politeness among middle school students. Many parents responded that middle schools tolerate "too much rudeness and incivility . . . and [that] appropriate standards of behavior are neither modeled nor monitored." Embedded in many of the parents' remarks was "a pervasive concern that middle level schools 'were out of control.' " What many middle grades educators see as normal early adolescent behavior is seen by some parents as chaotic and even dangerous.[13]

Middle-level teachers and principals should collaborate directly and frequently with parents to develop standards for student conduct. The standards should provide sufficient guidance to reassure the community that middle schools care about behavioral issues yet allow enough flexibility so that each school can respond to the unique aspects of its own students. Adults should be visible during passing times, lunch periods, and other times of the day when students are moving about. And the behavior should be monitored, not just observed. Students should become involved in setting the behavioral tone of their school and should be more active in creating an environment in which civility is the norm.

(See also Appendix 13-H, "Civility, Ethical Behavior, and Social Consciousness: Needs and Commitments for Students, Parents, and Teachers," at the end of this chapter.)

# Health, Safety, Resilience, and Civility

- **The relationship between a healthy body and a healthy mind is well documented.** Yet the issue is rarely addressed except on testing days. Many young adolescents still come to school without breakfast only to see vending machines loaded with soda and candy. Yet they are overly concerned with their body image. Teachers complain that students are too tired or hyperactive to learn effectively. Size up your school's approach to student nutrition as to what is known about proper diet, emotional balance, and mental acuity. What messages are being sent to students? Are they consistent? What food choices are being offered? Are sodas, sweetened beverages, or high-fat snacks offered in the vending machines? What dining facilities are available? How much time do students have to purchase and eat their meals? Are the students involved in deciding which foods and beverages are offered? What do you think should be done to improve the situation? Work with a few colleagues who share your concerns. Present your recommendations for change at a faculty meeting.

- **Data from the annual California Healthy Kids Survey has consistently shown that middle grades students watch many hours of television, eat many high-fat snack foods, and participate in very little exercise.** As your school assesses the health, nutrition, and exercise needs of its students, what has it discovered? Are a significant number of your school's students living a "couch potato" lifestyle? What can your school do to encourage a healthier lifestyle for its students? Are there ways that students can be encouraged to develop a regular program of vigorous physical exercise? Are there ways in which your school can help students to monitor their own nutrition and exercise—to set goals for themselves and to do what needs to be done to meet those goals? How can your school increase the health and fitness of its staff while doing the same for all students?

- **Sleep can be an important element in ensuring students' health and intellectual development.** Unfortunately, many middle school students either get an inadequate amount of sleep or sleep in a room with lots of other stimulation, such as television sets, computers, stereos, and video games. As a result, some adolescents are at risk of sleep deprivation. Sometimes this situation occurs because of inadequate parental supervision. What can your school do to help all its students to get the sleep that they need for their physical and intellectual growth? How can you help students and their parents to monitor the situations in which students sleep? What can your school do to ensure that all students come to their classes well rested and with a full reservoir of energy? How can we help our students and their families come to value the role that sleep plays in assisting students to reach their maximum potential?

## Health, Safety, Resilience, and Civility (Continued)

- **The implications of research on the importance of building youth assets as a deterrent to high-risk behavior is almost overwhelming.** Has your school examined the research? Have youth-asset inventories been done to identify students who may need help? What additional actions might be taken? Share your thoughts with your colleagues. Present your recommendations to your principal.

- **Does your school have a district-developed, comprehensive violence prevention and response plan?** Such a plan should address identifying warning signs, responding to imminent danger, and providing for prevention and intervention strategies developed together with appropriate community services and agencies. If a plan exists, suggest a staff review to ensure that everyone understands it, is effectively implementing it, and can make recommendations to strengthen its provisions. If no plan exists, take aggressive action through proper channels to have a plan developed.

- **Although middle schools generally have a positive climate, concerns about civility and related issues are well founded.** Review Appendix 13-H, "Civility, Ethical Behavior, and Social Consciousness: Needs and Commitments for Students, Parents, and Teachers," at the end of this chapter and discuss it with colleagues, students, and parents. Explore ways in which you might improve student behavior. Involve parents in your efforts.

- **Is your school a healthy place in which to work for many hours each day?** Are there qualitative issues that trouble you? If so, bring them to the attention of your principal.

# State's Children Fare Poorly in U.S. Survey

by Melissa Healy

This report is the first, most comprehensive of a series of private efforts to gauge the effects of welfare reform on families across the nation. Adults and children in 44,461 households were interviewed.

California's children, especially youths from low-income families, are more likely to be in poor health, have no usual source of health care, and live in families where parents worry about putting food on the table than are those in other states, according to the first survey of families' well-being conducted by the Urban Institute.

Researchers found that in the 13 states they studied, the financial, physical, and emotional health of families varied enormously. On the first two measures, financial and physical, California came in below average.

On the third measure, psychological well-being, researchers found that Californians, both wealthy and poor, were in line with their counterparts elsewhere. Ten percent of the state's children were found to be living with parents who felt "highly aggravated" about their children. About 28 percent of California's children from low-income families were living with parents who appeared to be in "poor mental health"—a percentage just above the national average. Low-income parents in California reported "behavioral and emotional problems" in 5.7 percent of their children six to eleven years of age and 7.8 percent of their children twelve to seventeen years of age.

From the *Los Angeles Times,* January 26, 1999.

# Appendix 13-B

# Food for Thought

## by Barbara K. Given

It could be said that learning begins in the stomach. When voters demand a return to the basics, they refer to reading, writing, and mathematics. From a neurobiological perspective, however, getting back to the basics pertains to the fundamental building blocks of the brain and body, and those building blocks begin with nutrition and its relationship to emotions and learning.

### Our Chemical Brains

Knowing how the brain functions can make a tremendous difference in how teachers address the emotional, social, cognitive, and physical learning of their students. . . . Helping young people establish healthful lifetime eating habits is particularly critical because chemicals primarily produced from substances consumed affect brain development and functioning. If parents and teachers ignore these realities and attend only to the basic facts of cognitive learning, students will fail to achieve intended academic results.

### Chemical Messengers

Chemicals released as responses to stress and food are of great concern to educators because both can effectively prevent higher-order thinking. During the evolutionary process stress hormones developed as a rapid response to danger; thus they are strong enough to overpower other chemicals associated with well-being, pleasure, and happiness. . . .

For example, researchers now know that sensory input travels to the brain's relay station called the thalmus and that the thalmus passes the messages in two directions. One goes to a cluster of cell bodies in each hemisphere called the amygdala; the second goes to the thinking neocortex. . . . If the amygdala's fast signals alert for self-protection, muscles tighten for fight or flight, and stress hormones (cortisol, epinephrine, and norepinephrine) increase blood flows to the muscles. Then the muscles release stored nutrition for rapid conversion to glucose, added energy, and strength.

Chronic stress causes the brain and body to deplete available nutrients, leaving nothing available for learning. Further chronic stress inhibits the growth of message receptors (dendrites) on brain cells and limits interconnections among neurons. This results in slow thinking, depressed learning, and even mental retardation. . . . Similarly, ingested proteins and carbohydrates undergo lengthy processes that convert them from food to brain and body chemicals. Certain foods produce high energy, whereas other foods create a calm demeanor.

### You Think What You Eat

The immune system, the endocrine system, and the brain contain many of the same types of chemicals and chemical receptors. . . . Thus it makes sense that when youngsters have nutritious foods available while studying, they eat as needed and consequently earn statistically higher test scores, demonstrate more positive attitudes toward school, and increase their reading speed and accuracy. . . .

Because many students need to snack, chew, drink, or bite while concentrating, nutritional intake at school is worth exploring, especially if students are hyperactive, sluggish, underachieving, apathetic, or irritable. . . .

From *Educational Leadership*, Vol. 56 (November 1998). Reprinted with permission from the Association for Supervision and Curriculum Development.

Concentration and learning are more than a result of eating; they are the results of particular kinds of food intake.

### Aspartame Can Be Less Than Sweet

Students usually think of eating as an enjoyable experience. However, because chemicals from foods create different reactions, this pleasant event can result in lethargy, panic, inattentiveness, or depression. This is true even though individuals may fail to associate what they eat with how they feel.

Aspartame (low-calorie sweetener) affects children in different ways on the basis of factors not yet clearly understood. But the chemistry of aspartame provides some clues. It is composed of methanol, aspartic acid, and phenylalanine. . . . Methanol (wood alcohol) is a toxic substance at extremely low doses that breaks down into formaldehyde. . . . Methanol can paralyze the optic nerve and cause blindness in low doses and death in larger amounts. . . . Thirteen piloting journals and military magazines warn pilots against the use of artificial sweeteners. Readers are urged to investigate the debate about aspartame on the Internet.

### The Critical Role of Protein

As a natural function of the stomach, enzymes act on protein foods, such as beans, grains, seeds, nuts, and animal products, to trigger the release of 21 different amino acids, including tyrosine. . . . Tyrosine travels through the bloodstream to the brain, where it [eventually] becomes . . . dopamine. . . . Dopamine produces . . . a general feeling of alertness, attentiveness, quick thinking, rapid reactions, motivation, and mental energy. . . .

Protein [also] holds water in the blood, and an insufficient protein supply causes fluids from inside the cells to seep out, causing sluggishness, limited concentration, stomach bloating, and the loss of essential salts and nutrients. . . . Unfortunately, adults seldom associate these negative conditions in students with protein deficiency. . . .

Fear of failure, isolation, and other mild to severe psychological or physical traumas convert dopamine-produced alertness to norepinephrine-controlled agitation and aggression in a matter of seconds. When inadequately nourished, students have great difficulty [in] tolerating frustration and stress because they have no protein stores to draw on. Instead, they exhibit apathy, nonresponsiveness, inactivity, and irritability. When that happens, their attempts to learn are sabotaged.

### Breakfast and Snacks

Students who eat a nutritious breakfast make fewer errors throughout the morning than those who skip breakfast. Those who skip breakfast tend to eat heartily at lunch and then feel sluggish during the afternoon.

Although the availability of appropriate foods could have a positive impact on student learning and behavior, schools rarely provide snacks or encourage parents to do so. Without question many students could profit from having access to healthful snacks throughout the school day, or at least at midmorning.

Students, parents, and teachers could use a checklist to monitor their emotional and behavioral reactions to food. This self-monitoring is one way to help students understand the relationship between food and learning. Clearly, students require a breakfast with high levels of protein for alertness and a balanced diet which includes complex carbohydrates throughout the day.

## Making Nutrition a School Issue

Although drastic changes in children's behaviors are often blamed on violent television programming and lack of parental guidance, nutrition is rarely mentioned.

There are no single answers to why children behave—or at least appear to behave—more negatively than in years past. One thing is certain: The challenges are to investigate numerous factors that influence brain development and to incorporate emerging knowledge about these relationships into schooling practices.

School administrators must do their part to ensure the availability of nutritious foods in the lunchroom, the vending machines, and the classrooms. If administrators ignore this responsibility, teachers may as well be whistling in the wind because students' eating habits are caught more than taught. Teaching students about foods and their relationships to behavior and achievement is important, but action by parents, school boards, administrators, and politicians is equally critical.

# Appendix 13-C

# Experts Try to Lighten Kids' Packs

Concerned about students carrying unhealthy amounts of weight in their book bags, some health care professionals are launching a campaign to get kids to lighten up. The trend of students carrying too much stuff in their backpacks is evident on any campus, according to chiropractors, physicians, and school administrators.

With more books, after-school activities, and less time between classes to go to lockers (some schools have eliminated lockers for security reasons), kids carry not just school supplies but also items ranging from gym clothes to cell phones. The result is increasing numbers of kids with head, neck, shoulder, and back pain.

"Backpacks have become self-contained life-support systems for adolescents," according to Howard King, a pediatric spine physician who is a clinical associate professor in orthopedics at the University of Washington Medical Center. "The guys who climb Mount Rainier and Mount Everest don't have as much weight on their shoulders, even with 45-pound packs, as these kids," King said, noting that climbers use packs with waist straps designed to transfer weight to their pelvises.

Chiropractic specialists hope to persuade students and their parents that backpacks should not weigh more than 15 percent of a student's body weight. These specialists add that common sense should tell us that a heavy load, distributed improperly or unevenly, day after day is indeed going to cause stress to a growing spinal column.

Doctors are seeing more patients at a younger age suffering from back pain, not from accident or other injury but from the stress of carrying backpacks that are too heavy or that are improperly loaded or worn. As one specialist put it: "As the twig is bent, so grows the tree!"

From *The Oregonian,* April 12, 1999.

Appendix 13-D

# Junior Zombies
## Today's Kids: Overscheduled and Overtired

by Katy Kelly

Most nights, Jennifer McCandless, 13, goes to bed at 9:30. Few teens would dream of sacking out so early; it's an hour when many settle down to do homework, call friends, or surf the Web. But McCandless is making an informed trade-off. If she stays up late, says the Portsmouth, R.I., eighth-grader, "I'm like a zombie, awake but not doing anything."

That describes too many of her peers, say researchers and doctors. From elementary through high school, kids need nine to 11 hours a night, say experts. But according to a recent report from the National Sleep Foundation, only 15 percent of adolescents say they sleep 8½ or more hours on school nights. A quarter usually sleep 6½ hours or less. Younger kids are skimping as well, says Will Wilkoff, a pediatrician in Brunswick, Maine, and author of *Is My Child Overtired?* "About 80 percent of my practice is not getting enough sleep."

**28/7?** He says the number of overtired patients has soared in the 25 years he has been in practice, as families try "to squeeze 28 hours of living into 24." Working parents, eager to spend time with their kids, let bedtimes slide. Homework and after-school activities rev kids up just as they should be winding down. Older kids may be coping with jobs and college applications.

All this juggling takes a toll. Tired students don't learn well. Car accidents are more likely for inexperienced teen drivers. Too little sleep can contribute to depression. Wilkoff even suspects that "some children who are labeled ADD or hyperactive are actually [acting] that way because they are tired."

Sleep-starved kids are likely to go deepest into sleep debt when they hit the teen years, says Mary Carskadon of Brown University School of Medicine, who studies the sleep patterns of adolescents (Jennifer McCandless was one of her subjects). She found that body clocks reset themselves around puberty, making the natural sleep time about an hour later. "We think there is a change in the sensitivity to light signals," she says. Watching TV or reading can keep a teen awake. "The book may not be stimulating, but the light sends a message to the brain," says Carskadon.

When a 10-year-old accustomed to bedding down at 9:30 p.m. becomes a 13-year-old who can't fall asleep until 10:30 p.m., the lost hour can be overwhelming, particularly if school starts at 7 a.m. "Teenagers should feel wide awake, energetic, and motivated," says William C. Dement, head of the Sleep Disorders Center at Stanford University. Lack of sleep ensures that few do.

Sleep research shows most teens can manage pretty well with 8½ hours a night during the week if they catch up on weekends, but younger kids should get the full nine to 11 hours. "Make those tough decisions and say, 'Jeepers, we're going to have to give up one or two of these activities,'" says Wilkoff. If a parent's work schedule means late dinners, feed young children earlier and "make breakfast the family meal."

School districts in a handful of states have shifted their schedules to give teens an extra hour or so of sleep. Hoping to make the trend national, Rep. Zoe Lofgren, a California Democrat, has introduced a bill that would help high schools with switchover costs. Lofgren was inspired by experience. Her daughter Sheila was 15 when she started wanting to sleep in. "It was like flipping a switch. All of a sudden, she couldn't get up," Lofgren says.

# Appendix 13-E

# Creating Healthy Environments for Youth

*The following are excerpts from an interview with William Damon, Professor of Education and Director of the Stanford Center on Adolescence; and Robert Roeser, Assistant Professor of Education, whose research includes studies of the mental health of children and adolescents.*

*Do the media reports of school tragedies give us any greater insight into either the causes of or solutions to this problem?*

> *Roeser:* First, we want to say that we are very sorry about these tragedies, the loss of innocent life, the pain felt by all those involved, and the wasted potential of young lives that were lost.
>
> *Damon:* The media often ask the wrong questions, such as "What went wrong with this particular kid?" or "What did this school or that parent not do?" These situations are complex, and to understand them requires much more knowledge of the situation, knowledge developed from a long-standing relationship with the student and his family."
>
> *Roeser:* I agree. The media often seem to focus on and blame the adolescent instead of considering the broader circumstances that contribute to violence among youth.

*Is violence among youth a serious problem in the U.S. today, or has its importance been exaggerated?*

> *Damon:* There's no question that it's serious. . . . Violence among youth has always occurred, though there has been a gradual increase in recent years.
>
> *Roeser:* We also know that the problem has different parameters today, one of which is the wide availability of handguns. This makes acts of violence among youth potentially lethal, as we've seen. In general . . . there is a high rate of assault and death among fourteen- to twenty-four-year-olds, especially in the inner city. One reason why recent incidents received so much attention may have been because they hap-

pened outside the cities in places where many Americans didn't expect them to.

*How does the approach that educators take on this issue differ from that of other experts?*

> *Damon:* There's definitely a different world view between people who respond only after something has happened and those who anticipate potential problems before they occur. . . . The educational approach focuses more on prevention. It asks, "What can we do to maximize the potential of this youthful population we're dealing with?" It seeks ways to engage youth . . . and to [give] hope for the future.
>
> *Roeser:* We could say we are oriented toward the *promotion* of health and well-being. The hope is that this approach will lead to less of a need for intervention or prevention.

*Are there certain behaviors that could be considered "warning signs" that a young person is having difficulty coping? What should parents and teachers look for?*

> *Roeser:* A lot of the kids who committed these horrible acts had given warning signs to their friends, such as telling them explicitly that they were contemplating such acts. Such verbal warning signs should be taken seriously by peers, teachers, and parents. If we want to promote the well-being of adolescents so such tragedies don't occur, it is important that adolescents spend quality time with adults as well as with friends their own age. All adolescents, and especially those with difficulties, need to have caring adults in their lives who can listen and provide guidance. . . . The question is not merely what are the warning signs of

From an article in the *Stanford Educator* (Fall 1998), by Robert Hass. Used with permission.

problems among youth, but are there any adults out there watching for them?

*Damon:* Let me add one thing. A teenager without interests that are constructive is at risk! If a student has nothing that he or she cares about apart from antisocial or self-destructive activities, that's the first thing I would look for.

*I doubt many parents would recognize a lack of interests as a serious warning sign.*

*Damon:* That's exactly why I'm saying this. The first job of a teacher and parent should be to get to know the young adolescent in a personal way and to cultivate something that she or he feels is worth getting out of bed for each morning.

*How do people find time to do this?*

*Damon:* This is an especially appropriate question in this modern era. I have my own solution to the problem, a community-level solution I call the "youth charter." It says that everyone is responsible for every kid in the community. What communities can do is to create a network of adults and institutions that take responsibility for all their kids. In practical terms it means that people need to get together with their neighbors, the police, teachers and principals, religious leaders, librarians, community workers, and so on and create forums where they communicate about the kids to make sure no kid falls between the cracks.

*Considering how little interaction occurs within communities today, how feasible is the youth charter concept? And why would anyone bother to watch out for anyone else's kid?*

*Damon:* You're correct that communities are very disorganized in this country. But people

living in them have a high level of motivation to live in a different way, to reestablish community relations. There's no stronger motivation than the welfare of your child and other children in the community.

*Is further research needed in the area of youth development, or do we already know what needs to be done, and we simply are not doing it?*

*Roeser:* We know a lot about what we need to do for kids to help them be successful both in and out of schools. Kids have basic psychological needs for competence, autonomy, and quality relationships. Successful school or after-school programs provide for these needs in a developmentally appropriate way. What we need now is more insight into how successful schools and programs work in different communities and what this can teach us about adolescent development.

*What things can schools do, as institutions, to help students grow and mature?*

*Roeser:* Schools can do what they are intended to do—provide environments that support adolescents' intellectual, social, and emotional growth. Schools can provide a nonjudgmental, noncompetitive learning environment in which kids can develop their competencies. They can provide opportunities for adolescents to develop a sense of personal autonomy and responsibility. They can provide team teaching or "schools within a school," a technique where groups of students and teachers remain together for the school day or a significant part of it, thus providing kids with a more intimate community within the larger, often impersonal environment of a school.

*How do smaller communities of learners benefit students?*

Roeser: Teams make possible thematic instruction across subject areas because teachers in small teams have more opportunity to collaborate. This can make school more interesting for kids. Teachers in teams may also get to know and trust their students more and to give them more responsibility for their own learning.

*And the research suggests these approaches can make a difference in young people's lives?*

Damon: We've learned that young people have an amazing potential if you find ways to provide them with supportive relationships.

Roeser: I don't think it's too far of a stretch to say that we can also lower dropout rates and enhance adolescents' mental health by designing schools appropriately.

*We are ending on a very positive note. Are there any other connections you'd like to make?*

Roeser: The painful tragedies that we began talking about have led us to recognize that, with concerted effort on the part of schools and community organizations, we can design environments that meet the needs of adolescents.

Damon: A lot of what we're doing to respond to the problem of youth violence is so punitive and negatively conceived that it only makes the problem worse. What we're calling for here is to reconceive the problem from a different perspective—one that gets us to think about how we can build up the capacities of young people and build them such a health system that violence can't get a foothold.

# Appendix 13-F

# Early Warning Signs of Violent Behavior by Students

There are early warning signs in most cases of violence to self and others, certain behavioral and emotional signs that, when viewed in context, can signal a troubled student. Early warning signs are a signal that a student needs help—now!

Psychologists emphasize several important principles to observe when early warning signs appear evident: (1) *do no harm*—early warning signs should not be used as a rationale to exclude, isolate, or punish a student; (2) *understand violence and aggression within a context*—there may be many antecedent factors, in the home and/or school, for students at risk of committing violent acts; (3) *avoid stereotypes*—it is important to be aware of false cues, including race, socioeconomic status, learning difficulties, or physical appearance; (4) *view warning signs within a developmental context*—know what is developmentally appropriate behavior so that supposed warning signs are not misinterpreted; (5) *understand that students typically exhibit multiple warning signs*—research confirms that most students at risk of aggression exhibit more than one warning sign repeatedly and with increasing intensity over time.

## Warning Signs

A good rule of thumb is to assume that warning signs, especially when exhibited in combination, indicate a need for further analysis to determine an appropriate intervention for the student.

- *Social withdrawal.* Withdrawal often stems from feelings of depression, rejection, persecution, unworthiness, and lack of confidence.
- *Excessive feelings of isolation.* The majority of students who appear isolated or friendless are *not* violent and may be in need of other types of specialized help. However, research also shows that such feelings can be associated with violent behavior and should not be ignored.
- *Excessive feelings of rejection.* Some aggressive students who are rejected by non-aggressive peers may seek out aggressive friends who, in turn, reinforce violent tendencies.
- *Being a victim of violence.* Research shows that students who have been victimized by others are sometimes at risk of becoming violent toward themselves or others.
- *Feelings of being picked on or persecuted .* Students who feel constantly teased, bullied, singled out for ridicule, or humiliated at home or school may, if not given adequate support, vent their emotions in possible aggressive behavior.
- *Low school interest and poor academic performance.* In some situations, such as those in which the low-achiever feels frustrated, unworthy, chastised, and denigrated at home or at school, acting out behavior in aggressive ways may occur. It is important to assess the emotional and cognitive reasons behind poor performance in school to determine the true nature of the problem.
- *Expression of violence in writings and drawings.* Many students express

From *Early Warning, Timely Response: A Guide to Safe Schools.* Washington, D.C.: U.S. Department of Education, Special Education and Rehabilitative Services, 1998.

themselves through drawings, stories, diaries, journals, poetry, and other expressive forms. Most are essentially harmless. However, an overrepresentation of violence that is focused on depictions of family members, peers, teachers, administrators, or others consistently over time may signal emotional problems and potential violence.

- *Uncontrolled anger.* Everyone gets angry. It's a basic human emotion. However, anger that is expressed frequently and intensely in response to minor irritants may signal potential violent behavior toward self or others.

- *Patterns of impulsive and chronic hitting, intimidating, and bullying behavior.* Students often engage in acts of shoving and mild aggression. However, some mildly aggressive behaviors, such as constant hitting or bullying of others, if left unattended, may escalate into more serious problems.

- *History of discipline problems.* Students with a history of chronic behavior problems both in school and at home indicate unmet needs. These problems may set the stage for more deliberate violations of norms and rules, defiance of authority, disengagement from school, and involvement in aggressive behavior directed toward peers and adults.

- *Past history of violent and aggressive behavior.* Unless provided with emotional support and professional help, students who have previously committed violent or aggressive acts are at significant risk of repeating such behavior. Prior aggressive behavior may have been directed at persons or expressed through cruelty to animals, firesetting, lying, vandalism, or other antisocial acts. *Research suggests that age of onset may be a key factor in interpreting early warning signs. Students who engage in aggression and drug abuse at an early age—before age twelve—are more likely to show violence later on than are students who begin such behavior at a later age.* In the presence of such signs it is important to review the student's history with behavioral experts and to seek parents' observations and insights in planning help.

- *Drug and alcohol use.* Apart from being unhealthy behaviors, drug use and alcohol use reduce self-control and expose students to violence . . . as perpetrators, as victims, or both.

- *Affiliation with gangs.* Gangs that support antisocial values and behaviors, including extortion, intimidation, and acts of violence toward other students, cause fear and stress among other students. Youth who are influenced by gangs, who emulate their behavior and values, as well as those who actually join a gang, may act in violent and aggressive ways in certain situations. Gang-related violence and turf battles are common occurrences in some communities and often lead to injury and death, frequently including innocent victims.

- *Inappropriate access to, possession of, and use of firearms.* Families can reduce inappropriate access to and use of firearms by their children through careful monitoring and supervision. Students with a history of aggressive, impulsive, or other emotional problems should not have access to firearms or other weapons.

- *Serious threats of violence.* Idle threats are a common response to frustration. *Alternatively, one of the most reliable indicators that a student is about to commit a violent act toward self or others is a detailed, specific threat to use violence.* Such threats must always be taken with utmost seriousness. Steps must be taken to understand and address the reasons for the threats and to prevent them from being carried out.

**Responses to Warning Signs**

Imminent warning signs of violent behavior require immediate response! *Physical aggression, destruction of property, rage, detailed threats of lethal behavior, possession of firearms and other weapons, or self-injurious behaviors or threats of suicide are each sufficient cause for immediate action.*

When warning signs or overt behavior indicate imminent danger, safety must always be the first and foremost consideration. *Immediate intervention by school authorities and possibly law enforcement agencies is needed when a student:*

- Has presented a detailed plan—time, place, method—to harm others
- Is carrying a gun or other lethal weapon

In situations where students exhibit threatening behavior, parents should be notified immediately after the safety of students and faculty members has been assured.

School personnel, parents, and other concerned citizens have the responsibility to seek assistance for troubled youth from appropriate agencies, such as child and family services and community mental health agencies.

School boards should also have policies in place which set forth a comprehensive violence prevention and response plan. These policies should provide clear direction for principals and teachers regarding:

- Identification of warning signs
- Reporting of warning signs
- Responses to imminent danger
- Provision of prevention and intervention strategies in close collaboration with parents and appropriate community services and agencies

# Appendix 13-G

# The Role of Parents in Helping to Create Safe, Violence-Free Middle Schools

Parents can help create middle schools where all students can pursue high academic standards in a safe, caring and challenging learning environment. Take these steps now:

✔ Discuss the school's discipline policy with your son or daughter. Show your support for the rules and help your child understand the reasons for them.

✔ Involve your son or daughter in setting rules for appropriate behavior at home.

✔ Talk with your son or daughter about the violence he or she sees on television, in video games, and possibly in the neighborhood. Help your child understand the real-life consequences of violence.

✔ Teach your child how to solve problems. Give praise when she or he follows through.

✔ Help your son or daughter find ways to express anger that do not involve verbally or physically hurting others. When you get angry, use it as an opportunity to model these appropriate responses for your child and talk about it.

✔ Help your child understand the value of accepting individual differences.

✔ Note any disturbing behaviors in your child. For example, frequent angry outbursts, excessive fighting and bullying of other students, cruelty to animals, fire setting, frequent behavior problems at school and in the neighborhood, lack of friends, and alcohol and drug use can be signs of serious problems. Get help for your child. Talk with a trained professional in your child's school or in the community.

✔ Keep open communication with your child, even when it is tough. Encourage your child always to let you know where and with whom he or she will be. Know your child's friends.

✔ Listen to your son or daughter if she or he shares concerns about friends who may be exhibiting troubling behaviors. Share this information with a trusted professional, such as the school psychologist, principal, or teacher.

✔ Be involved in your child's school life by supporting homework, talking with his or her teachers, and attending school functions, such as parent conferences, open houses, PTA meetings, and other school activities.

✔ Work with your child's school to make it more responsive to *all* students and to *all* families. Share your ideas about how the school can encourage family involvement, welcome *all* families, and include them in meaningful ways in their children's education.

✔ Encourage your school to offer before- and after-school programs. These usually involve the need for extra financial resources. Take part in helping to identify them by working closely with your school's principal.

✔ Volunteer to work with school-based groups concerned about preventing school violence. If no such group exists, offer to form one. Find out if there is a violence prevention group in your community. Offer to participate in the group's activities.

✔ Talk with the parents of your child's friends. Discuss how you can work together to help ensure the safety and well-being of your children in their varied activities.

✔ Ask your employer if there are provisions for parents to have time off to attend parent conferences which focus on helping you to understand and support your child.

From *Early Warning, Timely Response: A Guide to Safe Schools.* Washington, D.C.: U.S. Department of Education, Special Education and Rehabilitative Services, 1998.

# Civility, Ethical Behavior, and Social Consciousness: Needs and Commitments for Students, Parents, and Teachers

| Students | Parents, Teachers, and Principals |
|---|---|
| • I have priorities in my life, including my friends, that may not be priorities for my parents and teachers. I need to be able to say what is important to me and to know that when I do, I will be heard with respect. | • I need to listen carefully to what my (children, students) have to say about what matters most to them. I need to show through my responses that I respect differences about priorities in our lives. We also need to talk about why our priorities differ. |
| • I need to ask for help when I need it. I also need to expect that my parents, teachers, and counselors will help me learn to think through and solve my problems without preaching to me, embarrassing me, or making me wish I had never confided in them. | • I need to realize that having my (children, students) come to me with a request for help is one of the highest kinds of respect I can be shown. I must honor this behavior by spending time responding with sensitivity and wisdom as I help her or him find answers to whatever the problem may be. |
| • I need to be able to attend a school that is safe and where I can learn without fear of being hurt physically or emotionally. I have an obligation to help create this kind of school through the things I say and do daily that influence the lives of my classmates and teachers. | • I need to do everything reasonably possible to observe and monitor the behavior of my (children, students) and to provide appropriate prevention and intervention before emotional crises develops. I cannot do this alone. As parents and teachers we must work together in providing a safe school. |
| • I need to be treated as a competent person whose opinions, knowledge, and values are respected. I know that I am a young adolescent and that I still have a lot to learn. But I expect my parents and teachers to support me as I try to be a responsible person at home and at school. | • I need to understand as fully as possible that my (children, students) are experiencing rapid developmental changes in their lives and that the unfolding of their minds and emotions is to be celebrated. When I can give praise, I will. When I believe guidance is needed, I will offer it in a responsible and caring way. |
| • I need to live life free of prejudices and stereotypes directed at me or others because of race, language, sexual preferences, or other types of differences which | • I need to work on my own tendencies to judge others on the basis of unfair criteria. I also need to face the fact that my (children, students) will pick up on my example far |

**Students** (Continued)

humans experience. I know it is not a perfect world and that the kind of life I am talking about begins with me.

- I need to be able to change my mind or make mistakes without fear of ridicule or punishment. I need to give others the kind of slack I want for myself—including my friends as well as my parents and teachers.

- I need to have acceptance from my parents and teachers, even when they do not approve of what I do at all times. I know that I must be responsible and accountable for my behavior and that there are consequences when I do something that must be punished. Even then, I need to feel I am still loved and cared for as a person.

- I have a right to demand that others change their behavior towards me when it violates my space or my personal integrity. I need the wisdom and strength to say "No!" to unreasonable or morally wrong requests without having to feel guilty. I must also be accountable for honoring the rights and values of others at all times.

- I need help in knowing when and how to share the hurts of my friends—and even their weird behavior—with my parents and teachers. I know that kids who do weird things, including threatening others or talking about how they are going to do some kind of violent thing, really need help. I could be the only one that would keep them from doing something stupid or

**Parents, Teachers, and Principals** (Continued)

faster than my words. I will seek to express true respect for others whatever their personal or social circumstances.

- I need to be less judgmental and more understanding of my (children, students). When I show respect, the chances are that I will receive it back. This is one of the best ways we can build a mature relationship.

- I need to remember that my (children, students) expect punishment when they do something wrong. But I must never give punishment in anger or send signals, by words or actions, of personal rejection that may lead to a break in our relationship.

- I need to accept responsibility for recognizing that young adolescents have a right to their own space and to honor this right to privacy. I also have a responsibility to discuss matters of personal ethics with my (children, students) and in the process to help build the inner strength which will allow them to behave morally and responsibly.

- I need to face up to the fact that the "code of honor" that keeps kids from telling threatening things they know about someone else is also present among adults. As a (parent, teacher), I need to examine my own life in this regard. I also need to take note of how often I watch things that are wrong rather than try to do something positive, honorable, and right to correct the problems. I will

| **Students** (Continued) | **Parents, Teachers, and Principals** (Continued) |
|---|---|
| far worse. But the "code of honor" thing can mean really hard consequences if it is broken. Why do kids have to carry this monkey on their backs? Why don't parents and teachers talk more about this? | spend more time with my (children, students), helping them to learn that there is a higher code of honor, when it should be invoked, and why it is the only way that one can live with a clear conscience throughout life. |
| • I need to know that my parents and teachers recognize that I am growing in my ability to learn many things about the world I live in. I sometimes have deep thoughts and feelings about the meaning of life. I am able to ask a thousand questions that I know neither my parents nor my teachers seem to want to hear: "Why am I here?" "Why is there suffering?" "Why do bad things happen to good people?" "Why are there wars?" "Why is there evil?" I would really like to get some answers or at least talk about these questions. But there are too many times when I start to think out loud that it seems as if the questions are out of bounds. I ask why. I have no good answer. | • I need to do a much better job of trying to deal with my own thoughts and feelings about big, unanswerable questions—at least unanswerable in some absolute sense. As a (parent, teacher), I must not be afraid to talk about the deeper meaning of life and all of the why questions because I feel threatened myself. What kind of a lesson does that teach my child or students? I need to realize that young adolescents do not expect perfect answers but do expect to be able to think about the larger meaning of so many things they are studying. Their schoolwork would be so sterile if it didn't raise questions about moral and ethical dilemmas: war, poverty, injustice, and even the awesomeness of life itself. I will do a better job of helping my (children, students) think big thoughts. After all, what is life really about? |
| • I need to have hope in the future, my future—that there is something out there worth trying to get. My friends and I often get depressed. Our parents and teachers say, "Oh, it's just from growing up!" I don't want to grow up feeling depressed. My friends and I often hide our real feelings behind noisy, weird behaviors, but underneath we wonder about a lot of things. | • I often wonder myself about what kind of world my (children, students) will inherit. It is more comfortable not to think about it too much. But that is a major cop-out. Too many kids act out their depression by high-risk behavior. As a (parent, teacher), I need to help my (children, students) know that life does hold many promises and to learn what it takes to achieve them. |

*"The bottom line is that there is just no way to create good schools without good teachers. . . . Success in any aspect of reform—whether creating standards, developing more challenging curriculum and assessments, implementing school-based management, or inventing new model schools and programs—depends on highly skilled teachers."*

—National Commission on Teaching and America's Future

# Standards-Based Professional Development at the School Site

A direct relationship exists between a school's effectiveness in implementing standards-based education and the knowledge and skills possessed by the school's professional staff. Therefore, the school must accept responsibility for providing a significant portion of the professional development required by its staff. According to Linda Darling-Hammond, Stanford professor and director of the National Commission on Teaching and America's Future, schools must, in the twenty-first century, have professional personnel who reflect the "wisdom of practice." She adds, "There is a simplistic notion of teaching that is just wrong. It is like going to the symphony, seeing the conductor wave the baton, and telling yourself, 'I can do that!'"[1]

 Recommendations 4, 5, 6, 12, 13

Standards-based instruction in the middle schools requires an increased level of professional preparation, including a sure grasp of academic content. However, although institutions of higher education should continue to help teachers succeed in an academic setting, many of the most important elements of effective teaching and administration must be learned on the job. Accordingly, the model to be followed will increasingly become like that found in teaching hospitals, where interns and seasoned practitioners grow together in their knowledge and skills, professional collaboration is the norm, and peer review is expected.

## Urgency of School-Based Professional Development

School-based professional development is critical to the success of the standards-based education. However, a cautionary note about professional development is offered by Hayes

Mizell as follows:

It is good that you want to learn as much as you can and develop and implement standards as effectively as possible. But I caution you not to make this an endless quest for "the answer." The technologies of standards implementation—rubrics, portfolios, benchmarks, authentic assessments, and even content and performance standards themselves—can become so complex that mastering them becomes the end rather than the means. Students will not perform at higher levels because your school system's rubrics are better than another school system's rubrics. They may perform at higher levels because both teachers and students understand the rubrics and their purpose and because they consistently use them to improve student performance. If teachers . . . are not actively using the technologies of standards implementation, the time they spend learning [them] will have been wasted. Make sure [you] understand these technologies and how to use them to increase student learning; but above all, make sure [you] are using the technologies to enhance student performance.

Mizell then discusses the "big contextual issue" of staff development:

I urge you to reexamine and agonize over how well [you] are using staff development resources. They are precious and often wasted. If your staff development is mostly about consciousness raising, exposure, inspiration, and transmitting information or points of view, go back to the drawing board. This staff development will not change teachers' attitudes or practices. . . . They will not teach differently or better unless your staff development focuses on strengthening their skills as teachers. . . . What teachers want and what they need is direct support in learning and using standards-

based instruction in difficult classroom contexts. Most staff development falls far short of meeting this need.[2]

Implementing Mizell's recommendations is hindered by the widespread isolation of professional staff in the school. That reality works against collegial professional development, the most effective way to advance beyond superficial learning. Only one of five teachers feels adequately prepared to work in a modern classroom. One of the primary reasons given for the shortcoming is that many teachers have few opportunities for professional development. The situation is described by U.S. Department of Education researchers as follows:

While doctors and lawyers routinely confer with colleagues, teachers often remain isolated in classrooms. Among teachers whose schools dedicate time for team planning, 40 percent say it improves their teaching "a lot." Another one-third say it improves their teaching "moderately." Yet in spite of these impressive findings, the practice remains uncommon in American schools. Through this study teachers are telling us the kinds of support they need— more peer collaboration, team teaching, and common planning periods. If we don't listen to them, we will shortchange our children and our teachers by hanging on to self-defeating practices.[3]

The research, conducted by the National Center for Educational Statistics in 1999, was based on a sampling of over 4,000 public school teachers. Only about 20 percent of the respondents said that they were confident in (1) working with students from diverse backgrounds, those with limited proficiency in

English, and those with disabilities; and (2) using modern technology in the classroom. Seventy percent praised a formal professional mentoring relationship as a significant help to teachers.

Anne Wheelock adds yet a third perspective, bringing together substance and setting. Arguing for important content learned in a collegial school environment, she writes that:

> A school culture that can rise to the expectations of standards-based reform must be a culture in which teachers share professional knowledge and skills, exchange ideas and information, and support and critique one another as they implement the best practices and press students toward producing better work more of the time. Without a network of professional relationships to nurture teachers' opportunities to learn, standards-based reforms will collapse under their own weight.[4]

## Emphasis on Collegial Professional Development

A community of learners that emphasizes professional collegiality is one the most important factors in teachers being able to weather change and take advantage of resources essential to educational reforms. School-based staff development is one of the most potent ways of building collegial norms among teachers and principals (see Figure 14-1). Colleagues who work together daily learn about one another's strengths and weaknesses and, perhaps most important, can develop relationships based on collaboration and trust. Such norms depend on colleagues who respect the confidentiality of their peers, are good listeners, facilitate reflective thought, are honest and open, respect new ideas and opinions, and are committed to one another's success.

The importance of a comprehensive, long-range, school-based professional development program for the middle grades is captured by Joellen Killion and Stephanie Hirsh as follows:

> Nearly a decade ago, the Carnegie Council on Adolescent Development called the years from ages ten to fifteen "the last best chance" to ensure that young people reach a fruitful adulthood. . . . But statistics show us that the nation has yet to heed fully the council's warning. Middle grade students tend to do less well on national exams, . . . and the inequities between high-achieving and low-achieving students deepen during the middle grades.

> The mortar that can fill this crack in the middle is competent and caring teachers—teachers who understand the needs of young adolescents, who establish a safe, nurturing learning environment, and who elicit a high level of performance through their own strong instructional practices and deep content knowledge. More than perhaps [in] any other area of education, the challenge of educating early adolescents requires caring, well-versed teachers who will balance standards of excellence with the provision of supportive surroundings.

> . . . For reasons ranging from collegiate preparation to personal preferences, these middle school specialists are still in short supply. The most effective and efficient way to increase their numbers is through high-quality, comprehensive staff development geared specifically to middle grades instruction. The time is ripe for this improvement. Theory and practice are just coming together to produce solid information to reform education in the middle grades.[5]

Figure 14-1

**Standards-Based Performance Standards for Teachers and Principals in Middle Schools**

*Teachers and principals in middle schools will:*

- **Possess** demonstrable professional competence.
- **Provide** caring emotional support for all students to develop positive educational values.
- **Maintain** emotionally and physically safe learning environments in the classrooms.
- **Implement** standards-based education in all areas of the curriculum.
- **Use** curriculum materials and assessment practices that are aligned with standards.
- **Provide** content and performance standards that are clear and free of jargon, including required academic performance levels, for students and parents.
- **Develop** scoring rubrics based on the consensus of colleagues in determining levels of student proficiency.
- **Make** scoring rubrics available to students and parents for all major assignments.
- **Provide** performance report cards based on standards.
- **Communicate** student progress to parents regularly and specifically, including the use of telecons and face-to-face conferences.
- **Develop** and use a wide repertoire of teaching strategies in response to varied student learning styles.

- **Provide** differentiated instruction, including the use of scaffolding, to assist students in learning to use knowledge and skills in practical ways.
- **Engage** students in tasks requiring complex reasoning that are expressed in speech or writing or in experiments, projects, artwork, models, or other appropriate means.
- **Assign** relevant and demanding homework linked to content and performance standards.
- **Establish** the development of basic and academic literacy for all students as the highest priority in each school.
- **Use** support personnel effectively, including aides, tutors, and adult volunteers.
- **Avoid** classroom interruptions, including intrusive passing bells and announcements over the loudspeaker.
- **Schedule** wisely the precious commodity of time.
- **Facilitate** student access to human services agencies or other appropriate helping organizations.
- **Plan,** implement, and evaluate regularly school-based initiatives focused on remedial programs for students.
- **Inform** students, parents, and the community about the basic and special efforts of each school to help all students meet or exceed district-mandated levels of academic proficiency.

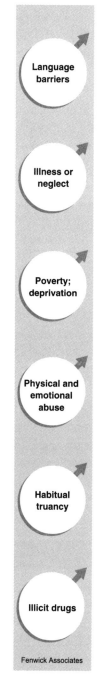

Late or transfer enrollment

Family transiency; discontinuity in schooling

Negative peer pressures

Malnutrition or overweight

Family dysfunction

Cumulative learning deficits

Language barriers

Illness or neglect

Poverty; deprivation

Physical and emotional abuse

Habitual truancy

Illicit drugs

Fenwick Associates

**Circles represent counterforces working against the efforts of students to succeed in school.**

## Characteristics of High-Quality Professional Development

Creating the kind of professional development environment just described is a compelling challenge in implementing standards-based education. The directors of the California Professional Development Program Consortia recommend that staff development should (1) allocate time for educators to pursue professional inquiry, reflect, mentor, and refine skills; (2) include the participants in the planning process; and (3) ensure that the development is long-term and site-based to encourage collaborative relationships.[6]

A set of quality criteria for professional development specifically targeted to middle schools has been published by the National Staff Development Council (NSDC), a non-profit professional association of approximately 8,000 educators. Represented on the council are the National Middle School Association, the American Association of School Administrators, the Association for Supervision and Curriculum Development, the National Association of Elementary School Principals, the National Association of Secondary School Principals, and the Edna McConnell Clark Foundation. According to the NSDC the effective middle-level professional development program accomplishes the following:

- Increases educators' understanding of how to provide school environments and instruction responsive to the developmental needs of young adolescents
- Facilitates the development and implementation of school-based and classroom-based management to maximize student learning
- Addresses diversity by providing awareness and training related to the knowledge, skills, and behaviors needed to ensure that an equitable and high-quality education is provided to all students
- Enables educators to provide a challenging, developmentally appropriate curriculum that engages students in integrative ways of thinking and learning
- Prepares teachers to use research-based teaching strategies appropriate to their instructional objectives and students
- Prepares educators to demonstrate high expectations for student learning
- Facilitates staff collaboration with and support of families for improving student performance
- Prepares teachers to use various types of performance assessment in their classrooms
- Prepares educators to combine student academic learning with service to the community
- Increases administrators' and teachers' ability to provide guidance and advice to adolescents
- Increases staff knowledge and practice of interdisciplinary team organization and instruction[7]

## Site-Based Professional Development Councils

To achieve high-quality professional development, each middle school is encouraged to create a site-based professional development council to oversee all professional development planning. The council should be composed of the principal; teachers; certificated support staff; paraprofessionals; community volunteers, such as tutors, mentors, and aides; and others who participate in the instructional program, including university interns. The professional development council should design and implement a comprehensive, high-quality professional development program embedded in the workplace to be closely related to the educators' work experiences.

Professional development councils should be funded appropriately and provided with a mission statement clearly defining their responsibilities, which may include:

- Conducting school-based professional development needs assessments
- Identifying professional development priorities based on those assessments and on the results of student assessments (Student achievement data related to standards should be used to identify and target professional development needs.)
- Planning curriculum to address professional development priorities
- Assigning instructional leadership roles
- Scheduling classes, seminars, or other appropriate learning environments
- Allocating resources, including compensation for instructional leaders
- Determining in-service credit conforming to district policies

- Negotiating compensation for faculty participation, including compensation for released time
- Overseeing schoolwide participation, including participation by noncertificated staff
- Coordinating with district-level personnel
- Coordinating with institutions of higher education
- Evaluating all phases of the program
- Providing periodic program reports to the faculty and the superintendent

## School-Based Professional Development Programs

School-based professional development programs should provide the expertise that teachers and principals may not have developed in their formal certification programs, especially the knowledge and skills needed to work effectively in standards-based education. Institutions of higher education cannot be expected to provide expertise with a site-specific focus. From among the priorities addressed in previous chapters, 41 have been selected for emphasis in middle school-based professional development programs. (See also Appendix 14, "Priorities in School-Based Professional Development," at the end of this chapter.)

# Professional Development

- **This chapter is premised on the importance of collegial relationships among teachers.** Yet study after study reveals that most of a teacher's professional day is spent in isolation from other colleagues. Although a lack of time to interact is undoubtedly an important part of this problem, it is not the only variable that contributes to a go-it-alone approach. What other factors are present? Which factors are unique to you? Which are widely present among the teachers you know? Can you suggest ways to introduce more collegiality into your school? Invite other teachers to join you in this process. Consider appropriate ways to share the results.

- **School-based professional development is the most effective way to gain knowledge and skills.** Evaluate your school's professional development program. What are its strengths? Its weaknesses? What can you recommend to ensure that you and your colleagues have the knowledge and skills needed to function professionally in a stan-dards-based middle school? How can the results of student assessments help you identify your professional development needs?

- **Consider the range of professional staff development priorities listed in the appendix to this chapter, including the model for organizing a schoolwide profes-sional development program thematically.** Identify your list of highest priorities among those suggested. Are any categories missing? If so, identify them. Share this information with your principal or school-based professional development council.

- **Do you have a professional mentor?** Are you a mentor to someone else? What are the most important qualities in a strong mentoring relationship? Consider first the role of the mentor and then the role of the person being mentored. Respond in the context of what mentoring might ideally be among professionals already engaged in their careers. Seek opportunities to discuss your thinking with others. If you do not have a mentor, whom might you invite to be your mentor? What would be required to have you take this step?

- **What would be your major priorities in communicating to an institution of higher education ways to strengthen teacher or administrator certification programs?** Develop a list of suggestions from your school and arrange to meet with the university dean of education to consider them. Explore ways in which your school might help implement some of your suggestions.

# Appendix 14

# Priorities in School-Based Professional Development

The following 41 items identify the specialized knowledge and skills needed by teachers and principals in middle school-based professional development programs. Each item provides opportunities for school-based professional development experiences emphasizing strong, enduring collegial bonds among faculty members within the same middle school. Learning experiences range from one-to-one mentoring relationships to schoolwide participation.

## 1 Middle School Philosophy, Policies, and Practices

Most middle school teachers have backgrounds in elementary or secondary education. That fact is not surprising because in formal credentialing programs a credential for teaching in the middle grades is not offered. Therefore, a concerted effort must be made to ensure that the focus of middle grades education and its underlying principles are fully understood by all middle school faculty. A deeply engrained, caring approach to students, together with high academic expectations, is a powerful formula for ensuring the success of standards-based education in middle schools. And reviewing and reaffirming the philosophy, policies, and practices essential for a middle school to succeed must be a continuing priority in professional development.

## 2 School Mission and Vision

Every school requires a mission statement clearly setting out the basic tenets of the school's educational philosophy and the way in which the school intends to translate that philosophy into daily practice. The statement should combine immediate reality with a vision of the future and be clear and consistent internally.

Standards-based middle schools must share their expectations for student achievement with all the students and their parents. They must also state what the school will do to help all students succeed. If a school's mission statement is to reflect quality and integrity, the school must work hard to achieve that goal. Once again, the process is ongoing, and the professional development efforts needed to sustain that process must also be constant.

## 3 Standards-Based Education: A Conceptual Framework

An understanding of standards-based education is required of all professionals, paraprofessionals, interns, student teachers, and volunteers involved in professional development programs in middle schools. To be included in that understanding are the meaning and role of content and performance standards; the urgency of working together to build a consensus on student assignments, rubrics, and levels of performance; and the assumptions about student achievement throughout the school.

## 4 Content Standards, Curriculum, and Instruction

An understanding of the close relationship between content standards, instructional materials, and teaching practices is essential. The complex processes involved should be practiced in a collegial setting—often among teachers who share the same subjects and grade levels. However, because the basic knowledge and skills required cross subject areas, all faculty can participate in school-site seminars that address generic issues.

## 5 Performance Standards and Assessment Practices

The development of a performance standard system requires intense collegial cooperation. Beyond the alignment or adoption of state performance levels and descriptors (see Chapter 2), teachers of the same grade level work together to develop benchmark assessments and scoring criteria for those assessments. Scoring student work based on exemplars and analyzing individual student data as well as collective student data is a collaborative, collegial process. Familiarity with the appropriate California frameworks is essential.

## 6 Generic and Subject-Specific Rubrics

The development of rubrics (scoring criteria) to assess student proficiency on performance tasks is a key component of a performance standard system. Without rubrics reflecting professional consensus on the quality of student work relative to content standards, standards-based education would falter. With consensus, the evaluation of a student's proficiency becomes consistent from one teacher to

the next. The opposite situation occurs when a student's proficiency is measured according to the subjective judgments of individual teachers. The result of the latter practice does not differ from the conventional grading practices of teachers working alone in their classrooms and establishing their own grading standards. Professional development programs must provide faculties with assistance in designing and working with generic rubrics (those that may apply across the curriculum), subject-specific rubrics, and task (standards)-specific rubrics.

## 7 Auditing Student Performance

Designing and using reasonably comprehensive audit trails for tracking student performance is yet another key element in implementing standards-based education effectively. A system must be implemented that allows parents easily to monitor their children's academic progress. In turn, the students should be given rapid, frequent feedback on their performance. Recordkeeping involves not only grades but also evidence of student work made available for inspection by parents, professional peers, and supervisors. Because standards-based education is a very open public process, careful documentation of student progress should be achieved through collegial planning, monitoring, and consensus building.

## 8 Reporting Student Performance

Developing student performance reports differs from determining and awarding conventional letter grades. Although new reporting formats may continue to use letter grades, the meaning of those grades differs significantly for students and parents. Developing or adapting new protocols and formats for reporting proficiency in the core curriculum requires the intensive collaboration of faculties, close communication with parents, and a close working relationship with central office personnel. Professional development in reporting on performance levels should ensure comprehensive understanding of the differences between conventional grading and performance reporting. Other issues involve ensuring facultywide consistency in using new reporting procedures and developing the essential skills needed to use manual or computerized reporting formats.

## 9  Performance-Benchmark Assessments/Assignments

An important part of standards-based education is performance-based assessments that help students develop those creative, problem-solving skills needed in today's global economy (see Chapter 3, Figure 3-2), such as portfolios, exhibits, projects, experiments, or other substantive activity allowing students to demonstrate academic proficiency. Developing performance assessments involves teaching teams and teachers of the same subject and at the same grade level. The generalized study of developing performance assessments, developing scoring rubrics, and identifying student exemplars (anchor papers) are considered a valid

focus of professional development for an entire faculty.

## 10  Developmental Characteristics of Young Adolescents

A thorough understanding of the developmental characteristics of middle grades students, a priority of staff development, is essential to providing a developmentally appropriate instructional program for them. Intellectual, physical, social, and emotional changes are more intense during early adolescence than at any other period in life except early infancy. These developmental changes take on new characteristics or may be expressed in different ways from one student generation to the next. Furthermore, new research continues to contribute to the body of knowledge about young adolescents. That information powerfully influences the development of effective teaching and learning strategies in middle schools.

## 11  Managing Classroom Behavior

Good classroom management is the foundation of good learning. However, a philosophy of teaching characterized by firmness, fairness, consistency, and a sense of humor is mere rhetoric without effective methods for applying that philosophy to the classroom. All teachers, but new teachers especially, need to revisit the tenets of effective classroom management. A teacher's first year is often made miserable because of the teacher's inability to manage student behavior and instructional goals effectively. As a result a significant number of teachers resign during their first three years of employment. And when good classroom management is lacking, the students and the well-being of the entire school suffer.

Beginning teachers require the support of other faculty and intensive supervision. Every effort should be made to prevent the teacher's first year from becoming a threatening experience. Most teachers new to the profession can succeed if they receive needed professional help. Site-based professional development support programs can provide the basis for achieving that goal. And schoolwide discipline policies help to bring consistency to student behavior. A system beyond the classroom needs to be in place to support the teacher.

New teachers should participate in seminar-type forums, discussing their work, identifying challenges, and developing solutions. Those who lead the forums should offer support and professional guidance. Beginning teachers should be given ample opportunities to observe instruction being delivered in other classrooms and to have their own work observed and critiqued by peers.

## 12  Collegial Crisis Management

Crisis management is a way of life in many schools. However, teachers and school administrators lack the opportunities afforded medical and legal professionals, who regularly confer with one another to analyze problems and decide on courses of action. This situation in the schools should not continue. Collectively, teachers and administrators should share their knowledge and skills as they address problems. Every school should have a crisis unit in which the individual teachers feel comfortable as they involve other colleagues in the search for solutions.

## 13  Teachers as Mentors, Advisers, and Friends

The roles of teachers as mentors, advisers, and friends require specific professional skills. Seminars devoted to an examination of those roles, including such matters as when to transfer problems to specially trained personnel, can prove to be invaluable for many teachers, including veteran teachers. The need is especially acute in middle schools, where most faculty are expected to assume leadership for advisory programs.

## 14  Teachers as Coaches, Principals as Coaches

Teachers as coaches to students are vital to ensuring each student's academic success. Coaching involves the collaboration of teacher and student. The teacher, much like the coach of an athletic team, offers support, assistance, and friendship. Presenting explanations, demonstrations, practice, and constructive feedback, the teacher as coach helps ensure that what has been learned becomes usable and provides a formal yet personal support system for students.

Like coaches, teachers seek to identify their students' abilities, talents, learning styles, and motivation that lead to success.

However, effective coaches (teachers) avoid being judgmental in assigning success or failure. Rather, they try to bring out the best in every student. They also work to foster cooperation and team effort.

The practice of teachers as coaches to other teachers and principals as coaches to teachers takes the power of coaching up to the collegial level of professional development. Teachers with their own peer coaches benefit from support and nonjudgmental feedback about their newly acquired standards-based practices. Because coaching represents a powerful instructional technique, its skills should be learned and practiced in a formal program of professional development.

## 15  Differentiated Instruction

Differentiated instruction provides many more ways for students to take in new information, assimilate it, and demonstrate what they have learned in contrast to instruction that merely aims at the average student through uniform lectures, activities, homework assignments, and assessments. But many teachers make few if any modifications for struggling or advanced learners. They deliver lessons at a uniform pace in a uniform instructional approach that is ineffective for many students and harmful to some. Struggling to cover too much material in too little time, teachers can easily fall prey to using this survival skill of one-size-fits-all instruction while their students may be falling by the wayside.

To overcome this ineffective approach, teachers need extensive professional development focused on determining what their students need and how to meet those needs. Some students need more repetition of the material to be learned, fewer ideas presented at a time, clearer homework assignments, more time to read instructions and to look up new vocabulary, or more direct monitoring by the teacher. Others require more individualized instructional guidance, such as a clearer explanation of what happened in an experiment or more time for independent, hands-on problem solving. And still others may benefit most from tutorial help or mentoring. A variety of strategies should be employed.

## 16  Multicultural Education and Equal Access

When principals and teachers are responsible for teaching culturally diverse students, they require specialized skills for working effectively in that environment. The term *multicultural education* encompasses certain fundamental commitments:

a. There is value in promoting cultural diversity.

b. Schools should be models for expressing human rights and respecting cultural differences.

c. Social justice and equality for all people should be made paramount in designing content and performance standards and curricular materials.

d. Schools should develop a deep understanding of democratic principles and the rights of all citizens.

## 17 Inclusive Classroom Teaching

The term *inclusive* here refers to classrooms in which students with a potentially wide range of abilities learn together. Inclusive classrooms reflect standards-based education's commitment to high levels of academic achievement for all students. To be effective in such a learning environment, teachers use a wide range of instructional strategies and learn how to differentiate instruction through strategies that respond to the students' varied abilities and learning styles. Professional development programs should provide opportunities for teachers to learn instructional techniques suited to the inclusive classroom, practice them, and interact with one another through peer observations and critiques.

## 18 Learning Styles and Classroom Environment

Appropriate responses to students' different learning styles and the need for flexible classroom arrangements to accommodate them can contribute directly to the quality of learning. Ideally, students should experience a classroom environment allowing them to carry out their work effectively. If students, for example, have visual or auditory deficits that are ignored, they may have difficulty in learning. Further, ill-conceived physical arrangements in the classroom may nullify efforts to use grouping practices designed to facilitate learning assignments. The primary professional development goals responsive to students' learning styles are

to help teachers modify their classrooms in response to the needs of individual learners and to design room arrangements to facilitate specific learning tasks.

## 19 Learning Deficits

Helping students with learning deficits in a standards-based classroom requires patience, wisdom, knowledge, skill, and systemwide support. Opportunities for professional development can be provided after a benchmark assessment is given and students with specific or standards deficits are identified. Extended collegial planning sessions focusing on strategies for these students and reporting back on measurable progress enrich standards-based practice and provide peer support. The primary goal of this professional development program is to ensure that students with learning deficits move toward their highest level of achievement.

## 20 Safety Nets for Students

Safety nets for students are essential because prevention and intervention demand much more than random responses. Planning for the early identification of students' difficulties, developing appropriate efforts to address those difficulties, and coordinating access to specialized assistance for students and parents should be made priorities in professional development programs. Just as academic standards have been raised for students, professional standards have been raised for teachers and principals to ensure that every student meets or exceeds defined proficiency levels. The challenges faced in staff development programs include not only producing a master plan for safety nets but also ensuring that all faculty members will help implement it.

## 21 Gifted and Talented Students

Gifted and talented education (GATE) students, who are well served by standards-based education, are continually challenged to excel. The inclusion of GATE students in heterogeneous standards-based classrooms does not necessarily impose additional instructional challenges for teachers.

Content standards are uniformly rigorous for all students. The performance level of *advanced* should reflect the highest quality of student work relative to the content standards. While *proficient* is the target for most students, all students, including GATE students, should be encouraged to attain the highest level.

Scoring criteria for the top level of points on a rubric or for the top performance level of collective work should reflect the highest creative and intellectual capacities of a student at the particular grade level. The top level is for excellent, thorough, and insightful work.

The same engaging performance tasks asked of all students should be sufficient for GATE students as they work toward the highest performance level. However, if a student is easily and conceptually achieving at the advanced level on most grade-level performance tasks, the

student may need enhanced performance tasks with enhanced rubrics or challenges beyond his or her grade-level standards. Developing enhanced tasks and rubrics to challenge their students should be the focus for professional development of GATE teachers who have students at this very high level.

## 22 Scaffolding

Given the large number of students still developing English-language proficiency, *scaffolding* (see the glossary) remains a dominant instructional tool. It should also be used with native speakers of English. Scaffolding may be used along the full continuum of learning—from acquiring basic knowledge and skills to understanding principles fundamental to a given discipline and the ability to use them in completing complex reasoning tasks. The most important elements of scaffolding are those listed in Chapter 10.

Because scaffolding is complex, developing the professional skills needed to implement it requires intense collaboration. In this effort peer observations and critiques are especially effective strategies to use.

## 23 Specially Designed Academic Instruction in English

Specially designed academic instruction in English (SDAIE) originated in earlier efforts to help second-language learners develop their English-language skills and simultaneously address grade-level content in the core curriculum. More recently, however, instruction exemplified by SDAIE has become increasingly popular in classes for students at all levels of ability in using English. The reason for this development is that large numbers of native speakers of English, in addition to the second-language learners, lack proficiency in academic language.

## 24 Interdisciplinary Team Teaching and Thematic Instruction

Interdisciplinary team teaching and thematic instruction are powerful tools for organizing standards-based learning experiences. Usually, interdisciplinary teams consist of two or more teachers specializing in different subjects who teach the same students within a common block of instructional time. Team members commit to working together to develop and teach interdisciplinary units. Their primary instructional objective is to focus standards-based content on specific themes. In successful interdisciplinary instruction the knowledge and skills associated with separate disciplines are used to allow students to develop a broader perspective about the major issues embedded in the theme.

## 25 Complex Reasoning

Another vital component of standards-based education is complex reasoning, which includes such skills as classifying, sequencing, drawing analogies, hypothesizing about cause and effect, comparing and contrasting, drawing inferences, evaluating, and summarizing. These and other comparable abilities are used in various combinations to solve problems, for example, or to conduct research, engage in sports, participate in performances, complete a work of art, or write original prose or poetry. Organizing instruction and assignments involving complex reasoning requires the teacher to have specialized skills.

## 26 Deep Learning

Deep learning, a quintessential part of effective standards-based education, involves ensuring that students have internalized new knowledge and skills and can apply them in several practical ways. For deep learning to occur, a sufficient amount of time must be spent on specific standards to ensure that they are mastered at or above a predefined level of proficiency. Deep learning requires an understanding of its principles and processes and the ability to use the processes to complete assignments.

## 27 Homework Assignments

Homework assignments should be a logical extension of classroom instructional practices. Students and parents should be helped to see the relationship between homework and the standards. Homework assignments are varied and call for students to use all levels of cognitive thinking.

## 28 Polishing and Refining Student Work

Students should be given ample opportunities to refine their work. Further, renewed attention should be devoted to the qualitative aspects of student work, such as neatness, accuracy, and completeness, and to the correct use of grammar and syntax in written work.

Professional development should focus on instructional processes that include extensive use of drafts, teacher commentary, and several revisions. When student work is evaluated, it should be measured against consensus-built rubrics with clear descriptors of performance-standard expectations. Students, parents, and teachers consistently and uniformly know "how good is good enough" and what needs to be done to do better.

## 29  Academic Literacy

Every teacher must teach reading and writing skills as a natural support and extension of their own content areas. All teachers should be familiar with the English–language arts content standards for the grade-level student they teach. This establishes the rigor they should expect and require from their students. In this publication much emphasis is given to *academic literacy,* the ability to use competently the specialized vocabulary for each subject offered. Students are helped to understand the difference between fluency in social language and proficiency in academic language, where meaning is derived from the formal, often technical language of specific subject matter. Only a limited prior association with ideas, events, or surroundings in the lives of students helps convey meaning.

Middle grades students should be helped to understand that they are entering a period during which academic literacy can deny access or provide limited or full access to advanced courses in high school and affect admission to college and attractive career options. To be able to help students achieve academic literacy, many teachers may require extensive training in learning to use effective strategies.

## 30  Service-Learning

The California Service-Learning Task Force has called for school districts to use service-learning to connect youths to their communities by integrating academic facts and standards while providing opportunities for students to demonstrate civic responsibility. Many opportunities for service-learning can be found within the schools. However, because service-learning strategies are very time-intensive, training and support are required for teachers willing to use those opportunities.

## 31  Time Management: School and Classroom

The wise use of time is one of the most critical dimensions of effective school and classroom management. Time lost means lost opportunities. The wise use of time involves maximizing the effectiveness of teaching and learning.

Extraneous factors compromising teaching and learning must be carefully identified and controlled. Intense professional efforts should be made to isolate practices that rob teachers of instructional time and help them develop options for resolving the problems.

## 32 Aides as Adjunct Teachers

The effective use of aides varies markedly among teachers. Many teachers are skilled in using aides; others are not. Often, the aides' roles and responsibilities are not clearly defined. Because each aide brings his or her own special talents to the role, those talents should be exploited through specific assignments and added training when needed. To develop good working relationships, both teachers and aides need opportunities for professional development. Seminars should be developed around topics that address the aides' responsibilities. Aides used to support instruction should be well versed in the content and performance standards for the classes in which they assist. And the aides, together with the teachers, should play a significant role in planning professional development opportunities.

## 33 Parents and Others as Community Volunteers

Parents, college students, and other community members who serve as volunteers need effective preparation and guidance. In the middle grades volunteers fill various roles, including those of tutor and mentor. Recruiting, screening, selecting, training, and supervising classroom volunteers are significant responsibilities. Professional development experiences should be provided for the staff who assume those duties and for the volunteers.

Although in nearly every community volunteers provide a large reservoir of talent, they are overlooked by most middle schools. This situation is sometimes explained as resulting from the wishes of young adolescents to keep parents away from school. The more likely cause is that volunteers do not feel welcome. Ways must be found to break down any barriers between the schools and volunteers. This issue should be addressed in professional development efforts so that strong, effective volunteer programs can be built in the schools.

## 34 Management of Classroom Paperwork

Inability to manage paperwork effectively, especially student assignments and grades, is the nemesis of many teachers. It robs them of personal time, delays invaluable feedback to students, and loses time that might otherwise be spent on effective instructional planning. Both new and experienced teachers often suffer from this problem. However, many solutions are available, including assistance from technology. Mentor teachers, instructional leaders, and others experienced in handling this problem have much to suggest. Teachers need time to learn techniques, try them, discuss their effectiveness, and gain from interaction with colleagues.

## 35 Lesson Planning and the Weekly Syllabus

Good lesson planning is essential to good teaching. Well-prepared teachers can see immediate benefits in their students' progress. Effective lessons in standards-based classrooms are derived from "backwards planning." The assessment of what students are expected to achieve (selected standards) and the evidence teachers need to gather from students have already been determined. Teachers scaffold their lessons and student learning while focused on the standards-based assessment target. The lessons include anticipatory sets: an introduction to the lesson to gain student attention and interest; statements of the lesson's goals and how they relate to the standards; formal teaching procedures and necessary instructional materials; independent practice by students under the guidance of the teacher; and extended learning in the form of activities to be completed in the classroom or as homework.

Teachers can prepare a weekly syllabus identifying the content standards to be addressed, to be followed by an outline of instructional activities and student assignments. Although simple, the format provides information useful in communicating with students, parents, and administrators. Some teachers staple completed homework assignments and test results to each student's weekly syllabus and file the information so that it can be reviewed easily for computing grades and preparing for conferences with parents. Some teachers post their weekly syllabus on their school's web page. The syllabus is also sent to parents. A weekly syllabus saves time, provides

clear guidance to students and parents, and serves as an immediately available reference for a substitute teacher.

## 36 California Subject-Matter Frameworks

Content and performance standards must be understood as related to curricular scope and sequence and instructional and assessment practices. Teachers should immerse themselves in the California frameworks that have been or are being developed for their respective disciplines. The frameworks address standards, grade-level considerations, instructional strategies, assessment practices, accountability issues, and other essential aspects of standards-based education. (See Chapter 1.)

## 37 Expanded Subject-Matter Knowledge

A deepening of subject-matter knowledge is essential if teachers are to hold students to high standards. If teachers have only a superficial understanding of the major principles and concepts embedded in the subjects they teach, they will provide mediocre instruction, and their students' learning will be compromised. School districts experiencing rapid growth find difficulty in recruiting well-prepared teachers. However, failure to offer a strong professional development program to improve the teachers' knowledge of subject matter is inexcusable. To provide such a program, the district can cooperate with an institution of higher education to combine the formal academic work of the college or university with the instructional realities of the classroom. Such programs should be designed to meet the standards required for academic credit.

### 38 Instructional Technology

Integrating instructional technology with teaching strategies provides an expanding opportunity to enrich students' learning experiences. The possibilities far exceed current efforts to realize that goal. Professional development should continue to familiarize teachers with the basics of computer hardware and software. But the larger instructional issues must focus on current realistic applications throughout the curriculum. Using technology, students can acquire multiple skills and a knowledge base that expands the narrow confines of their classrooms.

Teachers must learn the skills required to enable students to locate information available through the Internet. Other essential knowledge and skills involve validating data sources and observing online protocols, including respect for intellectual property. Professional development programs should include teachers and selected students, aides, and volunteers.

### 39 Instructional Seminars

Teachers should be provided with frequently scheduled, carefully planned seminars that address the challenges of implementing standards-based education.

Mentor teachers, the principal, curriculum specialists, guest professors, and instructional leaders should participate in this professional development effort.

### 40 Book Clubs for Educators

Research findings repeatedly identify isolation and the lack of personal and collegial reflection as pervasive problems among teachers. Faculties can cope with this problem through professional dialogue centered on books whose themes have universal significance for educators. This idea is simple yet powerful. School-based book clubs may choose titles from a potentially broad offering of classic or contemporary books. The process is intended to be enjoyable and informative, maximum flexibility being allowed in the choice of books and the organization of reading groups.

### 41 Professional Reflections

Teachers and administrators, individually and collectively, must deal with the many issues affecting their day-to-day duties. Only then can problems be solved and classroom instruction refined. Each of the preceding priorities must embrace the importance of reflective thinking. Journaling, sharing with a mentor or other trusted colleague, or delving into a good book are only a few of the possibilities available. Although the processes and insights associated with reflective thinking are often essentially private matters, members of the same faculty should encourage one another and share ideas and insights whenever appropriate.

## Thematic Organization of School-Based Professional Development Programs

The following models suggest possibilities for organizing clusters of professional development topics (as already discussed) based on specific themes. Examples of two themes are shown in graphic models titled "Standards-Based Education" (Example A) and "Learning Communities" (Example B), together with suggested topics that address each theme. The graphic models are intended to emphasize the inherent relationship among selected topics. However, the selection of topics for each model is arbitrary. Other topics could have been added, and some topics might not have been included. Such decisions depend on needs at each school site. The school site's *professional development council* can play a significant role in this matter.

Other clusters of topics grouped around themes are also included, although not de-

picted in the graphic model. Again, the selection of topics in relation to particular themes is arbitrary (although, it is hoped, logical). Those planning school-based professional development programs should be completely flexible in mixing and matching professional development topics based on sample themes or in creating new themes and organizing topics based on them in any way that meets the needs of a given faculty. Moreover, the professional development topics are not intended to be exhaustive. Many other possibilities exist and should be developed as appropriate.

*Note:* The numbers that appear in Example A and Example B on the following pages correspond to the numbers appearing in this appendix.

Example A, "Standards-Based Education," is designed to show how professional development topics can be organized by major theme as a prelude to planning organized faculty learning experiences. Example B concerns learning communities. However, any combination of topics that responds to the needs of teachers and administrators in a particular school is appropriate. The creation of new topics and themes is always in order.

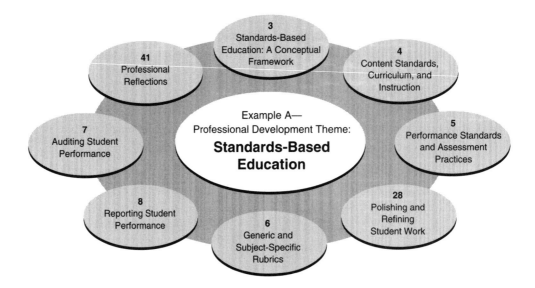

Example A—
Professional Development Theme:
**Standards-Based Education**

3
Standards-Based Education: A Conceptual Framework

41
Professional Reflections

4
Content Standards, Curriculum, and Instruction

7
Auditing Student Performance

5
Performance Standards and Assessment Practices

8
Reporting Student Performance

6
Generic and Subject-Specific Rubrics

28
Polishing and Refining Student Work

Other themes and topics are suggested below:

**Standards-Based Middle Schools**
- Middle School Philosophy, Policies, and Practices
- Standards-Based Education: A Conceptual Framework
- Interdisciplinary Team Teaching and Thematic Instruction
- Inclusive Classroom Teaching
- Multicultural Education and Equal Access
- School Mission and Vision
- Professional Reflections

**Instruction**
- Standards-Based Education: A Conceptual Framework
- Alignment of Standards, Curriculum, Instruction, and Assessment
- Differentiated Instruction
- Interdisciplinary Team Teaching and Thematic Instruction

- Scaffolding
- Specially Designed Academic Instruction in English
- Multicultural Education and Equal Access
- Professional Reflections

**Assessment and Performance-Standard System**
- Standards-Based Education: A Conceptual Framework
- Alignment of Standards, Curriculum, Instruction, and Assessment
- Performance Standards and Performance Tasks
- Benchmark Assessments
- Polishing and Refining Student Work
- Generic and Subject-Specific Rubrics
- Scoring Student Work
- Reporting Student Performance
- Auditing Student Performance
- Professional Reflections

Example B—
Professional Development Theme:
**Learning
Communities**

- **30** Service-Learning
- **41** Professional Reflections
- **18** Learning Styles and Classroom Environment
- **13** Teachers as Mentors, Advisers, and Friends
- **11** Managing Classroom Behavior
- **16** Multicultural Education and Equal Access
- **14** Teachers as Coaches
- **20** Safety Nets for Students

Other themes and topics are suggested below:

**Student Diversity**
- Developmental Characteristics of Young Adolescents
- Differentiated Instruction
- Learning Styles and Classroom Environment
- Scaffolding
- Specially Designed Academic Instruction in English
- Safety Nets for Students
- Inclusive Classroom Teaching
- Multicultural Education and Equal Access
- Professional Reflections

**Classroom Management**
- Content Standards, Curriculum, and Instruction
- Reporting Student Performance
- Auditing Student Performance
- Lesson Planning and Weekly Syllabus
- Managing Classroom Behavior
- Managing Time: School and Classroom
- Collegially Based Crisis Management
- Professional Reflections

**Paraprofessionals and Volunteers**
- Middle School Philosophy, Policies, and Practices
- Standards-Based Education: A Conceptual Framework
- Aides as Adjunct Teachers
- Parents and Other Community Volunteers
- Characteristics of Young Adolescent Students
- Managing Classroom Behavior
- Inclusive Classroom Teaching
- Professional Reflections

**Curriculum**
- Standards-Based Education: A Conceptual Framework
- Standards, Curriculum, and Instruction
- New California Subject-Matter Frameworks
- Expanded Subject-Matter Knowledge
- Deep Learning
- Complex Reasoning
- Professional Reflections

**Teachers as Classroom Managers**
- Parents and Other Community Volunteers
- Aides as Adjunct Teachers
- Managing Time: School and Classroom
- Managing Classroom Behavior
- Auditing Student Performance
- Lesson Planning and Weekly Syllabus
- Homework Assignments
- Managing Classroom Paperwork
- Professional Reflections

# Notes

**Chapter 1**

[1]*Caught in the Middle: Educational Reform for Young Adolescents in California Public Schools.* Report of the Superintendent's Middle Grades Task Force. Sacramento: California Department of Education, 1987.

[2]Anthony Jackson and Gayle Davis, *Turning Points 2000: Educating Adolescents in the 21st Century.* A Report of Carnegie Corporation of New York. New York: Teachers College Press, 2000.

[3]*Turning Points: Preparing American Youth for the 21st Century.* Report of the Task Force on the Education of Young Adolescents, Carnegie Council on Adolescent Development. New York: Carnegie Corporation of New York, 1989.

[4]Jackson and Davis, *Turning Points 2000.*

[5]*What Work Requires of Schools.* Report of the Secretary's Commission on Achieving Necessary Skills (SCANS). Washington, D.C.: U.S. Department of Labor, 2000, pp. B-1, C-1, vii, xviii, 2-3, 19.

[6]New Standards: Performance Standards and Assessments for the Schools. A joint project of the National Center on Education and the Economy and the Learning Research and Development Center, University of Pittsburgh.

[7]*Fact Book 2000: Handbook of Education Information.* Sacramento: California Department of Education, 2000, pp. 54, 58.

[8]*Every Child a Reader. Report of the California Reading Task Force.* Sacramento: California Department of Education, 1995, pp. 7-8, 13, 15-16.

[9]*Improving Mathematics Achievement for All California Students. Report of the California Mathematics Task Force.* Sacramento: California Department of Education, 1995, p. iii.

[10]*Mathematics Equals Opportunity.* White Paper Prepared for U.S. Secretary of Education Richard W. Riley. October 20, 1997. Washington, D.C.: U.S. Department of Education.

[11]*Fact Book 2000,* pp. 29-30.

[12]*Caught in the Middle.*

**Chapter 2**

[1]Adapted from Linda N. Hansche, "Checklist for Content Standards," in *Handbook for the Development of Performance Standards: Meeting the Requirements of Title I.*

Washington, D.C.: U.S. Department of Education and the Council of Chief State School Officers, 1998, p. 14; adapting from Ruth Mitchell, *Front-End Alignment: Using Standards to Steer Educational Change, A Manual for Developing Standards.* Washington, D.C.: The Education Trust, 1996, pp. 22–23.

[2]Douglas Reeves, *"Standards Are Not Enough: Essential Transformations for Successful Middle Schools."* Workshop given for the California Department of Education, Sacramento, October 16-17, 2000.

[3]Robert Marzano, *Transforming Classroom Grading.* Alexandria, Va.: Association for Supervision and Curriculum Development, 2000.

[4]*Reading/Language Arts Framework for California Public Schools, Kindergarten Through Grade Twelve.* Sacramento: California Department of Education, 1999, pp. 157–160.

**Chapter 3**

[1]*Testing, Teaching, and Learning: A Guide for States and School Districts.* Edited by Richard F. Elmore and Robert Rothman. Washington, D.C.: Committee on Title I Testing and Assessment, National Research Council. Washington, D.C.: National Academy Press, 1999.

[2]Joan Ardovino, John Hollingsworth, and Silvia Ybarra, *Multiple Measures: Accurate Ways to Assess Student Achievement.* Thousand Oaks, Calif.: Corwin Press, 2000.

[3]Richard J. Stiggins, *Classroom Assessment for Student Success.* Washington, D.C.: National Education Association, 1998.

[4]*Testing, Teaching, and Learning.*

[5]Letter from State Superintendent of Public Instruction Delaine Eastin and State Board of Education President Monica Lozano to school district superintendents, December 1, 2000.

[6]G. Wiggins and J. McTighe, *Understanding by Design.* Alexandria, Va.: Association for Supervision and Curriculum Development, 1998. Quoted in Anthony Jackson and Gayle Davis, *Turning Points 2000.*

[7]*Testing, Teaching, and Learning.*

## Chapter 4

[1]"Quality Counts 2001: A Better Balance," *Education Week*'s Fifth Annual 50-State Report Card. *Education Week* (January 10, 2001), 14.

[2]*Testing, Teaching, and Learning.*

[3]Senate Bill 1X, Ch. 3, Stats. 1999.

[4]Mike Schmoker, *Results: The Key to Continuous School Improvement* (Second edition). Alexandria, Va.: Association for Supervision and Curriculum Development, 1996.

## Chapter 5

[1]*Turning Points: Preparing American Youth for the 21st Century.* Report of the Task Force on the Education of Young Adolescents, Carnegie Council on Adolescent Development. New York: Carnegie Corporation of New York, 1989.

[2]*This We Believe: Developmentally Responsive Middle-Level Schools.* A position paper prepared by the National Middle School Association. Columbus, Ohio: National Middle School Association, 1995.

[3]*Exemplary Middle Schools.* Research Summary No. 4. Columbus, Ohio: National Middle School Association, 1999.

## Chapter 6

[1]William W. Purkey and John M. Novak, *Inviting School Success: A Self-Concept Approach to Teaching and Learning.* Belmont, Calif.: Wadsworth Publishing Co., 1993.

[2]*Turning Points: Preparing American Youth for the 21st Century.* Report of the Task Force on the Education of Young Adolescents, Carnegie Council on Adolescent Development. New York: Carnegie Corporation of New York, 1989.

[3]James J. Fenwick, *The Middle School Years.* San Diego: Fenwick Associates, 1993.

[4]Anne Wheelock, *Safe to Be Smart: Building a Culture for Standards-Based Reform in the Middle Grades.* Columbus, Ohio: National Middle School Association, 1998. See also Martin Haberman, "The Pedagogy of Poverty Versus Good Teaching," *Kappan,* Vol. 72 (April 1991).

[5]Anne Wheelock, *Safe to Be Smart.*

[6]Ibid.

## Chapter 7

[1]James J. Fenwick, "Managing Middle Grade Reform: An America 2000 Agenda." Sacramento: California Department of Education, 1992.

[2]*Prisoners of Time.* Report of the National Education Commission on Time and Learning. Washington, D.C.: U.S. Government Printing Office, 1994.

## Chapter 8

[1]*From Library Skills to Information Literacy: A Handbook for the 21st Century.* Prepared by the California Media and Library Educators Association. Castle Rock, Colo.: Hi Wilson Research and Publishing, 1994.

[2]June Hodgin and Caaren Wooliscroft, "Eric Learns to Read: Learning Styles at Work," *Educational Leadership,* Vol. 54 (March 1997).

[3]Carol Ann Tomlinson and M. Layne Kalbfleisch, "Teach Me, Teach My Brain: A Call for Differentiated Classrooms," *Educational Leadership,* Vol. 56 (November 1998).

## Chapter 9

[1]Thomas L. Shortt and Yvonne V. Thayer, "Block Scheduling Can Enhance School Climate," *Educational Leadership,* Vol. 56 (January 1999).

## Chapter 10

[1]*Reading/Language Arts Framework for California Public Schools, Kindergarten Through Grade Twelve.* Sacramento: California Department of Education, 1999, p. 19.

[2]*Reading/Language Arts Framework,* pp. 234–35.

[3]R. Scarcella, "Effective Language Instruction for English Learners." Paper presented at the Standards-Based Evaluation and Accountability Institute for English Learners and Immigrant Students: A Focus on English Language Development, sponsored by the California Department of Education, Santa Barbara, Calif., December 4, 2000; R. Gersten and S. Baker, "What We Know About Effective Practices for English-Language Learners," *Exceptional Children,* Vol. 66, No. 4 (2000), 459–70; L. Wong Fillmore and C. Snow, "What Teachers Need to Know About Language." Available on the Center for Applied Linguistics Web site <*www.cal.org/ericll/teachers/teachers.pdf*>.2000.

[4]California Reading and Literature Project (binder materials for the California Professional Development Institute for Teachers of English Learners, 2000).

[5]R. Gersten and S. Baker, "What We Know About Effective Practices for English-Language Learners," *Exceptional Children,* Vol. 66, No. 4 (2000), 459–70.

[6]*Reading/Language Arts Framework,* p. 279.

[7]P. M. Greenfield, "A Theory of the Teacher in the Learning Activities of Everyday Life," in *Everyday Cognition: Its Development in Social Contexts.* Edited by B. Rogoff and J. Lave. Cambridge, Mass.: Harvard University Press, 1984, pp. 117–38.

[8]S. Dutro, "Reading Instruction for English Language Learners: Ten Pedagogical Considerations" (California Reading and Literature Project, 2000, binder materials).

[9]Aida Walqui-van Lier, "Sheltered Instruction: Doing It Right" (1992; California Reading and Literature Project, 2000, binder materials).

## Chapter 11

[1]Anne Wheelock, *Safe to Be Smart: Building a Culture for Standards-Based Reform in the Middle Grades.* Columbus, Ohio: National Middle School Association, 1998.

[2]Robert C. Calfee and Cynthia L. Patrick, *Teach Our Children Well: Bringing K–12 Education into the 21st Century.* Stanford, Calif.: Stanford Alumni Association, 1995.

## Chapter 12

[1]*A Matter of Time: Risk and Opportunity in the Nonschool Hours.* Report of the Task Force on Youth Development and Community Programs, Carnegie Council on Adolescent Development. New York: Carnegie Corporation of New York, 1992.

[2]*Service-Learning: Linking Classrooms and Communities.* Report of the Superintendent's Service-Learning Task Force. Sacramento: California Department of Education, 1999, p. 38.

[3]*Service-Learning: Linking Classrooms and Communities.*

## Chapter 13

[1]Fred M. Hechinger, *Fateful Choices: Healthy Youth for the 21st Century.* New York: Carnegie Council on Adolescent Development, 1992.

[2]National Sleep Foundation, *Wake Up Call to Educators.* *<http://206.215.227.10/nsf/whatsnew/teen_sleep_news.html>*.

[3]*Los Angeles Times*, March 17, 1999.

[4]Cindy Rodriguez, "Even in Middle School, Girls Are Thinking Thin," *The Boston Globe Online,* November 27, 1998.

[5]Ridgley Ochs, "For Teens, Bloom of Youth Isn't So Rosy." Excerpted from *Newsday, Los Angeles Times*, January 26, 1999.

[6]Nancy Shute, "Go Out and Play," *U.S. News and World Report*, April 6, 1998.

[7] National Sleep Foundation, *Wake Up Call to Educators.*

[8] Ibid.

[9]*Early Warning, Timely Response: A Guide to Safe Schools.* Washington, D.C.: U.S. Department of Education, Special Education and Rehabilitative Services, 1998.

[10]*California Safe Schools Assessment, 1998-99 Results: Promoting Safe Schools.* Sacramento: California Department of Education, 1999.

[11]"Turning It Around for All Youth: From Risk to Resilience," *Digest, ERIC Clearinghouse on Urban Education*, No. 126, August 1997.

[12]Blyth D. Benson and E. Roehlkepartain, *National Report on Public School Students in 450 Communities.* Minneapolis: Search Institute, 1995.

[13]Ronald D. Williamson and J. Howard Johnston, "Responding to Parent and Public Concerns About Middle-Level Schools," *Bulletin of the National Association of Secondary School Principals*, September 1998.

## Chapter 14

[1]Linda Darling-Hammond, *The Right to Learn: A Blueprint for Creating Schools That Work.* San Francisco: Jossey-Bass, 1997.

[2]Hayes Mizell, "Standards in Context." An address given before the Council on Basic Education, Dallas, November 17, 1995.

[3]Kirk Winters, "Teacher Quality: Report on Teacher Preparation and Qualifications." Internet news release by the U.S. Department of Education, January 28, 1999.

[4]Anne Wheelock, *Safe to Be Smart: Building a Culture for Standards-Based Reform in the Middle Grades.* Columbus, Ohio: National Middle School Association, 1998.

[5]Joellen Killion and Stephanie Hirsh, "A Crack in the Middle," *Education Week,* Vol. 17 (March 18, 1998).

[6]"Elements of High-Quality Professional Development." Developed by the California Professional Development Consortia. Sacramento: California Department of Education, 1996.

[7]"National Staff Development Council's Standards for Staff Development" (Middle-level edition). Oxford, Ohio: National Middle School Association, 1997.

# Glossary

**academic enrichment center.** Usually an after-hours academic program serving students with a broad spectrum of interests and abilities. It should be viewed as an extension of the regular school program, not merely as a catch-all for middle grade students whose needs may not be addressed in other after-hours programs.

**academic literacy.** An advanced level of literacy enabling students to achieve deep learning of the more complex knowledge and skills embedded in and defined by grade-level content standards. For this level of learning to be achieved, the fundamental elements of academic literacy focuses directly on content and performance standards.

**accountability.** The extent to which an individual, group, or institution is held responsible for actions or performance. In education, schools and districts are now held accountable by providing evidence of student learning and achievement and school improvement.

**active learning.** Learning in which instructional strategies engage students intellectually and physically as they pursue given classroom assignments. Active learning is the opposite of passive learning, in which one-way communication from teachers to students is the norm. Active learning involves substantive changes in the ways students and teachers work together, shifting the focus of classroom instruction from teaching to learning. In such classrooms, students are engaged in learning activities such as gathering data, defining issues, stating problems, generating and testing hypotheses, drawing conclusions, reporting and defending their work. *One of active learning's most basic aims is to create independent learners.* Active learning is directly responsive to the developmental characteristics associated with early adolescence.

**advisory program.** A special type of group guidance experience in which students meet together in small groups with the same teacher or counselor over an extended period of time, often for two or more years. A strong, trusting relationship nurtured between students and their advisor allows them to deal with sensitive issues and concerns. Students gain emotional strength, self-knowledge, and social skills through their participation in well-defined advisory programs. (See also **teacher-based adviser/advisee program.**)

**analytic scoring.** Evaluation of student work across several dimensions of performance rather than on the overall quality of student work. In analytic scoring the crucial elements of response are identified and scored separately. For example, analytic scoring of a historical essay might include scores of the following dimensions: use of prior knowledge, application of principles, use of original source material to support a point of view, accuracy, and composition. An overall impression of quality may be included in analytic scoring.

**API.** The *Academic Performance Index (API)* is the cornerstone of the Public Schools Accountability Act (PSAA). The API ranks school performance, sets growth targets, and provides similar-school comparisons. The API is a single number on a scale of 200 to 1,000, indicating how well a school has performed academically the previous school year. Although initially based on the results of the Stanford 9, additional factors, when available, will be included in the calculation of the API.

**assessment.** The processes used to collect information about student progress toward educational goals. The particular form of an assessment depends on what is being assessed and on the uses to which the results of assessment will be applied. Assessments can range from small-scale assessments used in the classroom by teachers to obtain day-to day information about student progress, through medium-scale assessments used by school districts to evaluate the effectiveness of schools or educational programs, to large-scale assessments used by state or national bodies to assess the degree to which large educational goals have been met.

**assessment system**. The combination of assessments into a comprehensive system that produces comprehensive, credible, and dependable information upon which important decisions can be made about students, schools, districts, or states.

**benchmark assessments/assignments.** Formative, uniform measure of student progress relative to standards. Standards-aligned assessments and assignments provide information about progress toward the end target. The term *benchmark assessments/assignments* in this publication refers to a common, grade-level, standardized administration of an assessment/assignment that provides results that are comparable for all grade-level students. These results give an objective basis for measuring progress and making decisions about individual students.

**bias.** A characteristic of a test that could reduce the chances for identifiable subpopulations to receive scores that accurately reflect their abilities to respond to the skill being measured. Common sources of bias may be related to language, cultural, or gender differences. For example, a mathematics word problem that contains difficult language may be biased against English language learners. Inadequate performance may be due not to a lack of mathematical ability, but rather to a lack of English language skills.

**block scheduling.** An arrangement of blocks of instructional time during the school day composed of any number of increments and scheduled flexibly to accomplish specific instructional goals. Combined with interdisciplinary team teaching, block scheduling provides one of the most effective uses of instructional time.

**chronological team.** A type of team teaching in which two or more teachers specializing in different subject areas share the same students but teach in different classrooms. It is the most basic model for team teaching.

**classroom assessment.** An assessment developed, administered, and scored by a teacher or group of teachers to evaluate individual student or classroom performance on a topic. Ideally, the results of classroom assessments are used to inform and improve instruction to help students reach identified standards.

**constructed response.** Constructed-response format. An assessment activity that asks students to construct a response, create a product, or perform a demonstration to show what they know and can do.

**content standards.** Stated expectations of what students should know and be able to do in particular subjects and grade levels. Content standards define for teachers, students, parents, and communities not only what is expected of students, but also what schools should teach.

**cooperative team.** A type of team teaching in which two or more teachers specializing in different subject areas share the same students. Instruction may or may not involve having all the students learn together in large or small groups. The teachers may plan together but usually focus on allocating time and organizing instruction within a block schedule rather than on developing interdisciplinary connections.

**core curriculum.** A curriculum clearly defined by sets of content and performance standards for each subject and providing students with access to the knowledge, skills, and values that all educated citizens should possess. The core curriculum emphasizes cultural literacy, scientific literacy, knowledge of the humanities, and an appreciation for the basic values that sustain our nation. It also includes the opportunity to acquire proficiency in reading, writing, speaking, and listening, which are systematically and continually reinforced in all learning experiences at every grade level. The core curriculum is designed to maintain the future academic and career options of all students and to prepare them to exercise their personal, civic, and economic rights and responsibilities as adults.

**criteria.** Guidelines, rules, characteristics, or dimensions that are used to judge the quality of student performance. Criteria indicate what we value in student response, products, or performances. Criteria may be holistic, analytic, general, or specific. Scoring rubrics are based on criteria and define what the criteria mean and how they are used.

**criteria-referenced assessment.** An assessment designed to reveal what a student knows, understands, or can do in relation to specific objectives or standards. In criterion-referenced assessments, it is possible that none, some, or all of the examinees will reach a particular goal or performance standard.

**curriculum alignment.** The process of matching the curriculum to the content standards assessed in a testing program to ensure that teachers will cover the material assessed.

**deep learning.** Learning that involves ensuring that students have internalized new knowledge and skills and can apply them in practical ways. For deep learning to occur, a sufficient amount of time is spent on specific standards to ensure that they are mastered at or above a predefined level of proficiency.

**differentiated instruction.** An approach to teaching in which instruction is tailored to meet the needs of individual students. Such instruction is designed to provide each student with access to a rigorous and standards-based curriculum. Instructional decisions are based on the results of appropriate and meaningful student assessments. Differentiated instruction helps to provide a variety of ways for individual students to take in new information, assimilate it, and demonstrate what they have learned. It may be contrasted with instruction that aims lessons at the average student in terms of instruction, activities, homework assignments, and assessments.

**dimensions.** Desired knowledge or skills measured in an assessment, usually represented in a scoring rubric or criteria.

**early adolescence.** A term used to describe the initial phase of the transition between childhood and maturity. Intellectual development accelerates for most children during early adolescence, with rapid growth occurring in the ability to engage in abstract thought processes. Examples include reasoning with hypotheses involving two or more variables; use of complex symbolic logic, such as that found in more advanced mathematics; insight into the sources of previously unquestioned attitudes, behaviors, and values; and ability to project thought into the future and to anticipate and express goals.

The gradual emergence of a significant body of knowledge about the uniqueness of early adolescence has given rise to schools more responsive to the scope, rapidity, and impact of the physical, intellectual, psychological, and social changes accompanying this period of human development.

**ELD.** The English language development (ELD) standards provide criteria for documenting the progress of English learners and serve as a guide for development of the ELD assessments. These assessments will measure the progress of English learners toward proficiency in English. Under AB 748 (Escutia) and SB 638 (Alpert), districts will be required to administer the ELD assessments to their English learners, beginning in spring 2001.

**end-of-course**. Examinations that are administered at or near the end of a course to determine whether students have met specified course content and/or standards.

**equity**. The concern for fairness (i.e., that assessments are free from bias or favoritism). An assessment that is fair enables all children to show what they can do. At minimum, all assessments should be reviewed for (a) stereotypes; (b) situations that may favor one group or culture over another; (c) excessive language demands that prevent some students from showing their knowledge; and (d) the assessment's potential to include students with disabilities or limited English proficiency.

**evaluation.** In most educational settings, the process used to measure, compare, and judge the quality of student work, schools, or a specific educational program.

**equal access.** An educational principle holding that all students must be provided with the

opportunity to master the most advanced curricula offered at each grade level. Instructional research and practice demonstrate that students do have different strengths and that they will invariably master the same skill or topic at different levels of sophistication and detail. However, equal access stresses the notion that all students should be pushed as far and as fast as possible, particularly in the core curriculum subjects, so that they may have the opportunity to achieve academically at the highest levels they are capable of attaining.

**exemplars.** Examples of student work produced from a common assignment or assessment. Samples are evaluated by using uniform scoring criteria. Those that clearly demonstrate performance at different levels of the scoring guide (rubric) are used as anchor papers. These anchor papers serve as guides in bringing objective consistency to all other work being scored.

**exploratory curricula.** A term used to define learning experiences that provide students with an introduction to previously unknown or nonexperienced areas of knowledge and skills and represent learning episodes of varied length and scope. Offerings in the exploratory curricula may or may not reflect optimal choices for students. Students' identifiable abilities or interests are not required for enrollment in exploratory courses. Use of exploratory curricula is particularly appropriate during the middle grades. Exploratory courses (and units within courses) are often used successfully to pique interest and curiosity, thereby affecting student motivation in core curriculum subjects. Exploratory offerings provide many students with the impetus to pursue specific academic and career options in high school and in postsecondary education.

**formative assessment.** An assessment that is an ongoing, diagnostic assessment providing information (feedback) to guide instruction and improve student performance.

**heterogeneous grouping.** The practice of organizing students for classroom instruction without direct reference to differences in academic ability among students as measured by standardized tests, teacher observation, or other comparable criteria. A popular synonym for heterogeneous grouping is *multiability grouping,* a term viewed by many as being more accurate and more consistent in discussions of human diversity.

**high-stakes assessment.** Testing that has strong consequences for the participants. A student's performance on a high-stakes exam might affect entry into a special class, college admission, or the awarding of a diploma or degree. The college board's SAT is an example of a high-stakes test.

**holistic scoring.** Evaluation of student work in which the score is based on the overall quality of the response or performance rather than on the scoring of multiple dimensions of performance (analytic scoring).

**homogeneous grouping.** The practice of organizing classrooms and groups of students according to intellectual ability as measured by standardized test scores, literacy levels, teacher perceptions, or general academic performance. Extensive research data show that poor and ethnic minority students are massively overrepresented in the lowest-ability groups or tracks. Research findings also indicate that ability grouping is often based on subjective judgments, occurs as early as the primary grades, and condemns the majority of students to the same ability group throughout the remainder of their school lives. Students in low-ability groups may suffer impaired self-esteem and achieve far below their potential ability.

***High School Exit Examination (HSEE).*** A graduation requirement, authorized by state law in 1999, that requires California public school students, beginning with the graduating class of 2004, to pass the *HSEE* in order to receive a high school diploma. The *HSEE* will cover the curricular areas of reading, writing, and mathematics and will be aligned with the state content standards adopted by the State Board of Education.

**IASA/ESEA, Title I.** The Elementary and Secondary Education Act (ESEA) of 1965, the largest federal program for promoting equity and excellence for at-risk students. ESEA was reauthorized by congress in 1994 through the Improving America's Schools Act (IASA), which created a program with four parts:

- Part A:  Improving Basic Programs
- Part B:  Even Start
- Part C:  Migrant Education
- Part D:  Education of Neglected and Delinquent Youth

A school becomes eligible for ESEA, Title I, Part A, funding when it serves a large number of students living in poverty.

**IEP.** Individualized education program. A written plan of instruction required by the Individuals with Disabilities Education Act (IDEA) for every school-age student receiving special education. The plan must include a statement of the student's strengths and weaknesses, long-term and short-term goals and objectives, and all special services required.

**inclusive classroom.** A classroom in which students with a relatively wide range of abilities learn together. It reflects standards-based education's commitment to high levels of academic achievement for all students.

**interdisciplinary team.** A type of team teaching in which two or more teachers specializing in different subjects share the same students, usually for extended blocks of core instructional time, and plan and teach together to integrate their branches of knowledge. Students assigned to interdisciplinary teams gain insight into the logical relationships between the various curricular areas and receive classroom assignments that combine the knowledge and skills derived from their teachers' specific areas of expertise. The use of such teams assigned to core instructional blocks is a distinctive feature of middle grades education. This approach may be contrasted with traditional junior high schools, which are typically departmentalized: students are assigned to separate classes, usually one period in length, for each subject, and teachers meet together according to subject-matter specialization rather than by team. In such schools planning is focused on the coordination of courses and course sequences rather than on direct instructional collaboration.

**learning deficit.** Within the context of this document, a term referring to students who are performing below a basic proficiency level and who may be several grade levels behind in standards content. The majority of students with learning deficits are not *learning disabled* but are behind academically for other reasons, such as a lack of or limited basic skills or academic literacy and/or possibly a *learning difficulty* or nonschool-related factors.

**learning disability.** A disabling condition in which a person with average intelligence is substantially delayed in academic achievement because of a processing disorder, not because of an environmental, an economic, or a cultural disadvantage.

**low-stakes assessment.** Testing that has few direct consequences for the participants. Such testing is generally used for diagnosis of individual students or to provide information for such purposes as instructional improvement or curriculum redesign.

**multiple choice.** A response format in which students select from two or more predetermined choices. *Enhanced* multiple-choice formats may involve questions that are linked and sequenced in a manner that provides more insight into features such as the student's prior knowledge or the particulars of the solution process used by the student.

**multiple measures.** The use of a variety of measures (e.g., standardized test results, classroom assessments, tasks and projects, grades, and teacher evaluation) to provide a complete picture of a student's academic achievement.

**NAEP.** The National Assessment of Educational Progress (NAEP), which is an ongoing, national assessment of what America's students in grades four, eight, and twelve know and can do in various academic subject areas. NAEP is administered by the National Center for Education Statistics of the U.S. Department of Education. California has participated in NAEP for nearly 30 years. One NAEP component provides states with a measure of their students' academic performance over time and a comparison to the results of other states and students nationwide.

**norm-referenced assessment.** An assessment in which individual or group performance is compared to the performance of a larger group. Usually the larger group, or "norm group," is a national sample representing a wide and diverse cross-section of students. Students, schools, or districts are then compared or rank-ordered in relation to the norm group.

**opportunity to learn.** Elements of the learning process that positively influence student achievement. Opportunity to learn (OTL) is what takes place in classrooms that enables students to acquire the knowledge and skills that are expected of them. OTL can include *what* is taught and *how,* by *whom,* and with *what* resources it is taught.

**peer advising.** The practice of placing students in one-to-one relationships to enable them to share insights, explore major issues, affirm positive personal and social values, acquire new self-knowledge, and experience the personal acceptance of valued peers. (See also **teacher-based adviser/advisee programs** and **peer tutoring.**)

**peer coaching.** The practice of grouping small numbers of students enrolled in the same class or course to encourage them to help each other stimulate and nurture thinking skills, particularly through problem posing and problem solving. Learning activities are organized by the teacher, who assumes the role of manager of the peer support group in which students question and critique one another. Characteristics of effective peer coaching include learning settings that foster intellectual growth in a secure environment where problems may be presented and rational problem-solving processes may be used to their greatest advantage. Peer support groups and coaching techniques may be used effectively by teachers in any subject area.

**peer tutoring.** The practice of using student volunteers to give one-to-one instruction to other students of the same age and grade. It is used to (1) reinforce regular classroom instruction; or (2) enable underachieving students to improve their basic skills or acquire knowledge ordinarily associated with learning expectations for earlier grades. Extensive research supports the effectiveness of peer tutoring for those being tutored and those providing the tutoring. This practice can lead to statistically significant achievement gains and enhanced academic motivation. Students who provide tutoring experience valuable intrinsic rewards, including enhanced self-esteem and the acquisition of positive social values associated with service to others.

**performance assessment.** Refers to testing methods that require students to write an answer or develop a product that demonstrates their knowledge or skill. Performance assessment can take many different forms, including writing short answers, doing mathematical computations, writing an extended essay, conducting an experiment, presenting an oral argument, or assembling a portfolio of representative work.

**performance standards.** Standards that identify levels of student achievement based on a demonstrated degree of mastery of specified content standards. California has identified five performance levels for its statewide standards-based assessments: Advanced, Proficient, Basic, Below Basic, and Far Below Basic.

**performance standard system.** A system with linking component parts: performance levels, performance descriptors, aligned assessments, scoring criteria, and exemplars of student work.

**reliability.** The degree to which the results of an assessment are dependable and consistently measure a particular student knowledge and skill. Reliability is an indication of the consistency of scores over time, between scores, or of scores across different tasks or items that measure the same thing. If scores from an assessment are unreliable, interpretations based on those scores—and subsequent decisions—will not be valid.

**rubrics.** A listing of specific criteria used to score constructed-response tasks in an assessment. A typical rubric contains a scoring scale; states all the different major traits or elements to be examined; and provides criteria for deciding what score to assign to student responses or performances. Scales may be quantitative (e.g., a score from 1 to 6) or qualitative (e.g., "adequate performance" or "minimal competency") or a combination of the two.

**scaffolding.** Support, guidance, or assistance provided to students prior to learning a new or complex task. A teacher scaffolds the task by engaging in appropriate instructional interactions designed to model, assist, or provide necessary information or background.

**school climate.** A term that refers to issues associated with the emotional health of individuals and the organizational health of the school as an institution. It is closely related to school culture but differs in important ways. School culture concerns traditional patterns of knowledge, beliefs, and values that serve as the basis for policy decisions, organizational practices, and human relationships in schools.

**school culture.** A term adapted from sociology and anthropology. It has become useful as an analytical tool for describing the intricate patterns of knowledge, beliefs, and values that serve as the basis for policy decisions, organizational practices, and human relation-ships in schools. Those patterns are often subtle and poorly understood yet exercise a profound influence on the lives of students, teachers, and other school personnel. The interrelationships that form the basis of school culture are usually institutionalized; that is, they are affirmed by tradition and are thus resistant to change. Research findings on the dynamics of social change show that efforts to reshape school culture (i.e., to introduce innovation) are often

met with arguments and reactions that contradict evidence supporting desirable and effective educational practices. The findings also indicate that persons with professional training and experience can still remain deeply attached emotionally to symbols, rituals, ceremonies, and traditions long after they have lost their original significance. The elements of school culture—rational or irrational as they may be—nevertheless represent the glue which binds a school together and, over time, provide a sense of continuity and purpose meaningful to students, teachers, and the community.

**scoring criteria.** See *rubrics.*

**SDAIE.** Abbreviation for <u>s</u>pecially <u>d</u>esigned <u>a</u>cademic <u>i</u>nstruction in <u>E</u>nglish. It was developed to help second-language learners improve their English-language skills while they focus on grade-level content in the core curriculum. More recently, however, the broad repertoire of instructional skills offered through SDAIE has become increasingly popular in classes for students at all levels of English-language ability, including native speakers of English.

**service-learning.** An instructional strategy by which students learn through active participation in organized service that meets the needs of a community. It is integrated into and enhances the academic curriculum of the students or the educational components of the community service program in which the students are enrolled. Not to be confused with *community service,* which has long been a part of school activity through service clubs, student government, and leadership activities. It is often an "add-on" that is not integrated into the core curriculum.

**service-learning center.** An academic program, usually after hours, designed to provide a planned, supervised setting to broker a wide range of experiences for students. Ideally, service-learning is integrated into the academic curriculum and provides opportunities to demonstrate civic responsibility.

**standards.** These are generally divided into two types: content and performance. Simply stated, content standards define *what* students should know or be able to do. Performance standards are derived from content standards and define *how* or *how well* students must perform. In other words performance standards set the level of mastery expected for the content standards.

**standardization.** A consistent set of procedures for designing, administering, and scoring an assessment. The purpose of standardization is to ensure that all students are assessed under the same conditions so that their scores have the same meaning and are not influenced by differing conditions. Standardized procedures are very important when scores are to be used to compare individuals or groups and the results affect important, high-stakes decisions. Some of the key elements that must be standardized in achievement testing are the time allowed to take the test, the materials provided to the student, the directions given to the student, and the amount and kinds of assistance that may be given to the student.

**student performance report.** A report that identifies the major categories of the content standards for English–language arts, history–social science, mathematics, and science as adopted by the California State Board of Education and reports student progress as a performance level. The performance level relative to specific sets of standards differs from a course grade that may include subjective factors.

**student performance levels.** Levels that indicate the quality of a student's academic work on a continuum that assumes that progression toward higher levels of academic achievement is both possible and expected. Students are expected to exhibit their proficiency through multiple measures of their ability. When state and local performance levels are aligned, they provide clear expectations for teachers and students.

**summative assessment.** A culminating assessment for a unit, grade level, or course of study providing a status report on mastery or degree of proficiency according to identified content standards.

**teacher-based adviser/advisee program.** A program supporting an ongoing relationship between a student and a caring adult that provides the student with security, advice, affirmation, and a positive role model. The major goals of an advisory program are to enhance student-teacher relationships, develop interpersonal skills, discuss school-related issues, build group cohesiveness and school spirit, foster affective growth and development, and present positive adult role models. Most advisory programs include a regular series of activities based on a curriculum designed to promote student development in areas that include character development, conflict resolution, and self-esteem.

**team teaching.** A teaching arrangement in which two or more teachers are assigned the same students for at least part of the school day, either in a single period or in multiple-period core blocks, and together plan at least a portion of the instruction.

This description fits many types of team arrangements. Among these are instructional situations in which team members:

- Teach the same students but at different times of the school day—seldom if ever teaching together at the same time.
- Teach the same subject at the same time but divide content areas according to

special interests or professional
preparation.

- Teach the same subject at the same time
  but divide students into ability groups, with
  team members taking responsibility for
  different levels of instruction.
- Teach different subjects without attempting
  to integrate the knowledge and skills
  associated with the subjects.
- Teach different subjects and integrate the
  knowledge and skills associated with each
  subject—as occurs in interdisciplinary team
  teaching.

**test.** A measuring instrument for assessing and
documenting student learning. The traditional
test is a single-occasion, timed exercise.

**validity.** The degree to which evidence and theory
support the interpretation of test scores entailed
by the proposed uses of the test. The process of
validation involves accumulating evidence to
provide a sound scientific basis for the proposed
score interpretations. It is the interpretations of
test scores for proposed uses that are evaluated,
not the test itself. For example, if a student
performs poorly on a reading test, how
confident are we that this score indicates poor
reading ability? How confident are we that a
low reading score requires special educational
interventions?

**written response.** A response format that requires
students to write or develop a response.

# Additional References

The following publication and web site data were provided by the Middle Grades and High School Networks Office. Questions about the materials should be addressed to that office at (916) 322-1892.

## Print Materials

Alexander, William, and Paul George. *The Exemplary Middle School*. Fort Worth, Tex.: Harcourt, Brace, Jovanovich, 1993.

Ames, Nancy, and Elizabeth Miller. *Changing Middle Schools: How to Make Schools Work for Young Adolescents.* San Francisco: Jossey-Bass, 1994.

Balfanz, R., and Douglas MacIver. "Transforming High Poverty Urban Middle Schools into Strong Learning Institutions: Lessons from the First Five Years of the Talent Development Middle School," *Journal of Education for Students Placed at Risk*, Vol. 5 (Winter 2000).

Bambino, Deborah. *Teaching Out Loud: A Middle Grades Diary*. Westerville, Ohio: National Middle School Association, 1999.

Beane, James A. *Toward a Coherent Curriculum.* Reston, Va.: Association for Supervision and Curriculum Development, 1995.

Benson, Peter L. *What Kids Need to Succeed: Proven, Practical Ways to Raise Good Kids.* Minneapolis: Free Spirit Publishing, Inc., 1994.

Constitutional Rights Foundation. *Active Citizenship Today.* Step-by-step guide for establishing and operating a service-learning program appropriate for middle grades students. Constitutional Rights Foundation, 601 South Kingsley Drive, Los Angeles, CA 90005. Phone: (213) 487-5590. Web site: *<www.crf.org>*.

*Curriculum and Evaluation Standards for School Mathematics*. Reston, Va.: National Council of Teachers of Mathematics, 1989.

Darling-Hammond, Linda. "The Role of Teacher Expertise and Experience in Students' Opportunity to Learn," in *Strategies for Linking School Finance and Students' Opportunity to Learn.* Washington, D.C.: National Governors Association, 1996.

Darling-Hammond, Linda, and B. Falk. "Using Standards and Assessments to Support Student Learning," *Kappan,* Vol. 79 (March 1997).

DuFour, Richard, and Robert Eaker. *Professional Learning Communities at Work: Best Practices for Enhancing Student Achievement.* Bloomington, Ind.: National Educational Service, 1998.

Eccles, J. S. "The Development of Children Ages 6 to 14," *The Future of Children*, Vol. 9, No. 2 (Fall 1999).

Education Commission of the States. *A Policymaker's Guide to Standards-Led Assessment. <www.ecs.org>*.

Education Trust. "Good Teacher Matters: How Well-Qualified Teachers Can Close the Gap," *Thinking K–16*, Vol. 3, No. 2 (Summer 1998). *<www.edtrust.org>*.

Eggert, Leona; Leila Nicholas; and Linda Owen. *Reconnecting Youth: A Peer Group Approach to Building Life Skills.* Bloomington, Ind.: National Educational Service, 1997.

Elmore, R. F.; P. L. Peterson; and S. J. McCarthy. *Restructuring in the Classroom: Teaching, Learning, and School Organization.* San Francisco: Jossey-Bass, 1996.

Felner, R.; A. Jackson; D. Kusask; P. Mulhall; and
N. Flowers. "The Impact of School Reform for
the Middle Years," *Phi Delta Kappan* (March
1997).

Fertman, Carl; George P. White; and Louis J. White.
*Service Learning in the Middle School: Build-
ing a Culture of Service.* Westerville, Ohio:
National Middle School Association, 1996.

*Front End Alignment.* Washington, D.C.: Education
Trust, 1996.

Fullan, Michael. *Change Forces: Probing the
Depths of Educational Reform.* New York:
Falmer Press, 1990.

Glidden, H. *Making Standards Matter.* Washington,
D.C.: American Federation of Teachers, 1998.

*Great Transitions.* Report of the Carnegie Council
on Adolescent Development. New York:
Carnegie Corporation of New York, 1996.

Hatch, Holly, and Kathy Hytten. *Mobilizing
Resources for District-Wide Middle Grades
Reform.* Columbus, Ohio: National Middle
School Association, 1997.

Hechinger, Fred M. *Fateful Choices. Healthy Youth
for the 21ˢᵗ Century.* Copyright 1992 by
Carnegie Corporation of New York. New York:
Hill and Wang, 1993.

Hodges, Randall. "Supporting Failing Students
Through Positive Peer Intervention," *Schools in
the Middle,* Vol. 9, No. 9 (May 2000).

Hodgkinson, Harold. "Reform Versus Reality,"
*Kappan,* Vol. 72 (January 1991).

Hoff, J. *Dynamics of the Empowered School:
Getting to the Core.* Pittsford, N.Y.: J. W. Hoff,
1993.

*Implementation of Middle Grades Reforms in
California Public Schools.* Compiled by James
J. Fenwick. Sacramento: California Department
of Education, 1993.

Jamentz, Kate. *Standards: From Document to
Dialogue.* San Francisco: Western Assessment
Collaborative, WestEd, 1998.

Lessow-Hurley, Judith. *The Foundation of Dual-
Language Instruction.* White Plains, N.Y.:
Longman Publishers, 1996.

Lewis, Anne C. *Figuring It Out: Standards-Based
Reforms in Urban Middle Grades.* New York:
The Edna McConnell Clark Foundation, 1999.

Lipsetz, J.; H. Mizell; A. Jackson; and L. M. Austin.
"Speaking with One Voice: A Manifesto for
Middle-Grades Reform," *Phi Delta Kappan,*
Vol. 7 (1997), 533–40.

Loveless, Tom. *The Tracking and Ability Grouping
Debate.* A Fordham Foundation Report, Vol. 2,
No. 8. Washington, D.C.: Thomas B. Fordham
Foundation, 1998.

Marx, Eva, and Susan Frelick Wooley. *Health Is
Academic: A Guide to Coordinated School
Health Programs.* New York: Teachers College
Press, 1998.

Marzano, Robert J., and John S. Kendall. *Implementing Standards-Based Education.* Washington, D.C.: National Education Association,
1998.

McTighe, Jay, and Steven Ferrara. *Assessing
Learning in the Classroom.* Washington, D.C.:
National Education Association, 1998.

*Middle Ground—The Magazine of Middle Level
Education.* Published five times each year by
the National Middle School Association.

Noddings, N. "Thinking About Standards," *Phi
Delta Kappan,* Vol. 3 (1997), 184–89.

Norton, John, and Anne C. Lewis. *Middle-Grades
Reform.* A Kappan Special Report. Phi Delta
Kappan International Web site:
*<www.pdkintl.org/kappan/kappan.htm>.*
June 27, 2000.

Oakes, Jeannie. *Keeping Track: How Schools
Structure Individuality.* New Haven, Conn.:
Yale University Press, 1985.

Oakes, Jeannie, and Amy Stuart Wells. "Detracking
for High Achievement," *Educational Leadership,* Vol. 55 (March 1998).

O'Neil, John. "Finding Time to Teach," *Educational Leadership* (November 1995).

*Outline for Assessment and Accountability Plans.* Sacramento: California Department of Education, 1999.

"Positive School Climate: Creating a Place Where People Want to Be," *Middle Ground—The Magazine of Middle Level Education,* Vol. 3, No. 2 (October 1999).

*Project ALERT.* Materials developed by RAND for classroom use. Project ALERT, 725 South Figueroa Street, Suite 1615, Los Angeles, CA 90017-5416. Phone: (800) ALERT-10. Web site: *<www.projectalert.best.org>*.

*Safe Schools: A Planning Guide for Action.* Sacramento: California Department of Education, 1995.

Scales, P. C.; N. Starkman; and C. Roberts. *Great Places to Learn: How Asset Building Schools Help Students Succeed.* Minneapolis: The Search Institute, 1999.

Scales, Peter L. "Care and Challenge: Sources of Student Success," *Middle Ground—The Magazine of Middle Level Education,* Vol. 3, No. 2 (October 1999).

Schukar, Ron; Jacquelyn Johnson; and Laurel Singleton. *Service Learning in the Middle School Curriculum: A Resource Book.* Boulder, Colo.: Social Science Education Consortium, 1996.

Schurr, Sandra. *Authentic Assessment: Using Product, Performance and Portfolio, Measures from A to Z.* Westerville, Ohio: National Middle School Association, 1999.

*Service-Learning: Linking Classrooms and Communities.* Report of the Superintendent's Service-Learning Task Force. Sacramento: California Department of Education, 1999.

Shartland, A. *Supporting Latino Families: Lessons from Exemplary Programs.* Cambridge, Mass.: Harvard Family Research Project, 1997.

Smith, Marshall, and Jennifer O'Day. "Systemic School Reform," in *The Politics of Curriculum and Testing.* Edited by S. H. Furman and E. Malin. New York: Falmer Press, 1991.

Spurlock, H. L.; R. L. Mumford; and S. Madhere. "Effects of Gender, Race, and Grade Retention on the Developmental Progression of Self-Efficacy Perceptions." Paper presented at the American Psychological Society Conference, New York, July 1995.

*Statement of NASSP Board of Directors Position on Standards and Assessment.* Reston, Va.: National Association of Secondary School Principals, 2000.

*Trying to Beat the Clock.* Editorial Projects in Education. Washington, D.C.: U.S. Department of Education, 1998.

*What Current Research Shows to the Middle Level Practitioner.* Edited by Judith L. Irvin. Columbus, Ohio: National Middle School Association, 1997.

Wheelock, Anne. "Standards-Based Reform: What Does It Mean for the Middle Schools?" New York: Edna McConnell Clark Foundation, 1995 (working paper).

*Working for Equity in Heterogeneous Classrooms.* Edited by Elizabeth G. Cohen and Rachel A. Lotan. New York: Teachers College Press, 1997.

## CD-ROM

*The Middle School Concept: Why It Works.* Westerville, Ohio: National Middle School Association, 1995.

## Web Sites

Association of School Curricula and Development. *<www.ascd.org>*

California Department of Education. Includes standards adopted by the State Board of Education. *<www.cde.ca.gov>*

California Department of Education. Nutrition Services Division. *<www.cde.ca.gov/nsd/nets>*

California Department of Education. Public School Accountability Act. *<www.cde.ca.gov/psaa>*

California Parent Teachers Association. *<www.capta.org>*

California School Leadership Academy. *<www.csla.org>*

California Subject Matter Projects. *<www.ucop.edu/csmp>*

California Teachers Association. *<www.cta.org>*

Center for the Future of Teaching and Learning. Research-based policy documents. *<www.cftl.org>*

Center for Youth as Resources. Provides small grants for students to plan and carry out service-learning projects. *<www.yar.org>*

Comprehensive Health Education Foundation. *<www.chef.org>*

Comprehensive School Reform Demonstration program. *<www.cde.ca.gov/iasa/csrd>*

George Lucas Educational Foundation. *<www.glef.org>*

The Hope Foundation. Professional Development, Breaking the Cycle of Violence. *<www.communitiesofhope.org>*

Learn and Serve America, U.S. Corporation for National Service. *<www.cns.gov>*

Michigan Schools in the Middle. Professional Development. Includes an online magazine for teachers. *<www.schoolsinthemiddle.org>*

Middle Level Leadership Research Study. *<www.mllc.org>*

MiddleWeb. Provides links to 10,000 resources for middle grades educators and policymakers. *<www.middleweb.com>*

National Association of Attorneys General and National School Boards Association. Joint Web site addressing school violence. *<www.keepschoolssafe.org>*

National Association of State Boards of Education. Order publications, including *Fit, Healthy, and Ready to Learn: A School Health Policy Guide.* *<www.nasbe.org>*

National Forum to Accelerate Middle-Grades Reform. *<www.edc.org/FSC/MGF>*

National Middle School Association. *<www.nmsa.org>*

National Service Learning Center Clearinghouse. *<www.umn.edu/~serve>*

National Staff Development Council. "How-to" resources in easy-to-read format; *What Works in the Middle: Results-Based Staff Development.* *<www.nsdc.org>*

National Youth Leadership Council. Organization that sponsors the annual National Service Learning Conference. *<www.nylcinfo@nylc.org>*

Northwest Regional Educational Laboratory. Includes catalog of the 60+ Obey-Porter School Reform Models. *<www.nwrel.org>*

Policy and Practice Demonstration Project. A national initiative launched by the W. K. Kellogg Foundation to engage more young people in service to others as a part of their academic life. California is one of five states selected for participation. *<www.Learningindeed.org/ppp>*

WestEd. Family and Community Partnerships Resources. *What It Takes to Work Together: The Promise of Educational Partnerships.* Reviews different kinds of partnerships, their benefits, and what elements are needed for them to be as effective as possible. *<www.wested.org>*

# Publications Available from the Department of Education

This publication is one of over 600 that are available from the California Department of Education. Some of the more recent publications or those most widely used are the following:

| Item no. | Title (Date of publication) | Price |
|---|---|---|
| 1372 | Arts Work: A Call for Arts Education for All California Students: The Report of the Superintendent's Task Force on the Visual and Performing Arts (1997) | $11.25 |
| 1467 | Aviation Education and Technology Resources for Teachers (2000) | 15.00 |
| 1515 | California Public School Directory, 2000 | 19.50 |
| 1504 | California School Accounting Manual, 2000 Edition | 25.00 |
| 1373 | Challenge Standards for Student Success: Health Education (1998) | 10.00 |
| 1409 | Challenge Standards for Student Success: Language Arts Student Work Addendum (1998) | 12.75 |
| 1435 | Challenge Standards for Student Success: Physical Education (1998) | 8.50 |
| 1429 | Challenge Standards for Student Success: Visual and Performing Arts (1998) | 12.50 |
| 1290 | Challenge Toolkit: Family-School Compacts (1997) | 9.75* |
| 1439 | Check It Out! Assessing School Library Media Programs: A Guide for School District Education Policy and Implementation Teams (1998) | 9.25 |
| 1281 | Connect, Compute, and Compete: The Report of the California Education Technology Task Force (1996) | 5.75 |
| 1520 | Coordinated Compliance Review Training Guide, 2001-2002 (2000) | 22.00 |
| 1476 | Educating English Learners for the Twenty-First Century: The Report of the Proposition 227 Task Force (1999) | 10.50 |
| 1509 | Elementary Makes the Grade! (2000) | 10.25 |
| 1389 | English–Language Arts Content Standards for California Public Schools, Kindergarten Through Grade Twelve (1998) | 9.25 |
| 1468 | Enrolling Students Living in Homeless Situations (1999) | 8.50 |
| 1244 | Every Child a Reader: The Report of the California Reading Task Force (1995) | 5.25 |
| 0804 | Foreign Language Framework for California Public Schools, Kindergarten Through Grade Twelve (1989) | 7.25 |
| 1382 | Getting Results, Part I: California Action Guide to Creating Safe and Drug-Free Schools and Communities (1998) | 15.25 |
| 1493 | Getting Results, Part II: California Action Guide to Tobacco Use Prevention Education (2000) | 13.50 |
| 1482 | Getting Results, Update 1, Positive Youth Development: Research, Commentary, and Action (1999) | 12.00 |
| 1064 | Health Framework for California Public Schools, Kindergarten Through Grade Twelve (1994) | 10.00 |
| 1477 | Helping Your Students with Homework (1999) | 9.25 |
| 1488 | History–Social Science Content Standards for California Public Schools, Kindergarten Through Grade Twelve (2000) | 9.00 |
| 1284 | History–Social Science Framework for California Public Schools, 1997 Updated Edition (1997) | 12.50 |
| 1245 | Improving Mathematics Achievement for All California Students: The Report of the California Mathematics Task Force (1995) | 5.25 |
| 1500 | Independent Study Operations Manual (2000 Edition) | 30.00 |
| 1258 | Industrial and Technology Education: Career Path Guide and Model Curriculum Standards (1996) | 17.00 |
| 1442 | Joining Hands: Preparing Teachers to Make Meaningful Home-School Connections (1998) | 13.25 |
| 1266 | Literature for the Visual and Performing Arts, Kindergarten Through Grade Twelve (1996) | 10.25 |
| 1457 | Mathematics Content Standards for California Public Schools, Kindergarten Through Grade Twelve (1999) | 8.50 |
| 1508 | Mathematics Framework for California Public Schools, Kindergarten Through Grade Twelve (2000 Revised Edition) | 17.50 |
| 1065 | Physical Education Framework for California Public Schools, Kindergarten Through Grade Twelve (1994) | 7.75 |
| 1314 | Positive Intervention for Serious Behavior Problems: Best Practices in Implementing the Hughes Bill (Assembly Bill 2586) and the Positive Behavioral Intervention Regulations (1998) | 14.00 |
| 1221 | Practical Ideas for Teaching Writing as a Process at the Elementary School and Middle School Levels (1996 Revised Edition) | 18.00 |
| 1462 | Reading/Language Arts Framework for California Public Schools, Kindergarten Through Grade Twelve (1999) | 17.50 |
| 1399 | Ready to Learn—Quality Preschools for California in the 21st Century: The Report of the Superintendent's Universal Preschool Task Force (1998) | 8.00 |
| 1171 | Recommended Readings in Literature, Kindergarten Through Grade Eight, Revised Annotated Edition (1996) | 10.00 |
| 1511 | SB 65 School-Based Pupil Motivation and Maintenance Program Guidelines (2000) | 10.00 |
| 1505 | School Attendance Improvement Handbook (2000) | 14.25 |
| 1496 | Science Content Standards for California Public Schools, Kindergarten Through Grade Twelve (2000) | 9.00 |
| 0870 | Science Framework for California Public Schools, Kindergarten Through Grade Twelve (1990) | 9.50 |
| 1445 | Science Safety Handbook for California Public Schools (1999 Edition) | 17.50 |
| 1452 | Service-Learning: Linking Classrooms and Communities: The Report of the Superintendent's Service Learning Task Force (1999) | 7.00 |

* Other titles in the *Challenge Toolkit* series are *Outline for Assessment and Accountability Plans* (item no. 1300), *Safe and Healthy Schools* (item no. 1299), *School Facilities* (item no. 1294), *Site-Based Decision Making* (item no. 1295), *Service-Learning* (item no. 1291), *Student Activities* (item no. 1292), and *Student Learning Plans* (item no. 1296). Call 1-800-995-4099 for prices and shipping charges.

**Prices and availability are subject to change without notice. Please call 1-800-995-4099 for current prices and shipping charges.**

| Item no. | Title (Date of publication) | Price |
|---|---|---|
| 1407 | Steering by Results—A High-Stakes Rewards and Interventions Program for California Schools and Students: The Report of the Rewards and Interventions Advisory Committee (1998) | $8.00 |
| 1472 | Strategic Teaching and Learning: Standards-Based Instruction to Promote Content Literacy in Grades Four Through Twelve (2000) | 12.50 |
| 1277 | Strategies for Success: A Resource Manual for SHAPE (Shaping Health as Partners in Education) (1996) | 15.00 |
| 1261 | Visual and Performing Arts Framework for California Public Schools, Kindergarten Through Grade Twelve (1996) | 15.00 |
| 1392 | Work-Based Learning Guide (1998) | 12.50 |
| 1390 | Work Permit Handbook for California Schools (1998) | 13.00 |
| 1381 | Workforce Career Development Model (1998) | 9.50 |

- - - - - - - - - - - - - - - - - - - - - - - - - - - - - - - - - - - - - - - - - - - - - - - - - - - -

# Order Form

BUSINESS HOURS: 8:00 A.M.–4:30 P.M., PST

# To order call: 1-800-995-4099

MONDAY THROUGH FRIDAY • FAX 916-323-0823

**FROM:**

SCHOOL/DISTRICT (if applicable)   ☐ PUBLIC   ☐ PRIVATE

NAME/ATTENTION

ADDRESS

CITY                STATE      ZIP CODE

(     )
DAYTIME TELEPHONE

PAYMENT METHOD:   ☐ CHECK (Payable to California Department of Education)
☐ VISA
☐ MASTERCARD
☐ PURCHASE ORDER

CREDIT CARD NUMBER

EXPIRATION DATE

AUTHORIZED SIGNATURE

| Item No. | Title | Quantity | Price each | Total |
|---|---|---|---|---|
| 1503 | *Taking Center Stage: A Commitment to Standards-Based Education for California's Middle Grades Students* | | $13.50 | |
| | | | | |
| | | | | |

**CHARGES**

| Purchase amount | Add |
|---|---|
| 0 - $15 | $ 5.95 |
| $15.01 - $30 | 7.95 |
| $30.01 - $50 | 9.95 |
| $50.01 - $100 | 11.95 |
| $100.01 - $150 | 13.95 |
| $150.01 - $200 | 15.95 |
| $200.01 - $250 | 17.95 |
| $250.01 - $300 | 19.95 |
| $300.01 - $350 | 21.95 |
| $350.01 and up | 6% of subtotal |

Mail completed order form to:

**California Department of Education**
**CDE Press Sales Office**
**P.O. Box 271**
**Sacramento, CA 95812-0271**

Or fax completed order form to:

**916-323-0823**

Visit our Web site:

**http://www.cde.ca.gov/cdepress**

**Note:** Mail orders must be accompanied by a check, a purchase order, or a VISA or MasterCard credit card number, including expiration date and your signature. Purchase orders without checks are accepted from educational institutions, businesses, and governmental agencies. Purchase orders and credit card orders may be placed by FAX (916) 323-0823. Telephone orders will be accepted toll-free (1-800-995-4099) for credit card purchases. Please do not send cash. Stated prices are subject to change. Please order carefully; include correct item number and quantity for each publication ordered. *All sales are final.*

| | |
|---|---|
| SUBTOTAL | $ |
| Calif. residents: Please add sales tax. | $ |
| Shipping and handling charges (See chart at left.) | $ |
| TOTAL | $ |

**PRICES AND AVAILABILITY OF PUBLICATIONS ARE SUBJECT TO CHANGE WITHOUT NOTICE.**

R00-108 003-0065-00 6-01 20M

# NOTES

# NOTES

# NOTES

# NOTES

# NOTES

# NOTES

# NOTES

# NOTES